REWRITING WOMANHOOD

THE PENN STATE ROMANCE STUDIES SERIES

EDITORS
Robert Blue • Kathryn M. Grossman • Thomas A. Hale • Djelal Kadir
Norris J. Lacy • John M. Lipski • Sherry L. Roush • Allan Stoekl

ADVISORY BOARD
Theodore J. Cachey Jr. • Priscilla Ferguson • Hazel Gold • Cathy L. Jrade
William Kennedy • Gwen Kirkpatrick • Rosemary Lloyd • Gerald Prince
Joseph T. Snow • Ronald W. Tobin • Noël Valis

Reconstructing Woman:
From Fiction to Reality in the Nineteenth-Century French Novel
by DOROTHY KELLY

Career Stories:
Belle Epoque Novels of Professional Development
by JULIETTE M. ROGERS

Territories of History: Humanism, Rhetoric, and the Historical
Imagination in the Early Chronicles of Spanish America
by SARAH H. BECKJORD

The Book of Peace
by CHRISTINE DE PIZAN
Translated and edited by Karen Green, Constant J. Mews,
and Janice Pinder with the assistance of Alan Crosier

Consensus and Debate in Salazar's Portugal: Visual and Literary Negotiations
of the National Text, 1933–1948
by ELLEN W. SAPEGA

REWRITING WOMANHOOD

*Feminism, Subjectivity,
and the Angel of the House
in the Latin American Novel,
1887–1903*

NANCY LAGRECA

THE PENNSYLVANIA STATE UNIVERSITY PRESS
UNIVERSITY PARK, PENNSYLVANIA

Library of Congress
Cataloging-in-Publication Data

LaGreca, Nancy, 1972–
Rewriting womanhood : feminism, subjectivity, and the angel of the house in the Latin American novel, 1887–1903 / Nancy LaGreca.
    p.   cm.
Includes bibliographical references and index.
Summary: "An historical and theoretical literary study of three Latin American women writers, Refugio Barragón of Mexico, Mercedes Cabello de Carbonera of Peru, and Ana Roqué of Puerto Rico. Examines how these novelists subversively rewrote womanhood vis à vis the prescribed comportment for women during a conservative era"—Provided by publisher.
ISBN 978-0-271-03438-6 (cloth : alk. paper)
ISBN 978-0-271-03439-3 (pbk. : alk. paper)
1. Spanish American literature—Women authors—History and criticism.
2. Spanish American literature—19th century—History and criticism.
3. Feminism and literature—Latin America.
4. Women in literature.
I. Title.

PQ7081.5.L35 2009
863'.5099287—dc22
2008034080

Copyright © 2009
The Pennsylvania State University
All rights reserved
Printed in the United States of America
Published by The Pennsylvania State University Press,
University Park, PA 16802–1003

The Pennsylvania State University Press
is a member of the
Association of American University Presses.

It is the policy of The Pennsylvania State University Press to use acid-free paper. Publications on uncoated stock satisfy the minimum requirements of American National Standard for Information Sciences—Permanence of Paper for Printed Library Material, ANSI Z39.48–1992.

This book can be viewed at
http://publications.libraries.psu.edu/eresources/978-0-271-03438-6

To *Anne and Roy*, for all their love and support,
and to the memory of *Rose and Josephine*, for providing me early examples
of women who thought and lived against the grain.

CONTENTS

Acknowledgments ix

Introduction 1

1
Women's Imagined Roles in Nineteenth-Century Mexico:
Seclusion in the Midst of Progress and
Early Feminist Reactions 28

2
Coming of Age(ncy):
Refugio Barragán de Toscano's *La hija del bandido* 53

3
Women in Peru:
National and Private Struggles for Independence 78

4
New Models for New Women:
Rethinking Cinderella's Virtues and Humanizing the Stepmother
in Mercedes Cabello de Carbonera's *Blanca Sol* 102

5
Women as Body in Puerto Rico:
Medicine, Morality, and Institutionalizations of Sexual
Oppression in the Long Nineteenth Century 124

6
Sexual Agency in Ana Roqué's *Luz y sombra*:
A Subversion of the Essentialized Woman   149

Conclusions   171

Works Cited   177
Index   195

ACKNOWLEDGMENTS

THIS PROJECT HAS BENEFITED from the support and insight of people I hold in the highest esteem. Many thanks to Naomi Lindstrom for reading an early version of this manuscript and providing, with good humor and encouragement, invaluable detailed feedback on the content and writing. I am grateful to my colleagues Benigno Trigo and Katie Arens for their knowledgeable guidance regarding the theoretical frame of the analyses.

I would like to thank Kimberly Hamlin, Virginia Higginbotham, Jacqueline Loss, and Belinda Mora for their warm encouragement. Special thanks go to Betsy Phillips for her feedback regarding the writing and organization during the final stages of the preparation of this manuscript. I am indebted to the two anonymous Penn State University Press readers whose thoughtful comments aided in fine-tuning the content of this book. I am grateful to my fine colleagues at the University of Oklahoma, who have offered their advice and support, and my graduate students, who have provided encouragement through their lively and insightful discussions on the works studied herein. In particular I would like to thank A. Robert Lauer and Pamela Genova for always being on call to offer advice, Lourdes Yen for her help as my research assistant, and Kathy Peters for her cheerful help with the many administrative tasks involved in moving forward with this project.

My deep appreciation goes to my husband, Jack Douglas Eure III, one of my most trusted readers, and to my brother Charles for his enthusiastic moral support.

Funding for this project was provided by the Continuing Fellowship, administered through the Graduate School of the University of Texas at Austin. Additional research and preparation in the final stages of this manuscript were made possible with a Junior Faculty Research Grant from the University of Oklahoma's Office of the Vice President for Research and a Faculty Enrichment Grant from the College of Arts and Sciences at the University of Oklahoma.

INTRODUCTION

Ahora bien, la marcada repugnancia que inspira a la mujer toda observación abstracta, profunda y prolongada, a causa de la invincible fatiga que a poco le sobreviene, pone bien de manifiesto la debilidad relativa de sus órganos cerebrales que corresponden a las funciones de abstracción. En cambio, la meditación concreta, la observación sintética de las cosas reales, admite en ella un ejercicio mucho más sostenido; lo cual indica una aptitud cerebral mayor para ese género de observaciones. . . . La poca energía y vigor de sus facultades abstractas y analíticas ocasiona que la inteligencia femenina aprecie mejor las diferencias de los objetos que sus semejanzas.

[Now then, the marked repugnance that any type of abstract, profound, and prolonged observation inspires in women, owing to the invincible fatigue that sets in shortly afterward, is an obvious manifestation of the relative weakness of their cerebral organs that control the functions of abstraction. Conversely, concrete thought, the synthetic observation of real things, allow them a more sustained activity; this indicates a greater cerebral aptitude for this kind of observation. . . . The abstract and analytical faculties' meager energy and vigor cause feminine intelligence to better appreciate the differences among objects, rather than their similarities.]
—Horacio Barreda, *El siglo XX ante el feminismo*, 1909

HORACIO BARREDA, SON OF THE ILLUSTRIOUS Mexican Positivist philosopher Gabino Barreda, edited the periodical *Revista Positiva* (Positivist Journal) from 1901 to 1913. His assertions about women's intellectual deficiencies appeared in the *Revista* and were part of the lengthy essay *El siglo XX ante el feminismo* (The Twentieth Century in the Face of Feminism), which drew upon "scientific" proof to denounce women's career aspirations outside the home, positing such activity as the downfall of civilized society. Barreda's evidence, gathered from his own observations and opinions rather than from scientific experimentation or study, denied women's capacity to think abstractly and to study for prolonged periods. His assertion implied that female members of society were incapable of becoming writers, artists, politicians, or intellectuals or of pursuing any vocation other than housewife or seamstress. Other intellectuals shared Barreda's views on the alleged weakness of women's cerebral organs, and this line of thinking affected national policy: the late nineteenth century saw a decline in women's access to education in many Latin American countries.[1]

This brief case study of Barreda is illustrative of attitudes throughout Latin America during the formation of the new republics. Historian Elizabeth Dore, in her article "One Step Forward, Two Steps Back" finds in emerging historiography on Latin American women's roles that, contrary to the commonly held belief that the long nineteenth century ushered in progress for women, their general conditions actually declined as the century wore on (2000, 5). While some reforms in the protection of women were beneficial (such as protection from physical abuse) and women gained more legal rights over their children, overall the ideological push to define gender norms in order to normalize "'proper' behavior" for women in health, education, employment, and social charity work only enforced traditional and retrograde notions of womanhood, while women's legal protection related to family land holdings was taken away with the liberal trend toward the commoditization of landed property (Dore 2000, 23, 5–6). Despite vigorous campaigns in their countries of origin to create narrow and restrictive definitions of womanhood, writers such as Refugio Barragán de Toscano (Mexico, 1846–1916), Mercedes Cabello de Carbonera (Peru, 1845–1909), and Ana Roqué (Puerto Rico, 1853–1933) were challenging these ideals both through the very act of writing and through their subject matter, which often portrayed women as savvy, proactive, and authoritative heroines who drive the course of their lives and their formation as agent-subjects.

Such activity was not without its costs—women novelists were often scorned by contemporaries for preferring the writer's desk to the hearth—and an aim of this study is to discover why middle-class women in nineteenth-century Latin America would risk tarnishing their reputations and bursting the protective bubble of domesticity to write in the male-dominated and public genre of the novel.

What makes these three women novelists' stories unique, urgent, and necessary is that they *dreamed new women* for a modern age in texts that focus on the sociology and psychology of women and in which the authors imagine alternatives to women's roles and feminized identities in a world that has not yet admitted them. Thus the fiction studied here is imaginative and creative, based on fantasy rather than the realities of nation building in the era. The reader discovers, then, that these novelists' reward was worth the risk

---

1. For details on the decline of women's education during the Porfiriato, see Chapter 1 of this study. Women's education in Peru and Puerto Rico is discussed in Chapters 3 and 5.

of ridicule: an important goal of their writing was to imagine (and invite readers to imagine) new definitions of womanhood. In so doing, they were liberating their sex from an oppressive domestic feminine ideal: the Angel of the House, in brief, the notion that a woman's virtue is measured by her dedication to domestic life, self-sacrifice, and servitude to her family.

Because the law denied women direct means of swaying public opinion (through, for example, voting or running for office), writing a novel was a way for the gentle sex to insert their voices into the national dialogue. Barragán, Cabello, and Roqué committed to press tales that included dynamic, intelligent, and desirous heroines, thereby contradicting national images of female passivity and abnegation. Like Simone de Beauvoir in France; Virginia Woolf in Britain; and later, fellow Latin Americans Rosario Castellanos in Mexico and Rosario Ferré in Puerto Rico, our nineteenth-century novelists and other women writers of their generation knew that the cultivation of the self was key to sparking feminist awareness (although they may not have used this term); they experienced the epiphany of recognizing one's oppressed condition, or "click" moment, as the U.S. feminist Betty Friedan appropriately termed it in *The Feminine Mystique* (1963). Barragán, Cabello, and Roqué were part of the group of women intellectual precursors to the feminist movement of the twentieth century because they represent early efforts to reclaim the female self and define womanhood in Latin America for a modern era.

The opening quote to this Introduction provides insight into the serious challenges that women novelists faced. Arguments such as Barreda's were used in public policy decisions to limit women's education to basic reading, some geography or other general culture, and the domestic arts. Not all public writing was taboo for women; flowery, often insipid poetic verses appeared sporadically in popular periodicals because poetry was considered a "feminine" genre fed by instinct, nerves, "la loca de la casa" (imagination), and feeling. Although there were women poets who cultivated the genre to a high artistic and intellectual level, such as the famed Cuban novelist, poet, and playwright Gertrudis Gómez de Avellaneda (1814–1873) and the well-known Puerto Rican patriot and poet Lola Rodríguez de Tió (1843–1924), poetry that appeared in women's periodicals often expressed the joys of motherhood, religious devotion, or some other chaste love in a simplistic and syrupy way that upheld patriarchal values.

To write a novel, however, was another matter entirely. It was believed that "women who wrote, expressing their thinking in public media such as newspapers and novels, were exposing themselves to mental incapacitation as a consequence of their weak constitution" (Zalduondo 2001, 168). Narration implied a degree of intellectual acumen only recognized in men, who were capable of constructing characters with some psychological depth, thinking through a plot line, creating suspense, and dreaming up picturesque descriptions and adventures. Furthermore, publishing a work of fiction often implied knowledge of the public sphere, risqué love affairs, and politics—themes off limits to women, who were obligated to guard their virtue and innocence from such worldly matters. Not least among the reasons women were not supposed to write prose was that it meant that they would have a public voice; a woman author held the attention of a reader for the course of several hundred pages. She had an audience. Indeed, she had power, because she earned an opportunity to pen her own version of the world and present this subjective alternative reality to a reading public. And, as Angel Rama roundly proves in *La ciudad letrada* (1983), the literate public was the ruling class.

The female novelist, then, challenged traditional beliefs of the ruling class in several ways: she was a threat to the domestic status quo, she proved wrong the notion that the female brain was incapable of abstraction and intellectual activity, and she forged a forum for her views. In a backlash, women who wrote prose were often referred to as unfeminine, virile, or unnatural for daring to let their creativity overflow onto the public page.[2] As the scholar of women's narrative of nineteenth-century Spain Lou Charnon-Deutsch affirms, "Book writing was defined as a manly occupation; if a woman

---

2. Gertrudis Gómez de Avellaneda's contemporaries struggled with the idea that a woman could write serious literature, as she did. In the case of Avellaneda and others, the highest praise contemporaries could offer was to call them "masculine." Her contemporaries often called her writing "virile." Cuesta Jiménez notes that the phrase *Es mucho hombre esta mujer*, which loosely translates as "This woman is quite a man" (1943, 14), was often used to describe Avellaneda. This praise, however, was a double-edged sword in that there was a fine line between such a statement and calling a woman writer *marimacho* (which Zalduondo translates as "butch"). The Peruvian writer whose work is the subject of Chapter 4, Mercedes Cabello de Carbonera, was often the target of slanderous remarks implying her masculine character. One critic, the Peruvian writer Juan de Arona (real name Pedro Paz Soldán y Unanue), is often quoted as having maliciously changed the novelist's name to Mierdeces Caballo de Cabrón-era (which loosely translates as "She was the dung of a bastard's horse"), an insult that is both scatological and animalizing, as Peluffo points out (Sánchez quoted in Peluffo 2002, 39). Examples of such denigration of women writers abound in nineteenth-century studies of literary history. The literary critic Virginia Cánova, who published a scholarly edition of the first known novel by a woman in Uruguay, *Por una fortuna una cruz* (1860) by Marcelina Almeida, cites scathing critiques of this novel by a contemporary who launches the insult, among numerous others, that "nada sabe, pero escribe todo" (Cánova 1998, 69) [she knows nothing, but writes about everything]. All translations are my own unless otherwise indicated and all diacritical marks and spelling are original.

made a mark in the literary world, it was for her *virile* style, a distinction that always bore a price" (1994, 8). The three women writers whose prose we will explore risked their protected middle-class existences and exposed themselves to the critique of many in order to crack, or perhaps even shatter, the ubiquitous social signifier of angelic womanhood.

The Pervasive Obstacle: The Angel of the House

The Angel of the House was the domestic ideal for women of the mid nineteenth century in the Hispanic world and in Europe.[3] It portrayed the perfect woman as the Christian, chaste, maternal guardian of the happiness and success of her children, husband, and other family members. Extreme self-sacrifice and stoic suffering for the good of others were its main principles. The scholar of women's literature and culture of Spain Bridget Aldaraca acknowledges that the *ángel del hogar* took "as a starting point the negation of the real presence of woman as individual, i.e., as an autonomous social and moral being" (1982, 67). Abnegation, and the denial of the self that inevitably followed, were key to preventing women from demanding rights and moving beyond their prescribed place, as a strong sense of self is necessary to inspire consciousness regarding one's oppression and to spark activism.

In the Latin American context, the literary critic Francesca Denegri notes that policy makers who defined the roles of citizens in the new republics deliberately excluded "las 'masas de color'" (people of color) at the same time that it redefined Woman and created the image of national family of European descent (1996, 79). The Angel of the House, then, had two

---

3. The Virgin Mary is an ideal example of the Angel of the House, evidenced by her endless mercy, maternal chastity, and servitude to God (the father figure) and Jesus Christ (the male child figure). In Latin American letters the chaste, childlike, obedient, adoring, frail protagonist of Jorge Isaacs's *María* (Colombia, 1867), a novel read across Latin America from the time of publication up until today, is a melancholy angel who frequently leaves her beloved's favorite flowers in his chambers. Twentieth-century examples of the Angel of the House would be the long-suffering, virtuous, beautiful woman of many Latin American soap operas who is saved by a handsome man from a higher social class when he chooses to marry her (for example, the protagonist of the popular 1980s Venezuelan soap opera *Cristal*), the perfectly groomed, subservient robots in the film *The Stepford Wives* (based on Ira Levin's 1972 novel of the same name), or the nurturing and ever-cheerful homemaker Mrs. Cleaver from the popular U.S. television show *Leave It to Beaver* (1957–63). Although these various manifestations of the feminine domestic ideal spring from different cultural contexts and have different aims, they share certain angelic qualities: they equate femininity with domesticity, fidelity, obedience, abnegation, passivity, and fragile beauty.

primary functions: to charge women with providing a perfectly relaxing and safe haven for their men who had to deal with the day-to-day challenges of an unpredictable environment in a newly formed nation in flux and, second, to conserve the bourgeois family space as an exclusively white one (81); hence the emphasis on the seclusion and "protection" of women, to ensure chastity and the selection of appropriately white reproductive partners. The scholar of Argentine women's culture Francine Masiello stresses the central place of the Angel in the House in national discourse and nation building, where leading nineteenth-century intellectuals such as Domingo Faustino Sarmiento "molded an image of the Argentine spouse and mother to suit their projects of state" (1992, 53–54). This conscious act of defining gender in the project of nation building is not unique to Argentina; periodicals and novels of the period link good motherhood and virtue to good citizenship consistently throughout Latin America and Spain. In the novels considered in this study, the Angel of the House is a master signifier that Barragán, Cabello, and Roqué take apart and reappropriate for the purposes of promoting women's agency, intellectual abilities, and participation in public life—aims that were not part of national discourses on women's place.

The phrase *Angel of the House* gained widespread use throughout Europe in the 1850s and its Spanish equivalent was also common in Hispanic literature of the nineteenth century. The literary critic Bonnie Frederick, in her book on nineteenth-century Argentine women writers *Wily Modesty* (1998), attributes the origin of the phrase to a didactic poem by English clergyman Coventry Patmore in 1858. Although the phrase itself appears to have originated in Victorian England, the basic tenets of the model had been advocated for women centuries earlier. Spanish readers devoured editions of Fray Luis de León's 1583 manual of comportment for women, *La perfecta casada* (The Perfect Wife), which included the basic principles of the Angel of the House: abnegation, humility, modesty, obedience, chastity, and enclosure within the home. The manual went through a minimum of seven editions from 1583 to 1872; the 1872 edition was printed in response to "la frecuencia con que la obra es buscada para regalo de boda" (Ginesta 1872, i–ii) [the frequency with which the book is sought to be given as a wedding gift]. In late nineteenth-century Spain the popularity of this extremely conservative guide for women was booming.

As noted by Aldaraca (1982), writing on women's domestic culture in Spain, de León's sixteenth-century text, like later similar texts, defines women's place within the home and views motherhood as woman's only plausible function, yet its arguments lack the Romantic, generally positive (if restrictive), view of womanhood that was common in the nineteenth century, laying bare the author's misogyny. For example, de León dedicates the whole of chapter 16 to the importance of women's keeping silent and having an agreeable nature. The frank reasoning he offers is that women are not intelligent and therefore should not speak: "El mejor consejo que les podemos dar . . . es rogar que callen, y que, ya que son poco sábias, se esfuercen á ser mucho calladas" (de León 1972, 158) [The best advice we can give them . . . is to beg that they keep quiet, and, considering they are not very wise, that they make an effort to be very silent]. Fray Luis de León viewed woman as an inherently simple and impulsive creature prone to laziness who was to be kept enclosed, busily tending to the economy of the household. Her desires, her dreams, and the activities of her daily life were all carefully detailed for her in *La perfecta casada*; her place was to be "protected" by the man whom she gratefully served.

Fray Luis de León's manual may have been one of the models for another manual of comportment for women with runaway sales figures, María del Pilar Sinués de Marco's 1859 book *El ángel del hogar* (The Angel of the House).[4] Sinués de Marco's manual title appears to be an early use of the term *ángel del hogar*, although it is not certain when or where the phrase originated in Spanish. While Sinués de Marco's rhetoric is softer and more sympathetic toward women than that found in *La perfecta casada*, the elements that define traditional womanhood are very similar.

Sinués de Marco (1835–1893) was a renowned award-winning literary figure in her day. She was a conservative and staunch defender of separate spheres for men (public) and women (domestic), yet her status as both woman and writer was in conflict with her own ideology. (One wonders how much time she dedicated to perfecting angelic domesticity herself, as she must have quite been busy maintaining a wildly successful publishing career.) An acquaintance of Sinués de Marco's comments that whenever a visitor arrived at the writer's home, she was always "dutifully sewing"; this appeared to be staged, as she was always sewing the same piece of cloth (Nombela 1909 quoted in Jagoe 1990, 474).

Sinués de Marco partially and indirectly addresses the disjunction between her life and the ideology of her writings in "De la literatura en la mujer" (About the Place of Literature in Women's Lives), chapter 12 of *El ángel del hogar*. Therein she acknowledges women's intellectual capabilities and

---

4. For a detailed analysis of the differences between Fray Luis de León's *La perfecta casada* and Sinués de Marco's *El ángel del hogar*, see Aldaraca 1991.

affirms that men deny women's intellect because of "su instinto orgulloso y egoista" (their proud and egotistical instinct) that cannot bear to see a woman surpass them (1859, 173). She then offers as proof of women's talent the Cuban writer Gómez de Avellaneda, whom Sinués de Marco believes to be the highest example of woman's brilliance. However, she goes on to point out that such singular talent is extremely rare, and that the typical aspiring *literata* (woman writer) in Spain is a repugnant creature to be taken as a negative example for all virtuous women. The *literata*, according to Sinués de Marco, is vain, superficial, selfish, spoiled, and lazy, and because of her horrible character, combined with her pride and high opinion of herself, she is simply ridiculous (1859, 177–78). Sinués de Marco adds that even virtuous women who long to write do so in vain, as the opportunities are so slim; the vocation is like chasing a "phantom." This idea, in sum, is the key to Sinués de Marco's strong recommendation that women abandon their dreams and find solace in married life: "¡Estraño delirio es, por cierto, el que hace abandonar la dulce dicha del hogar doméstico para correr detrás de un fantasma, que raras veces ve realizado el hombre y que nunca alcanza la débil mano de la mujer!" (177) [It is certainly a strange delusion, that which makes women abandon the sweet happiness of the domestic hearth to chase after a phantasmagoric dream, one that is rarely achieved by man and that the weak hand of woman never attains!]. In a rhetorical gesture that is often repeated in Sinués de Marco's writing, she defends women as inherently good, intelligent beings worthy of happiness, but recommends squelching their desires and submitting to patriarchal norms as the only way to feasibly attain well-being—and avoid the inevitable suffering that comes with going against the rules of patriarchal society.

Sinués de Marco's chapter on "the place of literature in women's lives" not only addresses the presumably dreadful character of the *literata*, but also places strong emphasis on the careful choice of proper reading materials for women. Keeping with a tendency of the times in Spain and Latin America, she condemns worldly readings for young women that teach them of passions, betrayals, and sin (she gives the example of the 1844 adventure novel *The Three Musketeers* by Alexander Dumas to illustrate this harmful fiction). However, the Spanish writer finds numerous positive benefits to be reaped from readings that cultivate delicate sentiments, goodness, and purity. One may infer that Sinués de Marco's own novels and articles are precisely what her tender young *lectoras* (readers) should consume. Thus we have a glimpse of Sinués de Marco's possible justifications for her do-as-I-say, not-as-I-do attitude: she justifies her own publishing because she has women's best interest, rather than her personal glory, at heart (thus, we may conclude, she exhibits the important characteristic of sacrificing her time and energy solely for the good of others). Sinués de Marco envisions herself filling a gap in literature by providing materials to make young women *ángeles del hogar,* as opposed to the woman writer who seeks self-aggrandizement through the publication of worldly and intellectual themes.

Although Sinués de Marco recognized women's capacity for intellectual work and the creative arts, her advice manuals and novels roundly contest any hope that women could ever fully dedicate themselves to these endeavors, regardless of any natural talent they might possess. Two of her novels, *El alma enferma* (The Sick Soul [1864]) and *La senda de la gloria* (The Path to Glory [1863]), portray female protagonists who face the conflict between cultivating their own talents and dedicating their lives to their husbands. In both cases Sinués de Marco recommends to her female readers that they submit to masculine authority (Sánchez-Llama 1999, 754). For example, the long-suffering protagonist of *La senda,* herself a talented painter, must stoically tolerate the physical abuse of her husband and signs his name to her own paintings for the sake of maintaining domestic peace (Sánchez-Llama 1999, 754). Sinués de Marco's novel sends the message that, for the virtuous woman, creativity should be channeled into making the best of her home life; hopes of fame and public recognition should be abandoned and she should focus instead on raising a family and keeping her husband happy.

Sinués de Marco directed two popular women's journals, one, which bore the same title as her manual, *El Angel del Hogar,* from 1864 to 1869 and the other, *Flores y Perlas* (Flowers and Pearls), from 1883 to 1884. She published more than one hundred books, which were mostly sentimental domestic novels illustrating Angels of the House in action, but her oeuvre also includes various manuals of comportment for women for different stages of their lives and collections of essays, poetry, and short stories (*Gran enciclopedia aragonesa*). Her collections of moralizing short stories *La ley de Dios* (The Law of God [1862]) and *A la luz de una lámpara* (By Lamplight [1862]) gained the support of ecclesiastic authorities and were required reading in primary schools for many years (Sánchez-Llama 1999, 752). Sinués de Marco's view of womanhood, available to readers by way of fiction, anecdotes, and essays—in both printed bound editions and popular magazines—made an indelible mark on her generation and those to follow, in Spain and beyond.

Sinués de Marco's *El ángel del hogar* is a compilation of didactic stories that served as a spiritual and practical guide for women from youth through marriage. The stories and essays in the collection were first serialized starting in 1857 in the Madrid periodical *La Moda de Cádiz* (The Latest Trends of Cádiz) (Jagoe 1990, 473). More than six hundred pages long, the volume contains dozens of stories written to teach women how to be obedient wives and self-sacrificing mothers, as well as cautionary tales about those who faltered in their domestic and religious mission. The ideal angelic woman is not focused inward on her own subjectivity, but rather outward to those around her. She is judged by her tenderness and virtue toward others: women should be "buenas y tiernas madres, hijas sumisas y amorosas, esposas irreprensibles" (21) [good and tender mothers, submissive and loving daughters, irreproachable wives]. Almost all the definitions and discussions of the Angel of the House speak of this model in terms of the woman's relationship to those around her: she is daughter, wife, and mother, rather than an individual independent of these patriarchal family ties. In addition to the stories, there are informative summaries that teach readers about the history of the monastic orders of Spain, to round out women's ecclesiastic knowledge.

The author of *El ángel del hogar* had good intentions when she published this weighty volume; although the collection upholds the damaging standards typical of nineteenth-century patriarchal mores, her goal is ultimately to protect women. She speaks as a woman who understands the "azarosa existencia de la mujer" (women's hazardous existence) and emphasizes the inherent burden and second-class status of women, which starts even before birth, as the entire family longs for a male offspring and fears the child will be female (Sinués de Marco 1859, 1). However, by teaching women to ignore their own desires and to achieve happiness by making those around them comfortable, this unrealistically perfect ideal kept women from actualizing their own identities. The angelic standard was a major impediment to women's liberation because it caused them to ignore the most basic step toward an early feminist activism: the cultivation of the self. Sinués de Marco clearly empathizes with her sisters, yet rather than criticizing the damaging standards, she advocates molding oneself to fit the perfect domestic model. In her attempt to help her sex, she glosses over the fact that the burden of perfection is, itself, a form of torment.

Sinués de Marco's influence in the Hispanic world was strong. Her articles appeared in the most respected periodicals of her day, in Spain and in the Americas (Jagoe 1990, 474). Women in Cuba and beyond could order a copy of *El ángel del hogar* through their subscription to the 1860 *Album Cubano de lo Bueno y lo Bello* (The Cuban Album of the Good and the

Beautiful), a women's journal directed by Gómez de Avellaneda (as Susana Montero [1993] reminds us, however, it should be noted that Avellaneda's publication included subversive materials in support of women's intellectual growth along with good nest-building tips). It is probable that Clorinda Matto de Turner, the Peruvian author and contemporary of Cabello, read Sinués's work because a passage from one of the essays is quoted in *Aves sin nido* (1889) and attributed to the "escritora española" (the Spanish [woman] writer), although Sinués de Marco is not named. There is little doubt that the ideal put forth in Sinués de Marco's writings concerning women's mission in life was known by literate women of the bourgeoisie across Latin America in the last quarter of the nineteenth century. The importance of the notion of the Angel of the House went beyond the intimate familial unit in Latin America. Print media of the 1800s and early 1900s in the region portrayed women as the vessels of national morality; it was believed that through their high moral and religious standards the nation could aspire to future generations of good citizens. Publications from the mid to late 1800s dedicated to cultivating women's domestic skills and hygiene, fashion, beauty regimens, religiosity, and dedication to the family, such as Cuba's *El Cesto de Flores* (The Basket of Flowers [1856]), Brazil's *Bello Sexo* (The Gentle Sex [1862]), Argentina's *El Album del Hogar* (The Home Album [1878]), and Mexico's *El Correo de las Señoras* (The Ladies' Post [1883–93]), were popular reading for middle-class women. Since women were responsible for purveying the patriarchal value system and rearing generations of citizens to keep progress in motion, their subscription to national ideals was of utmost importance.

The Angel of the House was a pervasively consumed model in nineteenth-century Latin America; women and men, Positivists and Catholics, liberals and conservatives were counted among its supporters. As my historical chapters (Chapters 1, 3, and 5) demonstrate, discourses praising the Angel of the House—or condemning those who strayed from the model—could be found in church sermons, ecclesiastic decrees, Positivist journals, women's periodicals (those directed by women as well as by men), nationalist essays, and novels. It is no wonder, then, that conscious women like the writers I study here attack the feminine ideal subtly yet surely in their narratives.

It is easy to see why the Angel of the House presented a problem to thinking modern women. Following this paragon of obedient virtue meant stoically ignoring one's personal desires and sacrificing one's dreams for the good of the family. And today, the model of the angelic woman still poses an obstacle to a feminist reading of texts of the period. To the twenty-first-century reader, the inclusion of a female character who exhibits some (even if not all) of its characteristics often masks authors' attempts at criticizing women's position in society. In some cases, as we shall see, the trope of the angelic housewife or daughter probably served the female author as a shield against negative criticism. In the analyses in Chapters 2, 4, and 6, I explore how the symbolic ideal of the Angel in the House is manipulated in each novel to allow the author to offer an alternative and unique female self, inviting women to look and think beyond the prescribed model and take control of their subjectivity through the fulfillment of their desires for travel, public activity, education, or adventure (to name a few of the subversive activities the heroines of our novels enjoy).[5]

Against the Grain: Women's Literary Culture and Women Novelists in Nineteenth-Century Latin America

The focus of this study is to trace specifically the reworkings of the Angel of the House signifier in three novels produced in Mexico, Peru, and Puerto Rico. To provide a context for these writers' literary ambitions it is useful to look at other examples of women's prose production from the mid-1800s to the dawn of the twentieth century.[6] While Barragán, Cabello, and Roqué stand out as three underrepresented novelists who wrote female characters with audacious levels of agency that simultaneously portray and

---

5. The crucial role of agency as a part of identity within society and as a vision for change (social, national, and historical) can be seen in Kristeva's idea of the *chora* as an essential part of the feminine. For further reading on Kristeva, see Arens 1998a, in which Arens focuses on Kristeva's *sémanalyse* as a critical historical analysis that emphasizes the roles of the subject and language; the chapter on Kristeva in Grosz 1989; and, for an introductory reading, the chapter on Kristeva in Moi 1988. Oliver 1993 is a reading from a philosophical perspective that navigates the ambiguities of Kristeva's discourse and examines how it can be used for feminist criticism. The *chora* is part of the semiotic realm, a complement to the realm of the symbolic, composed of pre-linguistic drives and rhythms, similar to the rhythm one may sense in music and poetry (Kristeva 1974b, 93–97)—it is the realm of social and personal sense that can be signified, but which the social order has not yet chosen to designate as significant. The chora plays an important role for women in the nineteenth century because, as Kristeva points out, the symbolic realm or the realm of language had been rendered to some extent inaccessible to women in these social historical settings. Yet below that surface of designations, a region of sense, the semiotic and the chora that is its physical presence, waits to emerge as signified. Kristeva defines the semiotic and the chora in *Revolution in Poetic Language* (1984, chap. 1).

6. The list of writers included here is an overview and is not intended to be comprehensive. I have chosen to include writers whose work has received some critical attention in the past twenty years and have given precedence to women writers whose work is available in recent editions

critique angelic virtue in order to recode social expectations, they were part of a growing number of women who found the courage and desire to defy convention by cultivating the intellect and publishing their work. The unearthing of many important nineteenth-century women writers from the Southern Cone has made a significant addition to the field in recent years, and slowly but surely scholars are rediscovering early women writers from Mexico and the Spanish-speaking Caribbean as well. Recent scholarship on early women writers provides critical and cultural studies of underrepresented women writers from across Latin America.[7]

The 1860s and 1870s Lima literary salon of the Argentine writer Juana Manuela Gorriti (1818–1892) is one of the best-known organized efforts to cultivate women's writing in Latin America in the era.[8] Gorriti was a prose fiction writer and essayist from a politically liberal family who left her residence in Bolivia after separating from her husband (later president of Bolivia) Manuel Isidro Belzú. She is perhaps best known today for her collection of short stories, many of them critiques of the Juan Manuel de Rosas dictatorship in Argentina, *Sueños y realidades* (1865) and the collection of writings *Panoramas de la vida* (1876).[9] Already an established writer when she arrived in Lima, Gorriti was the driving force behind the meetings. The *veladas*, or late-night gatherings, began after the evening meal and often stretched into the early hours of the morning. The veladas included piano and other musical recitals, poetry recitation, improvisations, anecdotes, and the recitation of essays, followed by discussions. Denegri points out that children were

---

for further reading. A discussion of women poets is outside the scope of this study; however, the following is a basic list of some of the most prominent nineteenth-century women poets: Gertrudis Gómez de Avellaneda (Cuba, 1814–73), Juana Borrero (Cuba, 1878–96), Lola Rodríguez de Tió (Puerto Rico, 1843–1924), Dolores Veintimilla de Galindo (Ecuador, 1830–57), Adela Zamudio (Bolivia, 1854–1928), Salomé Ureña de Henríquez (Dominican Republic, 1850–97), and Delmira Agustini (Uruguay, 1886–1914). See the following works by and about women poets in Latin America: Orjuela 2000; Caillet-Bois 1958; Flores and Flores 1986; Campuzano 1997.

7. Some examples are Jiménez 1999b; Campuzano 1997; and González Ascorra 1997. Two recent works particularly dedicated to early women writers' essays, Meyer 1995 and Gloria da Cunha 2006, also deserve mention.

8. The literary critic Graciela Batticuore's (1999) study and anthology *El taller de la escritora* provides context to these history-making meetings as well as original documents read by participants. See also Denegri 1996. Several compilations of critical articles on history and gender are very useful for nineteenth-century feminist literary studies; see French and Bliss 2007 and Vidal 1989.

9. Selections of Gorriti's prose have been translated into English by Sergio Waisman and edited by Francine Masiello (Gorriti 2003). For a brief sketch on Juana Manuel Gorriti, see Mazquirán de Rodríguez's entry in Marting 1990. For critical studies on Gorriti's prose, including her historical critiques, fantastic elements of her fiction, and her place in nineteenth-century Argentine prose, see Guerra 1985, 1987a, 1987b; Lichtblau 1959; Fletcher 1993, 1994; Urraca 1999; and Barrera 1996.

welcome at the meetings, creating an even more diversified space relative to the masculine elite version of the intellectuals' club; the various discourses of the veladas (familial, private, political, and literary) were intermingled and coexisted to form a new, truly alternative community that began to surpass the popularity of the exclusively male literary clubs of Lima (1996, 121–23). The intellectual elite of Lima, made up of both women and men, attended the meetings. These included the well-known Peruvian writers Matto de Turner; Cabello; Ricardo Palma (1833–1919); and the intellectual, politician, and literary critic Manuel González Prada (1844–1918); among many others.

One of the many intriguing features of the veladas is the public and publicized aspect of their existence. The literary scholar Graciela Batticuore notes that the veladas began when a reporter overheard Gorriti mention that she would like to start a literary group and published this information in the Lima newspaper: "Los cronistas no sólo promueven la realización del evento sino que acompañan cada encuentro con la reseña detallada de las actividades, la publicación simultánea de muchas de las producciones leídas en la velada y la interpretación del rol social que este círculo de intelectuales se dispone a ejercer" (Batticuore 1999, 27) [The reporters not only set in motion the beginnings of the event, they also follow up each meeting with a detailed review of the activities, the simultaneous publication of many of the writings read during the velada, and an interpretation of the social role that this circle of intellectuals sets out to fulfill]. The reviews in the Lima newspaper *El Comercio* (Commerce) stressed the high attendance rate by Lima intellectuals; the importance of the event to Peru's national body of literature; and the variety of their content in terms of genre, themes, and styles of the readings and events (Batticuore 1999, 201–23). This woman-centered group, with Gorriti as the undisputed leader, became an integral part of the national literary scene of late 1870s Lima society. It is important to note that male intellectuals often approved of women's erudition, but *only* as a supplement to the latter's domestic skills and viewed education and critical thinking as ways to make women smarter and more apt homemakers, as well as better role models for the future generations of Peruvians (Denegri 1996, 82–83). Despite the fact that there may have been patriarchically driven motives for the public acceptance of women's cultivation of letters within the veladas (namely, that "civilized," somewhat learned mothers produce good future citizens), the experience of community for these women writers allowed them to flourish and they became examples for future generations of women intellectuals.

Several of the participants in Gorriti's veladas would go on to become accomplished writers, and some would make important contributions to early feminist causes.[10] The initiation of the woman-centered press (a press owned and operated by women, for women) across Latin America during this period was part of this important early feminist wave.[11] For example, Gorriti and the Peruvian writer Carolina Freire de Jaimes (1844–1916) founded the weekly publication *El Album* (The Album [1874]), which provided a forum for women's writings and discussions on women's topics.[12] The Peruvian writer and pedagogue Teresa González de Fanning founded one of the most academically rigorous schools for girls in Peru and made girls' education an important mission of her life's work (Batticuore 1999, 229). Fanning also went on to write the novel *Regina*, which won an award in the international literary competition of the Athenaeum of Lima in 1886 (Batticuore 1999, 229). Matto de Turner, an important Peruvian novelist whose work is widely studied today, used her tenure as editor of the daily newspaper *La Bolsa* (The Stock Exchange) in 1883 to advocate higher standards for women's education (Berg 1990, 304).[13]

---

10. One writer whose name does not commonly appear associated with Peruvian women writers born in the nineteenth century, but who nonetheless deserves mention for her literary contributions, is Zoila Aurora Cáceres (1877–1958), who married the well-known Guatemalan *modernista* writer Enrique Gómez Carrillo. This absence may be because of the later dates of Cáceres's publications or because she spent most of her life abroad, in Germany, France, and Spain. Cáceres stands out for being one of the few women prose writers of the *modernista* movement (Latin America's first autochthonous literary movement, which was in vogue between 1888 and 1920). Her work most typical of *modernismo* is her novel *La rosa muerta*, published in Paris in 1914 (Cáceres 2007), which deals with medical themes and a woman's sexual awakening at the hand of her gynecologist. The theme of this novel may make Cáceres sound very liberal; however, demonstrating a contradictory nature typical of modern women between two eras, she was a staunch Catholic who objected to other religious cults being allowed into Peru. Cáceres also published a travel narrative, a history of famous women, and a memoir of her life with Gómez Carrillo. Most of her work appears after 1910. Cáceres was an activist for suffrage and other rights for women.

11. In addition to the information in this Introduction and the historical chapters of this study on the early woman-centered presses in Latin America, for the history of the feminist press in Latin America, see studies by Bergmann et al. 1990 and Greenberg 1990; for women's periodicals in Mexico, see Herrick 1957.

12. Freire de Jaimes published dramas; poetry; and two short novels, *El regalo de bodas* (1887) and *Memorias de una reclusa* (Batticuore 1999, 228).

13. Matto de Turner's work is still studied today, in particular for her status as an early *indigenista* writer and for her 1889 novel criticizing clerical abuses and defending the cause of indigenous Peruvians, *Aves sin nido* (2004; trans., 1996). Berg has published critical editions of Matto de Turner's novels *Indole* (Character [1891]) (Matto de Turner 2006b) and *Herencia* (Heredity [1895]) (Matto de Turner 2006a). For a thorough critical study of the indigenous novel and on Matto de Turner's fiction, see Cornejo Polar 2005. See also Ana Peluffo's (2005) insightful study *Lágrimas andinas*, which

She then gained the editorship of the prestigious Lima literary weekly *El Perú Ilustrado* in 1889, but was forced to resign when, in her absence, a story was published about the life of Christ that alluded to an amorous attraction between Christ and Mary Magdalene (Berg 1995, 83). Matto was burned in effigy and excommunicated, and her writing was prohibited for consumption by the Archbishopric of Lima. After Nicolás de Piérola's troops sacked her home for political reasons in 1895, Matto fled for Argentina; there, she founded and edited the bimonthly magazine *El Búcaro Americano* (The American Urn), which specialized in publishing women's writing. Cabello, who is discussed at length in Chapters 3 and 4 of this study, became a successful writer, publishing several high-selling novels and many essays, including the prize-winning *La novela moderna* (The Modern Novel).[14]

As we can see in the case of both Gorriti and Matto de Turner, there was significant communication and intellectual exchange between Argentina and Peru. Gorriti's homeland produced several important women writers who are gaining recognition today. Although Frederick points out eight women writers who make up the "Generation of '80" in Argentina (1991, 282), I will highlight a few who have received critical attention

---

delves into Matto de Turner's strategic use of sentimentality to insert her discourse into the national program for liberal reform. Denegri 1996 also includes a chapter on Matto de Turner's Romantic discourse and struggle for entry into the national discourse. For an analysis and overview of Matto de Turner's essays, see Berg 1995.

14. Today *Blanca Sol* is the best-known work by Cabello. The rising number of critical studies on the novel inspired a 2004 edition, edited and with an introduction by María Cristina Arambel-Guiñazú and a 2007 edition with an introduction by Oswaldo Voysest. Interest in Cabello's work has led to other recent editions of her novels. Cabello's first novel was the 1886 *Los amores de Hortensia, biografía de una mujer superior* (Hortensia's Loves: Autobiography of a Superior Woman); however, this novel is not readily available today, even in specialized archives (Mazquiarán de Rodríguez 1990, 96). In 1886 she also published *Sacrificio y recompensa* (Sacrifice and Reward) (Cabello 2005), which won a gold medal from Athenaeum of Lima, and 1889 saw the publication of *Las consecuencias* (Consequences) (Cabello 1889b). A 2005 edition of *Sacrificio y recompensa* has recently appeared; contemporary interest in this novel likely arose as a result of the similarities between the character Elisa in this novel and the later, more fully developed character of Blanca Sol. Cabello's last novel, written in 1892, *El conspirador: Autobiografía de un hombre público* (The Conspirator: Autobiography of a Public Figure) (Cabello 2001) is considered a veiled critique of the presidency of Nicolás de Piérola (Peru, 1839–1913), who served during 1879–81 and 1895–99; the novel exposes, in the form of a fictional autobiography, the moral corruption and decline of Peru's political system. The discovery of evidence on video of the political corruptions of the Peruvian president Alberto Fujimori and his advisor Vladimiro Montesinos in 2000 inspired a 2001 edition of *El conspirador* (Voysest 2001, 5). Cabello is a nineteenth-century woman writer, along with Gorriti, Matto de Turner, and others, who is making her way into discussions on Latin American narrative in the nineteenth century.

in recent years.[15] The work of the feminist literary critics Masiello, Lea Fletcher, and Frederick have helped to bring these writers' work back into focus.

Juana Manso (1818–1875) was born in Argentina but later lived in Uruguay and Brazil. She started the scholarly and cultural organization the Ateneo de Señoritas (Young Ladies' Athenaeum) in 1841 and directed the early feminist journals *Jornal das Senhoras* (Ladies' Journal), *Album de Señoritas* (Young Ladies' Album), and *La Siempreviva* (The Everlasting Flower).[16] Through her essays and the founding of women's journals and schools for girls, Manso was a staunch advocate of women's education and participation in national literary production. The 1882 travel narrative of the Argentine Eduarda Mansilla de García (1838–1892; sister of the writer Lucio Victorio Mansilla and niece of the dictator Juan Manuel de Rosas) *Recuerdos de viaje* (Travel Memoirs) has seen a revival in a 2006 edition. The narrative tells of Mansilla's time abroad in Washington, D.C., with her diplomat husband and offers a woman's perspective on North American culture and mores, while at the same time shedding light on Argentine culture from a female viewpoint. As Masiello points out, an important facet of the narrative is Mansilla's wonder at the liberty of "yankee" women (1992, 83). The Argentine writer and activist Emma de la Barra (1861–1947) published five high-selling novels in Argentina, all of them largely forgotten until recently. In 2005 the specialist in Latin American women's writing Mary Berg edited a scholarly edition of de la Barra's 1905 novel *Stella* (originally published under the pseudonym César Duayen), which is a love story that also grapples with Argentina's transition into modernity and the role of women in this process. Thanks to the literary critics mentioned above, Argentine women writers are reappearing in nineteenth-century literary studies with ever greater frequency.[17]

One of Colombia's most prolific writers of the nineteenth century was a woman, Soledad Acosta de Samper (1833–1913) (Ordóñez 1977, 233), yet her work is largely unknown among Hispanists today. Specialists in women writers and nineteenth-century Colombian literature, however, have brought

---

15. The other women writers featured in Frederick's (1991) study "In Their Own Voice" are Elvira Aldao de Díaz (1858–1950), Agustina Andrade (1861–91), Silvia Fernández (1857–1945), Lola Larrosa de Ansaldo (1859–95), Josefina Pelliza de Sagasta (1848–88), and Edelina Soto y Calvo (1844–1932).

16. For more information on the feminist press in Argentina during this period, see Azua 1988.

17. Berg (1990, 1995, 2003, 2004) has published several critical articles on Emma de la Barra (pseud. César Duayén).

this multifaceted intellectual back into focus over the past fifteen years and now she is among the more frequently studied women writers of the era.[18] Acosta de Samper's literary career spanned half a century, and her oeuvre covers many genres: she translated works from French and English into Spanish and published prose fiction (historical, psychological, and fantastic); news articles; biographical articles; essays on women's social roles and education, science, religion, and history; travel narratives; and her own letters (Encinales de Sanjinés 1997, 229; Ordóñez 1997, 233). Like many women thinkers of her time, she was in favor of increasing women's education, and as a means of providing positive role models for young women, she published a collection of more than four hundred biographies of famous women throughout history, *La mujer en la sociedad moderna* (Woman in Modern Society [1895]).[19] She is perhaps best known today for her collection of short novels and narrations from the 1860s that were collected under the title *Novelas y cuadros de la vida sur-americana* in 1869 (of which a 2006 edition, edited and with an introduction by Flor María Rodríguez-Arenas, is currently available). Many of the stories in the collection are about the lives of women who face and overcome the challenges before them, and in Acosta de Samper's narratives, rising above these obstacles often includes the act of writing (González Ascorra 1997, 55–56). Through her biographies of successful, ambitious women and positive examples of fictional heroines taking control of their lives, Acosta de Samper sought to empower her Colombian sisters.

The hispanophone Caribbean produced several women prose fiction writers of importance. The aforementioned Cuban-born poet, dramatist, and novelist Gómez de Avellaneda appears to be the only woman writer of the nineteenth century who has achieved a steady place in the literary canon of Hispanic letters.[20] Gómez de Avellaneda's novels deserve mention for boldly

---

18. In 2005 Iberoamericana published an extensive compilation of critical studies, edited by Carolina Alzate. This collection includes more than five hundred pages of scholarship on the Colombian writer by respected scholars of nineteenth-century Latin American letters and women's writing such as Mary Berg, Lucía Guerra, Nina Scott, and Lee Skinner. Jiménez 1999b and Campuzano 1997 contain studies on Acosta de Samper, as does González Ascorra 1997. See also Ordóñez and Osorio 1997, a collection of critical studies.

19. A fully reproduced digital and searchable online edition of the original 1895 edition of *La mujer en la sociedad moderna* is available online at http://books.google.com.

20. At the time of writing Gómez de Avellaneda is the woman writer appearing most frequently on the Ph.D. and master's reading lists of top-ten-ranking programs in Hispanic literature in the United States, according to the latest available data from the *Gourman Report* (Gourman 1996), whereas many of the works by women writers listed in this section are rarely considered required reading (although this is changing over time, as scholars highlight women writers' central importance in filling in the gaps of the male-dominated canon in terms of nationhood, national identity,

taking on the onus of defending women's intellect and autonomy early in the century. Although she is best known for her 1841 abolitionist novel *Sab* (a passionate defense of the virtuous and noble character of a mixed-race slave), her 1843 novel *Dos mujeres* (Two Women), originally banned from Latin America for presenting an illicit love, is an unambiguous championing of a talented, beautiful, intellectual, and fiercely independent woman who is scorned by society for her relationship with a married man. Insightful book-length critical studies exist on Gómez de Avellaneda's work, such as Beatriz Pastor's *Fashioning Feminism in Cuba and Beyond: The Prose of Gertrudis Gómez de Avellaneda* and Florinda Álzaga's *La Avellaneda: Intensidad y vanguardia*, as well as dozens of critical articles.[21] There is still much work to be done on this prolific and brilliant writer; in particular, her numerous plays, which were performed in Madrid to rave reviews, have received little critical attention.[22]

Two significant women novelists from Puerto Rico have gained some critical recognition over the past two decades. Over the course of her long life, Carmela Eulate Sanjurjo (1871–1961) produced seven novels, twelve biographies, thirteen essays, a collection of short stories, a book of poetry, and twenty translations (Jiménez 1999, 181). Like her contemporary and compatriot Ana Roqué, she was a firm supporter of and activist for women's suffrage and equality, as well as a defender of women's ability to form part of the intellectual elite. The only work of Eulate Sanjurjo's that has received significant attention is *La muñeca* (The Doll [1895]), a story that criticizes the superficial, vain socialite who lives only to maintain her good looks and manipulate those around her. Roqué, the subject of Chapters 5 and 6 of this study, established several schools, scholarships, and vocational programs for girls as well as a feminist periodical, *La Mujer* (Woman). Her scholarly interests were varied, ranging from the natural sciences to literature, and she

---

and cultural meaning). In several cases, she was the only woman writer listed as required reading in the nineteenth century. Her poetry and her 1841 abolitionist novel, *Sab*, are often included in the nineteenth-century sections of general anthologies and literary histories of Latin American literature.

21. For further reading on Gómez de Avellaneda, see Araujo 1993; González Ascorra 1997; Guerra 1985, 1987a, 1987b; S. Kirkpatrick 1990; LaGreca 2006a, 2006b, 2007; Lindstrom 2007; Picón Garfield 1992.

22. Another eloquent and aristocratic Cuban-born woman whose work merits brief mention is María de las Mercedes Santa Cruz y Montalvo, la condesa de Merlín (countess of Merlín, 1789–1852), as she is known in Spanish. La condesa de Merlín published her memoirs and travel narratives, originally written in French. The work most often studied is the 1844 travel narrative of her return visit to Cuba after several decades living in Europe, *Viaje a la Habana* (Voyage to Havana). Several works of importance have been published concerning this fascinating historical figure in recent years, including Méndez Rodenas 1998; Campuzano 1997, 2004; and Molloy 1996.

published nonfiction books on geography, botany, grammar, and pedagogy that were used for many years in Puerto Rico. Her best-known work of fiction is the 1903 novel *Luz y sombra,* under consideration in Chapters 5 and 6 of this study. She also published several collections of short stories that, unfortunately, are not available in recent editions as of this writing.

Considering the central place of Mexican literature in the history of Latin American letters, the dearth of information available on nineteenth-century Mexican women prose writers merits correction.[23] Ana Rosa Domenella and Nora Pasternac's collection of critical studies and anthologized writings *Las voces olvidadas* is an important step toward filling this gap.[24] The collection contains one of the few essays on Barragán, along with some of her prose selections, and also points out several of her contemporaries who were accomplished writers during their time. Barragán is the earliest novelist Domenella and Pasternac list, while María Néstora Téllez Rendón (1828–1887) is the second woman known to have published a novel, *Staurofila, precioso cuento alegórico* (Staurofila, a Valuable Allegorical Tale) in 1889. Téllez Rendón was a blind schoolteacher, and *Staurofila* was a didactic tale that she told her students. The literary critic Gloria María Prado recognizes elements of Romanticism as well as mysticism and biblical allusions in the narrative, which features a female character, Staurofila, who is compared to both Eve and the Virgin Mary in the burdens she must bear (1991, 38). The Mexican prose writer and poet Laura Méndez de Cuenca (1853–1928) is not studied today; outside Domenella and Pasternac's compilation there are very few sources available on her. However, Méndez de Cuenca was an established member of intellectual circles in her time. She attended the meetings of the Ateneo de la Juventud (Athenaeum of Youth), a Mexican intellectual group that formed as a reaction against the Positivism of the Porfirio Díaz dictatorship, and made the acquaintance of many young writers and intellectuals of her day, including the Mexican poet Manuel Acuña (Domenella, Gutiérrez de Velasco, and Pasternac 1991, 118). She published essays and poetry in Mexico's most important newspapers and served as professor and director of the normal school of Toluca. Her publications include a "novela de costumbres mexicanas" (novel of Mexican customs),

---

23. Although she was not a novelist, Laureana Wright de Kleinhans (Mexico, 1846–96) deserves mention for starting two important feminist journals in Mexico that advocated women's suffrage and equality, *Violetas de Anáhuac* (Violets of the Anáhuac, 1884) and *Mujeres de Anáhuac* (Women of the Anáhuac, 1887).

24. Other women writers in Domenella and Pasternac's study either published their work after about 1910 or wrote in genres other than the novel.

El espejo de Amarilis (Amarilis's Mirror [1902]), and a collection of short stories, *Simplezas* (Simplicities [1910]), which is a series of seventeen short stories that are dated between 1890 and 1909. The short fictions focus on the dark side of a woman's existence and, in line with the dates of the writing, harbor influence from Naturalism and some momentary shades of *modernismo*.

The current state of the field shows a marked concentration of nineteenth-century women writers hailing from the Southern Cone and the Caribbean. It is possible that women in the mining nations of South America and in the international port cities of the Caribbean enjoyed more cultural exposure than those in other regions, thereby gaining greater access to novels, theater, and opera (several of high culture's forms of storytelling). However, this hypothesis does not explain the scarcity of information on women prose fiction writers from Mexico, as Mexico City, along with Buenos Aires, was a principal literary center in the late nineteenth century. It is likely that texts by Central American and Mexican women writers exist and have yet to be discovered by scholars. Certainly there is more archival work to be done to locate and evaluate texts by early women writers who have been forgotten over time.

The objective of the study at hand is to bring back into focus the work of three writers from three different regions of Latin America who were widely read in their countries of origin and to trace the surprising overlaps in the symbolic rewritings of womanhood through their prose. The particular novels I have chosen by Barragán, Cabello, and Roqué lend themselves to deciphering the ways in which these writers manipulated specific aspects of the Angel of the House in order to expand definitions of womanhood so to include agency, wit, intellect, and the freedom to act on one's desires without invoking society's scorn. These similarities serve as evidence of thinking women's desires to criticize, each in her own way, the ubiquitous Angel of the House as a damaging national model put forth for women separated by thousands of miles, yet united by the gender politics and ideology of their day.

Author and Text: The Unconscious and the Symbolic in *La hija del bandido, Blanca Sol,* and *Luz y sombra*

Although archivists in the state of Jalisco, Mexico, recognize the value of Barragán's novel *La hija del bandido* (1887) and published a local limited edition in 2004 and despite the fact that she is, at the time of writing, the earliest woman known to have written a novel in Mexico, Barragán is mostly absent from mainstream and feminist scholarship alike.[25] The same can be said of Roqué's *Luz y sombra* (1903); fortunately, Lizabeth Paravisini-Gebert's 1994 critical edition of *Luz y sombra* includes a rigorous introductory study and analysis. Since the dawn of the twenty-first century, Cabello has received increasing critical attention, particularly because of her use of Naturalism for feminist ends. Scholars such as Oswaldo Voysest, Lucía Guerra, Juan Armando Epple, Ana Peluffo, and Gonzáles Ascorra have published compelling studies on Cabello's novels.[26] A scholarly edition of *Blanca Sol* (1888), with a critical introduction by María Cristina Arambel-Guiñazú, was published in 2004 and another appeared in 2007 with an introduction by Voysest.

What distinguishes these novels from others by Latin American women authors from the nineteenth century is not that their primary focus is to propose or amend nationalist agenda, or to present a purely didactic story to young readers, but rather that they are more concerned with the identity politics of women. The division that I indicate is not black and white, as we know that national and private agendas overlap in subtle and intricate ways in novels of the period; however, one may speak of certain qualities that the novels of Barragán, Cabello, and Roqué share. While their subject matter may include messages that underline a need for social reform, specific sociopolitical issues are not the primary focus of their narratives and are not addressed overtly, as they are, for example, in the novels of Matto de Turner, who wrote in opposition to clerical exploitation and in defense of indigenous Peruvians, and in the work of Gorriti, whose fiction points out the need to reform women's material well-being or criticizes the Argentine dictatorship of Juan Manuel de Rosas by emphasizing the suffering of women and children. The novels of Barragán, Cabello, and Roqué offer three excellent, clear examples of novels by women writers that focus on the sociology and psychology of a central protagonist, rather than on their place in geopolitics; these authors have chosen to imagine alternatives to women's roles and feminized identities in a world that has not yet admitted them.[27] That is not to say that other women writers were not concerned with identity and gender

---

25. María Zalduondo's 2001 study of Barragán is the only in-depth work available at the time of writing. Zalduondo's scholarly edition of *La hija del bandido* (2007) is a readily available, glossed edition of the novel.

26. For an overview of criticism on Cabello, see Chapter 3 of this study.

27. Feminist literary scholarship on Latin American writing in the past twenty-five years has productively explored the role of women writers in the formation of a national identity. Jean Franco's (1989) *Plotting Women* is a cross-temporal study of women's struggle for interpretive power in Mexico.

politics, but rather that Barragán, Cabello, and Roqué offer up heroines who challenge very specific tenets of the Angel of the House, inviting readers to reimagine their prescribed roles and assert themselves as individuals.

By writing in a subversive and circuitous manner, Barragán, Cabello, and Roqué participated in the ongoing effort by women writers of the last quarter of the nineteenth century to insert their own ideals of womanhood into mainstream culture. Speaking to the reader's unconscious, they sought to imagine new women's voices and to tell of new dreams in poetic form so that they, like the repressed material of the dream, could force their existence into consciousness.[28] Logic tells us that these authors, aware of the negative criticism

---

It focuses on the nation-building process from the Aztec Empire through the modernization of Mexico. Franco analyzes the silencing effect of nationalism on women's writing and intellectual activity and the ways in which women represented themselves as gendered subjects in the construction of national identity. Also regarding women novelists and prose writers in Mexico, Domenella and Pasternac's (1991) aforementioned compilation of critical studies *Las voces olvidadas* is an important addition to the literature; it includes essays by various literary critics on little-known women writers, along with excerpts of their fiction and essays. Argentine women authors of the nineteenth century have enjoyed more critical attention in recent years than those of any other country in Spanish America. There are three major critical works on women's writing in Argentina, probably the result of the rediscovery of texts by Argentine authors such as Gorriti (1819–92), Eduarda Mansilla de García (1838–92), and Manso (1819–75). In *Between Civilization and Barbarism*, Francine Masiello, like Franco, is interested in women's "struggle for access to the symbolic realm that determines the cultural imagination of a nation" (1992, 2). The volume covers the early nineteenth century up to the 1930s. Lea Fletcher's (1994) compilation *Mujeres y cultura en la Argentina del siglo XIX* (Women and Culture in Nineteenth-Century Argentina) includes literary as well as sociological studies; the first part of her study focuses on women writers and their texts, while the second part contains studies on women's social, political, and cultural context in nineteenth-century Argentina. The authors in Fletcher's compilation analyze themes in women's fiction and poetry discuss biographical elements of their writing, and explore the place of the woman writer in the literary history of Argentina. Bonnie Frederick's (1998) *Wily Modesty* identifies women's construction of an authorial self that pretends to take on the self-abnegating role of the Angel of the House to appease male critics—a strategy that Barragán, Cabello, and Roqué also employ to greater or lesser degrees. Frederick believes that the strategy of "wily modesty" enabled women to have a better chance of forming part of the national literature. She terms this tactic "speaking up with eyes lowered" and the "rhetoric of femininity" (11). Frederick examines how male critics' reception of women's writing led to the marginalization of women authors by excluding them from the canon. One of the more recent studies on a nineteenth-century woman writer is Anna Peluffo's (2005) monograph *Lágrimas andinas: Sentimentalismo, género y virtud republicana en Clorinda Matto de Turner* (Andean Tears: Republican Sentimentalism, Gender, and Virtue in Clorinda Matto de Turner). Peluffo's project examines how Matto de Turner employs sentimentalism to insert her concerns regarding the status of women and indigenous peoples into the national discussions of social policies in Peru.

28. Psychoanalytic theory provides tools to discover desires and intentions in narrative and makes a viable connection between the unconscious and language; thus it has much to offer in the search to uncover women intellectuals' symbolic battles. Freud's chapters in his 1904 *Psychopathology of Everyday Life* reflect an inseparable link between words and the unconscious; he grapples with

and scorn their critiques of society could provoke, did not voice their concerns directly. Yet their narratives show how concerns regarding women's place in the symbolic order are subtly woven into the authors' discourses, paralleling the way our unconscious weaves our everyday worries into our mental narratives while we sleep.[29] Just as our dreams offer cues from the unconscious that we do not have during waking hours that can help us to decipher the nature of our desires and fears, these women authors give their readers subtle cues to facilitate the liberation of women through development of their identities.

The various types of theory that inform my literary analyses (psychoanalytic, philosophical, anthropological, and so on) help reveal how Barragán, Cabello, and Roqué highlight and deconstruct the myths behind traditional visions of female identity, as they move to designate the unspoken senses of the semiotic.[30] The historical context of each writer is also an integral part

---

subconscious meaning of forgetting proper names, foreign words, and word order, as well as other types of mistakes in speech, reading, and writing (Freud 1994, 3–55). As Lacan reminds us, dreams have the structure of a form of writing, and in adults reproduce the "simultaneously phonetic and symbolic use of signifying elements, which can also be found in the hieroglyphs of ancient Egypt and in the characters still used in China" (1977, 57). The connection between the symbols of the written language and the hidden desires of dreams is apparent in Freud's and Lacan's thought; writing can structure the unconscious workings of the mind and also serve as a medium by which the unconscious is expressed. Lacan further lists many rhetorical tools of literature that reveal the intentions of oneiric discourse, in which desires are expressed: "Ellipsis and pleonasm, hyperbaton or syllepsis, regression, repetition, apposition—these are the syntactical displacements; metaphor, catachresis, autonomasis, allegory, metonymy, and synecdoche—these are the semantic condensations in which Freud teaches us to read the intentions—ostentatious or demonstrative, dissimulating or persuasive, retaliatory or seductive—out of which the subject modulates his oneiric discourse" (58). Twentieth-century feminist theorists have criticized Freud and Lacan for ignoring female sexuality or aligning it with a phallocentric notion of sexuality, for example, Freud's concept of penis envy. Luce Irigaray's (1985) *Speculum of the Other Woman* is just one example of this critique. Here I use Freud and Lacan's elaborations on the subject and language to explore the parallels between the unconscious mind and writing. For theories of feminine desire I draw on Julia Kristeva's thought later in the study, as Freud and Lacan have limited use in this area.

29. Lacan and Kristeva refer to the shared social understanding as the *symbolic order:* a realm or discourse of spoken and written language which, more broadly, includes sets of social as well as linguistic signs. Lacan discusses the symbolic in his lecture "On a Question Preliminary to Any Possible Treatment of Psychosis" (1977, 180–97). For more on Kristeva's view of the symbolic order, see selections from "Women's Time" (Kristeva 1986, 199–200). The symbolic order is a system of signs in which the women writers I study here hope to participate and alter. This symbolic system known as the symbolic order is different from Foucault's definition of discourse, for example, in that it not only comprises print culture, social gestures, and art, but also broader symbolic signs such as the placement of bodies in society (such as the number of female bodies in the senate or the fact that women are free to walk in public spaces).

30. For an overview of current feminist theory written by U.S. and Latin American Hispanists and a discussion of current debates on the application of foreign theory to Latin American texts, see LaGreca 2006.

of this exploration. In the chapters that follow we will see how these authors subvert the traditional myths of the symbolic order and replace them with new visions of women that can move out from individual (female) subjects' isolated imaginaries into the symbolic order in general.

Obstacles to the Reading of Nineteenth-Century Female Subjectivity

There are several problems associated with the project of deducing female subjectivity from texts. The first, and most obvious, problem for modern readers is trying to reach across temporal and cultural boundaries to reveal notions of identity and uncover what we think authors wanted to express. Frederick and the critic Janet Todd, among others, have voiced this concern when looking at women's writing from the nineteenth century. The logical solution is to use the tools we have at our disposal: the fictional text and historical documents. Working from the text and available historical and social documents puts the reader back in touch with an 1800s reality and provides insight into the writer's position as an intellectual female subject who grappled with imposed limitations.

A second concern for feminist literary critics is the problem of generalizing a concept of female identity to an entire culture. The critical theorist Denise Riley challenges the overgeneralization of the term *woman* in her 1988 critical feminist work *Am I That Name?* while theorist Judith Butler's *Gender Trouble* reminds us that gender itself is a complex and constantly evolving situation that cannot be divorced from its political and cultural setting. I do not attempt to discover a single, unified, coherent type of womanhood put forth by Spanish American women, as Gilbert and Gubar have done in the case of nineteenth-century British women's writing.[31] Perhaps more fitting to analysis of one country's literature, such generalizations would level the specific internal histories of the various countries in which my authors lived. However, it is possible to use theory to uncover the strategies of reconstruction of female identity from a specific cultural context. While I use the Angel of the House as a common theme that allows comparisons between the works, I look at how the trope is manipulated differently in each particular context and in light of each country's history.

---

31. See Gilbert and Gubar 1979.

Chapter Summaries

Rewriting Womanhood tells a story about the plight of real women and the writers who attempted to better their lives through fiction; the real women and the fiction, then, are two sides of the same coin. I have included two chapters for each novel that I explore: one on the history of women in the country and time period of each author and the second on the imaginary early feminist journey brought to life in the novels.

Chapter 1 reveals Mexican women's domestic seclusion and limited opportunities for intellectual growth in Porfirian Mexico (1876–1911). This overview sheds light on the theme of exuberant freedom and travel in Refugio Barragán's *La hija del bandido*. This lively novel presents the coming-of-age ritual (the fifteenth birthday, or *quinceañera*) as a catalyst for agency, rebellion against the father, and the heroic acts of a girl dynamo.

The advancement of women's education in nineteenth-century Peru was a precarious project that seemed to change with every new political wave, yet never seemed to set sail. Understanding this historical context (the topic of Chapter 3) brings into focus Cabello's literary project, which focuses on women's paltry education, in *Blanca Sol*. On a symbolic level Cabello's narrative manipulates the patriarchal trappings of the Cinderella fairy tale to blur the boundaries between female "virtue" and "evil" in a more humanizing way, while emphasizing the role of proper education in determining these traits in both sexes. Agency and desire also play a central role in the development of Cabello's intriguing title character.

The historical and cultural story of colonial Puerto Rico and Ana Roqué's novel *Luz y sombra* are the subjects of Chapters 5 and 6. In Chapter 5, I outline the social policies in Puerto Rico that focused on repressing and containing women's bodies. Roqué's discursive efforts to legitimize female desire and pleasure in a symbolic order that marginalized and pathologized the sexualized female body respond to these repressive social practices.

To conclude my discussion, I point to certain generalities and differences characterizing the fight for identity and agency shared by these women in Latin American fiction. By discovering the ways in which Latin American women authors between 1887 and 1903 conceived and strategically wrote alternative creations of female subjectivity, we can begin to define a formalized, specifically Latin American brand of feminism for a modern era that was in germination in the second half of the nineteenth century and flowered over the following decades.

In the analyses that follow, images of fictional women are subversive alternatives to those in predominant literature of the period. These distortions of mainstream womanhood redefine *female subjectivity* because they rewrite the process of creating an individual as an imagined subject within an alternative social formation. The formation of such a subject, according to Lacan, occurs when an individual confronts and learns to deal with others or a symbolic other (an other in the mind or social consciousness, also denoted by Other, or *grande Autre*).[32] This is precisely the process that women writers undergo when they confront the ethereal specter of the Angel of the House, as we shall discover.

32. As his translator Alan Sheridan notes, Lacan avoids defining terms explicitly in his writings and lectures and instead lets the reader gather meaning from the use of the terms in context (Lacan 1977, vii). For this reason, and the complexity of the writings, secondary sources on Lacan are very useful. I suggest Grosz 1990 and the introductions by Juliet Mitchell and Jacqueline Rose to Lacan 1982. For the novice Lacanian scholar, Leader and Groves 1998 gives a basic outline of Lacanian principles and terms, complete with illustrations. For a postmodern perspective that mixes interpretations of Alfred Hitchcock with Lacanian theory, see Žižek 1992a or 1992b. For a Lacanian interpretation of desire and historicism, see Copjec 1994.

1

WOMEN'S IMAGINED ROLES IN NINETEENTH-CENTURY MEXICO: SECLUSION IN THE MIDST OF PROGRESS AND EARLY FEMINIST REACTIONS

BETWEEN 1810 AND 1821, women in Mexico temporarily put aside their primary duties as wives and mothers to take part in the Wars of Independence. Wartime provided an opportunity for women to break out of their domestic routines in order to work for a higher cause: freeing New Spain. The scholar of Chicana studies Elizabeth Salas in her book on *soldaderas* (women soldiers) in the Mexican military has found that women participated in the struggle for independence by fighting in battle as well as serving as spies, caretakers of soldiers, providers of provisions, recruitment agents, and financial contributors.[1] Women were also deployed as "seductresses" by both the royalists and freedom fighters to seduce the opponent's troops into deserting and joining the opposing army (Kentner 1975, 92). According to Salas, Mexican women put the frustration borne of their limited options and rights into the war effort, and thereby hoped to prove themselves strong, capable citizens to be taken seriously as part of the new national project (1990, 26). Although the efforts of some wealthy donors would be rewarded with gifts of property after the victory was won, most women who helped directly or indirectly in the battles found their situations did not change very much in the new republic and, in some ways, worsened over the course of the nineteenth century.

Mexico's founding fathers drew up the Mexican Federal Republic's constitution in 1824. The decades that followed brought a succession of internal struggles for power as well as foreign interventions. The United States

---

1. A comparison with the participation of women in Peruvian independence, outlined in Chapter 3 of this study, will show that Peru's "gentle sex" participated in wartime activities similar to those of women in Mexico. The historian Evelyn Cherpak's findings add further evidence of widespread activity by women in the wars of independence. Cherpak's case study of Gran Colombia (a colonial territory that is today Colombia; Venezuela; Ecuador; Panama; and parts of Costa Rica, Peru, Brazil, and Guyana) reveals that, as in Mexico and Peru, women took part in combat, espionage, missions to aid troops, nursing those injured in battle, and hosting meetings. They also donated their wealth and supplies (1978, 220).

invaded Mexico between 1846 and 1848 and took a wide expanse of its northern territories, which today make up a large part of the western and southwestern United States, while France under Napoleon III invaded and overthrew the liberal Mexican president Benito Juárez to instill the French emperor Maximilian from 1864 to 1867. This instability would subside for a time beginning in 1876, the date that marked the tenure of José de la Cruz Porfirio Díaz in power.

During the Porfiriato (the term used to refer to the presidency of Díaz) foreign firms built railroads, bridges, and a telegraph system, while Mexican- and foreign-owned factories imported machinery to raise the level of production of goods to European and U.S. standards.[2] In part because of the reduction of the national debt, and apparent political stability, Mexico played a more visible role in the international arena. International recognition was manifested in an increase in trade and diplomacy, which in turn led to a growing cultural sophistication and cosmopolitanism in urban centers. The opening of national and cultural borders brought in examples of mobile and independent women travelers from the United States and Europe.

Foreigners came to Mexico in large numbers for business, diplomatic service, and adventure (Meyer and Sherman 1991, 450). Mexico, in turn, went abroad, ideologically and literally. Díaz's group of advisors and politicians (called the *científicos,* because they followed various forms of the scientifically driven social philosophy Positivism) emulated the French technocratic republic for modernization. The word *afrancesamiento* (which means "Francophilia") was used to refer to Mexico's and many other Spanish American countries' eye toward French philosophy, science, medicine, fashion, art, and architecture.[3] In Mexico French influence was not just an abstract trend; it had a concrete legacy that came from the French occupation midcentury. Being a member of the Mexican elite effectively meant having a French education, either through attending school in France or receiving an education in French arts, letters, and sciences elsewhere. The new nation was reaching out internationally to establish itself within Western modernity, and France was the center for the arts and, along with the United States, scientific and sociopolitical thought.

---

2. The Mexican president José de la Cruz Porfirio Díaz lived from 1830 to 1915 and ruled for two terms, 1876–80 and 1884–1911.

3. Mexico's officials did not, however, share French leaders' preoccupation with workers' conditions. Tenorio-Trillo notes that during the World's Fair in Paris of 1889, France's congresses on social issues were sparsely attended by Mexican representatives (1996, 24).

While cosmopolitanism and major improvements in the national economy and infrastructure were appearing, Mexico's urban centers suffered the common ills of modernization: wide-scale disenfranchisement of the masses and a decline in the living conditions of the working classes. The alleged progress of the Porfirian era almost exclusively benefited a growing bourgeoisie and the elite. Agricultural and urban workers suffered in abject poverty, while signs of wealth sprang up in urban centers, particularly in Mexico City. To achieve the appearance of peace necessary for such developments, Díaz used the military and police to crush opposition and to keep bandits in check so as to make cities and roadways as safe as possible.[4] Minimizing crime in Mexico City and maintaining a semblance of safety were imperative for attracting foreign investors and creating the appearance of a stable democracy. Díaz's political corruption and his administration's efforts to concentrate wealth in the upper classes, among other causes, led to the Mexican Revolution, which ousted him in 1911.

As Mexican society became more cosmopolitan, a smattering of education for well-heeled women that did not emphasize critical thinking continued to be regarded as a prestigious reflection on their husbands. Within the role of model homemaker, perceived to be of utmost social importance, women were meant to be somewhat cultivated, yet largely unthinking, domestic beings who served as paragons of morality and propriety for their children. Hence a common characteristic of feminine education in all classes was that it was conceived to reflect well upon or provide utility to others, rather than built on developing areas of interest for women's growth as individuals; for example, a woman's fine piano playing could add prestige to her father's or future husband's home, but the moment it began to interfere with the care of her children or domestic responsibilities, she was viewed as faltering in her role and ceased to live up to the self-abnegating ideal of the Angel of the House. The development of one's abilities as an autonomous agent who thinks critically, acts upon society, and engages in public life was reserved for upper-class men, as women were thought to be too delicate and incapable of such activity.

This view of women as industrious yet ornamental keepers of the home did not arise in the Porfiriato; colonial Mexico's first novelist, José Joaquín Fernández Lizardi (1776–1827), recognized and criticized the superficiality of women's academic formation in the early 1800s in his novel *La educación*

---

4. For historical information on bandits in Porfirian Mexico and for an analysis of their role in Barragán's novel, see Zalduondo 2001.

de las mujeres o la Quijotita y su prima: Historia muy cierta con apariencias de novela (The Education of Women or the Quijotita and Her Cousin: A Very True Story That Resembles a Novel [1818]). Although Lizardi believed that women could be useful outside the home, he still envisioned limited roles: "reconoce en las mujeres dones administrativos y manuales, pero no intelectuales, y jamás se le ocurre proponerles ejercer las profesiones liberales ni adquirir un saber de tipo intellectual" (Carner 1987, 104) [he recognizes administrative and manual talent in women, but not intellectual talents, and never would it occur to him to propose that they pursue professions in the liberal arts or acquire intellectual knowledge]. Dominant discourses consistently portrayed the woman intellectual as a selfish person who would end up unhappy. In 1856 an anonymous writer published an overtly misogynist article in the newspaper *El Monitor Republicano* (The Republican Monitor), in which he mockingly critiques *talentacias* (bluestockings), intellectually curious women, who "eat little, pay no attention to their appearance, constantly bemoan the ignorance of the masses, and consider themselves unfortunate because one lifetime is not enough to read even a millionth part of what has been written" (quoted in Macías 1982, 16). This was clearly a reference to the growing number of women who were interested in education instead of, or in addition to, becoming self-sacrificing housewives. Similarly, in 1894 the Mexican modernist poet Manuel Gutiérrez Nájera satirizes a young woman from the University of Cambridge for winning a mathematics competition, in which she excelled over all her male colleagues: "Esa laureada señorita no se casará," he explains, because "una esposa fuerte en multiplicación es un peligro" (quoted in Zalduondo 2001, 44) [This celebrated young woman will not marry; a woman strong in multiplication is a danger]. As Zalduondo reminds us, his words bring to mind a Spanish saying of unknown origin: "Mujer que sabe Latín, ni encuentra marido, ni tiene buen fin" (The woman who knows Latin does not find a husband, nor does she come to a good end). Although the poet's words may not indicate his personal opinion, they mark the unease with which many men of the era viewed exceptionally intelligent women—women who were not just bright or witty in social exchanges, but who carried out notable, extradomestic accomplishments (45).

Women's participation in the workforce and access to public schooling in the Porfirian era were invariably a function of hegemonic ideas of national progress. For instance, if girls' elementary education improved, it was to proliferate prudent and decisive, rather than frivolous and materialistic, mothers of future generations (Macías 1982, 8). As the historian Françoise

Carner puts it, it was assumed that "las mujeres educadas, especialmente las de las clases altas, proporcionarán a la sociedad dentro del rol de educadoras activas e ilustradas de sus hijos, una base sólida para la socialización adecuada de éstos y la transmisión de los valores sociales y morales, y el progreso de la nación" (1987, 104) [educated women, especially those of the upper classes, in their roles as active educators and enlighteners of their children, would offer a solid base for their appropriate socialization, the transmission of moral and social values, and the progress of the nation]. If women entered the workforce, it was because low-paid labor was needed for office work and other menial or time-consuming labor that did not yield high income and was not intellectually stimulating; as men generally sought work with higher pay to support their families than what this "feminine" work provided, women's participation in the workforce was not considered a competitive threat to men, and thus their exit from the home was tolerated to some extent (10).[5] My point here is that bourgeois women, like working-class Mexicans, were generally considered tools of the Porfirian push toward progress, which benefited a small elite and foreign investors. As one historian simply communicates, the "condition of women was . . . a concern that Mexican Científicos did not seriously consider" (Tenorio-Trillo 1996, 24). In the section on antifeminist discourse, we see that Díaz's advisors, the *científicos,* were indeed somewhat concerned with the status of female members of society—insofar as they attempted to maintain the angelic standard in the face of outside threats, such as suffrage and feminism.

The primary difference between women's roles before and after the Porfiriato is that in the last quarter of the century there was a surge in middle-class women working outside the home in low-level office and technical jobs. Another distinguishing characteristic of the Porfiriato was that education became more secular and women's legal rights and access to public education were reduced, as I will detail shortly. Particular effort was exerted to keep women from gaining equal footing with men socially, legally, and in the workplace. Political voice was completely out of women's reach as they, like women in many European and North American countries of the 1800s and early 1900s, were not allowed to vote or hold any type of government office.

5. For instance, Macías notes that during the Porfiriato, "women were especially encouraged to become primary schoolteachers, because teaching of young children required enormous dedication, but received minimal compensation" (1982, 10). She adds that elementary schoolteachers received less than two pesos per day, which was barely enough money to support one person without additional income from the woman's family (10).

The Porfiriato reversed gains in women's education, as a brief history of women's education during this period shows. Postindependence enlightenment ideals midcentury included women's education, which was generally limited to catechism, reading, writing, and some basic math (Carner 1987, 96). After years of considering the construction of a secondary school for girls in a changing political environment, liberals were finally able to open one in Mexico City in 1869 and several more like it in provincial areas in the next five years (Macías 1982, 10). The director of the schools heard demands from female students for courses of study in pharmacy, medicine, and other "masculine" professions, but these fields were not open to women. Many worked as schoolteachers and could be certified to teach secondary school.

As the century marched into the Porfirian era and Díaz and his *científicos* achieved progress in industry and trade, women's access to higher education was limited. The historian of women's culture in Mexico Anna Macías notes that after 1889, graduates of the women's Normal de Profesoras (Normal School) received two years fewer instruction than before 1889 and were licensed to teach only primary school, rather than primary and secondary, as had previously been the case (1982, 11). Macías finds that women's desire to study was strong; the number of female students willing to enroll in higher education consistently exceeded available spots and more than one thousand women were enrolled in vocational school by 1899. Despite women's diligence and demands for greater opportunities, the Porfiriato consistently limited its female citizens' access to higher-paying careers in the sciences and humanities, while primary teachers were not paid even enough to support one person (10–11). Apparently, for women, progress meant being sheltered from excessive knowledge and too much contact with "worldly seductions" (Moreno and Elizalde 1909, 150). Although several pioneering female scholars graduated from medical school and one from law school at the end of the century, these were the exceptions to the rule. (The law graduate received particular criticism, as there was actually a need for women doctors, but law was strictly controlled by men. She was forbidden to practice criminal law, because it was "improper," and alternatively, she concentrated on civil law [Macías 1982, 12].)

Ladies of the upper classes in the Porfirian era were prepared to be just cultivated enough to be able to carry on polite conversation without appearing ignorant and perhaps entertain guests by singing or playing a musical instrument; being mothers of future generations of ruling-class Mexicans meant having an ornamental education to make a favorable impression on visitors and reflect well on their families. They were literate and were taught embroidery and domestic arts and perhaps French or English; some literature; drawing, music, or both; and the basic notions of geography, geometry, and astronomy (Moreno and Elizalde 1909, 27).

It was commonly believed that providing a broad but very superficial education to women added prestige to the family. A cultivated young lady could attract a desirable suitor more easily than one who lacked social grooming, as this meant she could be a better role model for her children; a mother's positive influence was considered paramount to modernizing and advancing bourgeois society. Thus women's education was suited to fit their imagined social roles: "values that were deemed eternal in women [delicateness, moral superiority, and spirituality] were readapted to the specific needs of the moment" (Tuñón Pablos 1999, 47). Studies beyond the elementary levels were reserved for young men; as the overview of masculinist discourse on women will show, anything beyond a very basic education for women was considered not only improper, but also a burden to their minds and a first step toward worldly evil.

Early modernization required female labor, and women took underpaid jobs in textile and tobacco factories and, if more educated, as office workers, telegraph operators, schoolteachers, porcelain painters, or workers in photography (Carner 1987, 105; Ramos Escandón 1987b, 154–58). Although careers for women existed, it was still often viewed as inappropriate for them to work outside the home unless absolutely necessary for survival, as in the case of those who were widowed or were granted the rare ecclesiastic separation (which did not permit remarriage) and therefore did not have a man to support them.[6] Working women often faced criticism if they had small children, because it was considered immoral to neglect the foremost feminine duty of child care. So, although modernization's demand for cheap labor was in conflict to some degree with the Angel of the House by requiring women's work outside the home, the domestic model was still considered the most important ideal of womanhood for the nation.

Mexico's laws in the 1800s reflected and enforced the national ideology of the Angel of the House. In many respects, married women maintained "the legal status of minors," as often a woman could take legal action only with the

---

6. Although it would seem that the death of a separated woman's husband could free her to remarry, I did not find any information on this particular scenario.

consent of her husband (Ramos Escandón 1987b, 147).[7] In the 1850s, married women (unlike minors), did, however, have the power to bequeath their property or take authority away from their husbands if it could be proved that the latter were mishandling their wives' money (Arrom 1985, 73). Women could use the recourse of ecclesiastic separation to distance themselves physically and legally in extreme cases, such as in instances of harsh physical abuse, forced prostitution, or the threat of contracting an incurable disease (such as leprosy) or if the man was a "pagan," but they could not remarry (206–8).[8] Note that, except in extreme cases, a man's infidelity was not a reason for separation.

Despite minor rights for female citizens, the Civil Code of 1870 legally enforced the tenet of wifely submission: in return for protection and economic support, the Code specified that a wife's obligation was to "obedecer a su marido así en lo doméstico como en la educación de los hijos y la administración de los bienes" (Civil Code of 1870 quoted in Ramos Escandón 1987b, 147) [obey her husband in domestic concerns as well as in their children's education and in the administration of property].

Women lost legal control over their property under Porfirio Díaz. The Napoleonic Civil Code of 1884 "deprived married women of any rights to administer or dispose of their personal property" and "married women . . . could not take part in civil suits, draw up any legal contract, or even defend themselves against husbands who squandered their money" (Macías 1982, 15). In response to the limitations on women's rights the Mexican law student Genaro García, who would later go on to become an important advocate for women's rights, presented his thesis "La desigualdad de la mujer" (The Inequality of Women) in 1891. García summed up women's legal situation by stating that the law maintained married women in the status of "imbecilitas sexus" (quoted in Macías 1982, 13) [an imbecile by reason of her sex].

The second half of the nineteenth century saw few advancements for single women. Widows had the greatest legal and financial freedom, as they had full control over their property and children upon the death of a

---

7. Arrom has specified the legal differences in some detail between the status of minors, slaves, and women under the law in Mexico through the middle of the 1800s (1985, 53–97). Although she argues that women were perceived as more deserving of rights than were slaves and children; that single women were released from their fathers' legal control, or *potestas* (93); and that women of all civil statuses were given more authority over their children in the 1850s, ultimately, married women were still subordinate under the law to their husbands in most cases. After the 1850s, however, under Porfirio Díaz's Napoleonic civil codes, women lost many of the rights that Arrom discusses, as I mention in the body of this chapter.

8. For detailed information on marriage and separation in the mid-nineteenth century in Mexico, see Arrom 1985, 206–58.

husband. (It is not surprising, then, that Barragán and Cabello, who were both forward-thinking writers in terms of women's personal liberties, were both widowed at a young age, while Roqué separated from her husband early on.) In the 1850s, single adult women were legally released from their fathers' authority and given control over children and, later, were granted rights similar to those of adult males in the Civil Code of 1884 (Macías 1982, 13). Despite these gains, economically and socially life without a male head of household must have been very difficult, given society's emphasis on marriage and chastity, combined with the financial burden of having to support oneself and perhaps a family on a woman's meager income. It would appear that under such a civil code, heiresses would also enjoy a high degree of personal autonomy, although it is likely that social pressure to marry would have been great (especially if the heiress could form part of a favorable family union to ensure the consolidation of wealth).

Virtue, for women, was an oppressive burden, and yet it was also a key to some small amount of authority in the general scheme of things. Moral goodness was one area in which women were generally perceived to excel over men; women could be more authoritative in spiritual concerns, charity, and sexual restraint. However, fixing inflexible roles for women within the angelic model, which focused on their reproductive capacity and sexual fidelity, was also a way of attempting to maintain patriarchal control, according to Carner: "El tremendo poder de su sexualidad y de su papel reproductivo debe ser controlado para conservar el orden social dentro de los parámetros fijados por la sociedad" (1987, 97) [The tremendous power of [women's] sexuality and their reproductive role had to be controlled in order to maintain the social order within the parameters set by society]. Ultimately, feminine virtue was a crutch that women could use to argue cases for social rights or stake a claim for separation, but when a woman's virtue was questioned, she was in danger or losing her rights (for example, women who "engaged in improper sexual activity were denied protection from sexual crimes" [Arrom 1985, 79]).

In addition to limited access to education, minimal legal rights, and restrictive policies vis-à-vis female virtue, clothing trends may have been a vehicle for keeping women from cultivating self-fulfilling activities. The Scottish travel writer and wife of a Spanish diplomat Fanny Erskine Inglis Calderón de la Barca claimed that Mexican women's feet were squeezed into shoes so small that they restricted walking and dancing; this was apt to keep women from becoming too adventurous (quoted in Tuñón Pablos 1999, 56). Another reference to feet advocates limiting their use: one of the women's "ten commandments" of being good Angels of the House was

"Do not study more with one's feet than with one's head" (59). (Of course the reference to studying likely implied studying female-appropriate subjects such as catechism or hygiene.) These references link desirability and obedience with immobility. The Mexican historian Carmen Ramos Escandón (1987b) speaks of women's physical and ideological restrictions in terms of a "double corset": the article of clothing pinched her waist and limited her movement and spontaneity, while the ideological corset enforced a strict morality, which entailed taking responsibility for the actions of others as well as for her own behavior (153). The social evidence of women's enclosure to ensure virginity and limited access to the public sphere in the 1800s and early 1900s in Mexico make Barragán's interesting novel and ambulatory heroine all the more intriguing, as I will discuss in the following chapter.

Mexican women's unchaperoned travel was apparently so rare that there are only indirect references to this topic. It was considered unacceptable, a stain on a woman's virtue (Carner 1987, 97–99). According to Carner, men had three ways of controlling their women's sexual activity (thereby protecting their honor): "el encierro, el chaperon y la interiorización de las normas de conducta adecuadas" (97) [enclosure, chaperoning, and teaching women to internalize appropriate norms of conduct]. Proper women remained indoors or ventured out only with a respectable escort such as a parent or relative. The historian of gender in Latin America Nancy Van Deusen has found in the context of Lima that *recogimiento* (seclusion)

> implicaba tanto una conducta controlada y modesta como el encierro dentro de una institución o dentro del hogar, y una actitud retraída y quieta. . . . El recogimiento implicaba un dominio de la sexualidad y la conducta femenina, lo cual se podía lograr por medio del encierro institucional o el aislamiento dentro del hogar. Por consiguiente, el término implica que las libertades sociales y los cuerpos de las mujeres debían ser controlados. (1999, 39)

> [implied controlled conduct and modesty as much as it implied enclosure within an institution or the home and a submissive and quiet attitude. . . . This seclusion implied dominance over feminine sexuality and conduct, which could be achieved by way of institutional enclosure or isolation within the home. Consequently, the term implies that women's social liberties and bodies must be controlled.]

Van Deusen expresses in terms of social policy the restrictive stance toward women that limited their mobility. The institutions to which she refers were at the time probably convents and *beaterios* (reform homes, run by nuns, for women temporarily separated from their husbands during ecclesiastical conjugal trials or reform for prostitution).[9]

The domestic sphere was women's purported natural domain, and their lives "normally excluded travel" (Tuñón Pablos 1999, 49). This was generally true, regardless of the political background of a woman's husband or father: "The common domain for nineteenth-century Mexican women was the home: among . . . federalists and centralists, Liberals and Conservatives, women devoted their efforts to maintaining peace and order in the private sphere, to keeping the world of reproduction safe" (47). This sentiment is echoed repeatedly in the 1909 treatises I will examine shortly. We can gain a better idea of women's level of mobility (or lack thereof) by looking at contemporary essays on their place in society. First I will present some of the subversive claims on the symbolic order, which may have sparked the impassioned reactionary defenses of the angelic standard that I will be analyzing.

Early Feminist Projects and Foreign Women Travelers

Despite patriarchal culture's almost complete prohibition of women's participation in the public sphere, Porfirian progress needed its female citizens for the underpaid work of blue- and white-collar jobs in factories and businesses, and a few, as I mentioned, even entered the forbidden areas of law and medicine.[10] In the 1880s to the early 1900s, lower- and middle-class women entered the workforce by the thousands, thus becoming more aware of their role as earners and of the inequality between the sexes outside the home. It was from the ranks of this emerging sector of educated bourgeois women that early feminism arose in Mexico.

---

9. *Recogimiento* was also a term for houses that took in marginal women (Franco 1989, xvii).

10. Most ruling-class men, even progressive liberals, did not envision major changes in women's roles. Ignacio Ramón was a noteworthy exception; he was an early advocate of sexual equality who wrote in the 1860s. As was often the case (even with early female feminists), his vision still located women in the role of mothers, and he saw equal education as a way to ingrain the value of education into the minds of their children. Nonetheless, some of his ideas were radical for the times: he condemned women's objectification as "machines of pleasure" and a "positive piece of luxury furniture" and, most notably, advocated their becoming "equal to men in teaching posts, tribunals, at the rostrum and possibly even on the battlefields" (quoted in Tuñón Pablos 1999, 62). The idea of

Women's journals were an important outlet for early feminist concerns. Between 1870 and 1910 several important publications appeared. In 1870, Rita Cetina Gutiérrez published *La Siempreviva* (The Everlasting Flower), whose name connoted the tenacity of the movement in the face of patriarchal resistance, and in 1873 *Las Hijas de Anáhuac* (The Daughters of Anahuac) appeared, this periodical nationalistically named for the Anahuac Valley where Mexico City is located.[11] *Albúm de la Mujer: Periódico Redactado por Señoras* (The Women's Album: Newspaper Written by Ladies) circulated from 1883 to 1889 and was a venue through which women voiced the concerns of their sex. One pioneer of feminism was the poet Laureana Wright de Kleinhans (1846–1896), an early suffragist and advocate of equal rights for women. In the 1880s, Wright de Kleinhans founded the feminist publication *Violetas de Anáhuac* (Violets of Anahuac), in which she reported gains in women's rights in Wyoming, Arkansas, Kansas, and Mississippi (Alvarado 1991, 15).

These early attempts at a women's movement did not seek to change women's roles drastically, but did articulate demands for the right to secular education and greater social recognition. The writings and organizing efforts of the well-known British Positivist John Stuart Mill (the author of *Subjection of Women* [1869]) and pioneers of suffrage Elizabeth Cady Stanton and Susan B. Anthony "were not hidden from Mexican society" (Alvarado 1991, 11). They were likely role models that inspired Mexican women to take action for their own causes.

In the early 1900s, feminists in Mexico began to flesh out an agenda. The feminist journal *La Mujer Mexicana* (The Mexican Woman [1904–8]) was a major step for organizing bourgeois women to create an actual and symbolic community in which to speak about sexual inequality. The publication was started by three highly educated Mexican women: Dr. Columba Rivera (Mexico's second woman medical doctor), María Sandoval de Zarco (Mexico's first female civil lawyer), and the normal school teacher Dolores Correa Zapata. Although suffrage was still not on the list of rights

---

women interacting with men as equals was unusual for the times, given their official subordination to men under the law and in education. Of the areas Ramón mentions, only primary school education was an exemplary field for women. (Primary school teachers, as many scholars have noted, often received official praise for their self-abnegation and dedication—that is, they performed an important, work-intensive, and motherly job, for little money, and thus ideologically fit within the Angel of the House model.) Genaro García, whom I mentioned, was another male Mexican thinker concerned with women's legal equality in the 1890s.

11. Translations for the names of journals in this section (with the exception of *Albúm de la Mujer*) are taken from Tuñón Pablos 1999, 80–81.

that women demanded, the following were concerns that the women contributors to the journal voiced passionately: the right to a single sexual standard (legal recourse for wives against unfaithful husbands), reformation of the 1887 Civil Code to grant married women more legal control over their property and the ability to sue and make contracts, higher wages for women workers, and more training for women to earn their own livings and share in Porfirian progress (Macías 1982, 14–15).

Although these early feminist desires did *not* include women's abandoning their traditional roles (they still wanted to be good wives and mothers), one contributor to the periodical *La Mujer Mexicana* stated in 1904 that the idealization of bourgeois and elite women as selfless, dutiful, and good was not enough; they needed to be able to earn more income to support themselves without the help of a man, if necessary (Esther Huidobro de Azua quoted in Macías 1982, 14). Thus it is during this era that women were recognizing that the praise and idealization that ruling-class men bestowed upon them for self-abnegation was a substitute for paying them living wages, granting them civil rights, and enfranchising them into the public sphere. Women were getting wise to the detrimental myth of the "eterno femenino" (the eternal feminine), to employ a phrase that the twentieth-century Mexican feminist writer Rosario Castellanos would later use in her play of the same name to describe the phenomenon that, ideologically, put women on a symbolic pedestal as a substitute for granting them financial, legal, and civil opportunities equal to those of men.

New models for womanhood came from at home and abroad. An important difference in the landscape of Porfirian Mexico in comparison with previous decades of the nineteenth century was the increased presence of foreign, independent, and ambulatory women. The presence of the wives and daughters of foreign investors and diplomats in Mexico altered the symbolic order in ways that may have affected how Mexican women viewed womanhood.[12] It is likely that Barragán was aware of the rise in foreign travel because in *La hija del bandido* the narrator makes specific reference to the increase in the attendance of foreigners at festivals. Several of these women, including Frances Erskine Inglis Calderón de la Barca, Helen Sanborn, and Fanny Chambers Gooch, left written testimony of their experiences in Mexico. Their writings give us valuable insight into their own

---

12. According to June Hahner's research, Mexico and Brazil were the most frequented destinations for European and North American travel in Latin America in the later part of the nineteenth century.

experiences as women and into the lives of Mexican women (perspectives that male travel writers such as Alexander von Humboldt could not offer).[13] These women wrote about courtship rituals, convent life, gender roles, housekeeping, servants, and dress, as well as politics and local customs.

At the same time that foreign women were insisting on touring Mexican cities and going to the markets unchaperoned and then writing about the confinement of Mexican women, Barragán was dreaming up her own independent heroine. The scholar of travel writing and English literature Indira Ghose notes that travel writing "serves to circulate stereotypes and images of the other and actively participates in the production of knowledge and the dissemination of the effects of power," and in terms of its effect on the other, it "serves as a mirror held up to the self" (1998, 2). Thus, by the 1880s, when Barragán was imagining an active female adventurer for her novel, a small percentage of Mexico's learned female elite were imagining their own alternative roles for their sex (possibly galvanized in part by the presence of more independent foreign women). This early feminist activity did not go unnoticed; masculinist contestations with the intention of stagnating these early surges of feminism and maintaining traditional roles were well under way.

Ecclesiastic Reactions Against Feminism: The Catholic Discourse of Moreno and Elizalde

The publication *La mujer* (Woman [1909]) carries the seal of the secretariat of the archbishop of Mexico City, which meant that vast numbers of Mexican women loyal to the Catholic Church would have placed their trust in its contents. This document is relevant to the study at hand because it brings into stark relief that dominant discourses of so-called modernity, whether Positivist and secular or church approved, vehemently upheld the Angel of the House just as passionately as they admonished women for attempting to develop their intellects. The document appears to be epistolary correspondence between

---

13. In 1843 the Scottish wife of a diplomat, Erskine Inglis Calderón de la Barca, published a collection of her writings, titled *Life in Mexico*, some of which appeared in a Mexico City newspaper the same year. From the United States, the Wellesley graduate Sanborn traveled extensively in Mexico and Central America in the 1880s, and later helped found the Instituto Internacional language school in Madrid. Sanborn published *A Winter in Central America* in 1884. Her compatriot Chambers Gooch Iglehart lived in Mexico intermittently from 1880 to 1887 and authored *Face to Face with the Mexicans*, published in 1887, the same year as Barragán's novel.

the Mexican poet and intellectual Antonio de P. Moreno (who writes in a spiritual, Romantic style) and his young protégé Domingo Elizalde.[14] The collection of letters, which are not individually dated, seems rather to be a didactic manual written in epistolary form, although I was not able to determine whether the letters were authentic or invented.

In the epistolary dialogue, Moreno defends women in response to Elizalde's critiques of them. The point of the exchange is that the delicate sex is very easily influenced by men or God toward good, but is also extremely vulnerable to evil (Cepeda 1909, vii). Women's easily impressionable nature must be taken seriously, since, Moreno asserts, they exert a profound influence on society as mothers. Thus men bear the burden of defining models for them as "vírgenes . . . esposas . . . madres" (Cepeda 1909, viii) [virgins . . . wives . . . mothers]. According to Cepeda, a contemporary who wrote the introduction to *La mujer*, Moreno's letters are an "estudio concienzudo acerca de la mujer y de su misión en la tierra" (v) [conscientious study about woman and her mission on earth]. His statement indicates that the publication expressed common beliefs about female citizens and their social responsibilities in the early 1900s.

Elizalde takes, or at least initially pretends to take, a Positivist outlook toward women (his message later becomes heavily religious). He claims to "juzgarle desde un punto de vista real, positivo y desapasionado" (8) [judge them from a real, objective, and dispassionate perspective]. He will throw open the doors of women's domain, the home, and, he exclaims, "á la luz de una razón fría y reposada y de una filosofía inflexible y severa, busquemos la causa de los males que se han apoderado del sér débil" (10) [by the light of cold and calm reason and of a severe and inflexible philosophy, let us search for the causes of the evils that have overcome the weaker sex]. The severe, cold, inflexible philosophy to which Elizalde refers seems to be Positivism; the letters appear to be staged to criticize the anticlerical policies of the Positivists by presenting them as purely rational, unfeeling intellectuals. It is not surprising that the published letters would not favor a Positivist stance,

---

14. The following is an example of the flowery, metaphoric, poetic style that characterizes Moreno's discourse: "Esto ya es un buen principio, y casi estoy por creer que, al llegar al término de nuestra discusión, estaremos enteramente acordes en nuestro modo de pensar, como lo estuvimos antes de que tu alma impresionable apurara las primeras gotas de hiel en que mojaste tu pluma para escribirme la carta que tanta pena me causó" (13) [This is already a good beginning, and I am almost ready to believe that, upon arriving at the end of our discussion, our modes of thinking will be in agreement entirely, as it was before your impressionable soul consumed the first drops of bile, into which you dipped your pen in order to write me the letter that caused me so much pain].

since Porfirian *científicos* generally believed that religion had little or no place in social policy.

Elizalde claims that one of the gravest mistakes women make is to neglect their moral education and that of their daughters, which entails avoiding flirtatiousness and vanity and instead cultivating modesty, humility, and self-abnegation (12). Moreno, in turn, agrees and only mentions academic education to question its importance relative to the indispensable teachings of "religion, morality, and duty." Elizalde adds that the role of women's education is "in a word, to take care of the heart, almost exclusively" (28, 30). Elizalde makes the distinction between *educación* (education, upbringing) and *instruir* (to instruct), in which the former deals with the heart and the latter deals only with the brain, the cultivation of the "intellectual faculties" (30). Needless to say, women were to be educated in matters of the heart rather than instructed intellectually; he scorns parents who teach their daughters math and science and neglect religion (31). Elizalde, in the end, champions religion as the savior of men and women, and as the panacea of society.

According to Elizalde, evil influences on women are fiction, journalism, Protestantism, and any other outside "theories." He likens the sources of entertainment and information to "un reptil que, astuto y arrastrándose, acecha á su víctima, ha penetrado el descreimiento en el hogar bajo la forma de la novela y del periódico, atacando desde luego el pudor de la mujer, lanzando después el soplo de su hálito sobre la llama de la fe, y queriendo, en fin, arrancarle el grandioso poder que le da la religión" (46) [a reptile that, astute and slithering, spies on its victim, and has infiltrated disbelief into the home by way of the novel and the newspaper, suddenly attacking women's chastity, then extinguishing with its breath the flame of faith, and seeking, finally, to wrench away the grandiose power that religion bestows upon them]. His words are in accordance with hegemonic ideology, which purported that women were not socially impotent, but rather held power in domestic, moral, and religious matters. This power only functioned within the angelic model; straying from it (by self-indulgently educating oneself with periodicals and novels, for example, as Elizalde notes) strips away the fragile legitimacy women could claim in society.

Besides including newspapers and novels, Elizalde expands the category of threats to woman's morality to a vast one: outside ideas and carriers of faiths other than Catholicism were also "slithering reptiles" waiting to dampen women's faith. He explicitly makes reference to the French Revolution (perhaps for women's prominent and notably nondomestic role in it) and the reforms, taken up by the United States, that had "demoralized" these societies (70). He specifically mentions "*Volterianismo*, . . . *Protestantismo, Racionalismo*, etc." as dangerous influences (71). The negative references to rationalism and the French deist *philosophe* and writer Voltaire (real name François-Marie Arouet [1694–1778]) are likely reactions against the political era in which Moreno writes, which is as dominated by science and Enlightenment ideals of reason as it is skeptical of religion.

These unwholesome philosophies, then, could "pervertir á la mujer por medio de falsas religiones, de teorías seductoras y de libertades que le concedían vivir á sus anchas, satisfacer sus deseos y despreciar todo lo que la ennoblece" (55) [pervert woman by means of false religions, seductive theories, and liberties that would allow her to live large, satisfy her desires, and reject all that ennobles her]. In this passage, development of one's identity and self-indulgence through worldly knowledge is explicitly adverse to the feminine ideal. This message is repeated in a section titled "Virtue in the Home," in which Moreno notes that errors women can make are often caused by "demoralization and free thought" and "individual liberty," which open the door to "worldly seductions" (150). The book Moreno recommends for female citizens is, in sum, the Roman Catholic Bible (14), although general reading on the improvement of one's domestic skills and other morally edifying and church-approved reading was likely acceptable.

It is thus the duty of men and God to keep women from being led astray: "la mujer, más que él, necesita de guía para emprender el áspero camino que la conduce al hogar, término natural y preciso de sus aspiraciones, á despecho de todas las teorías que se inventen en contrario para deslumbrar á la que debe ser astro" (5) [woman, more than man, needs a guide to set forth on the harsh road that directs her to the home, the natural and precise goal of her aspirations, despite all the theories that are invented to the contrary, in order to confuse she who is meant to be a leading light]. The final tone is that of a protective shepherd who must look over the flock of women who are to be the gentle caretakers of Mexico's children.

Positivist Antifeminist Rhetoric: Redefining Progress for Women

Although the following antifeminist discourse has a very different tone and style from *La mujer's* religious rhetoric, the fundamental symbolic role that it defines for women in society is the same: that women's strengths are self-abnegation, morality, and nurturing others; that they are best at being wives and mothers; and that any foreign ideology that contradicts this is dangerous. The principal differences in the following essay I will examine are that the rhetoric is scientific, women's strengths and weaknesses are biologically defined, and contradictory ideology (such as feminism), in line with Positivist rhetoric, is not evil poison to the soul, but rather "unhealthy" and "unnatural," given women's *organic* constitution. It is also communicated within the nationalist rhetoric of the *científicos,* rather than in a religious tone and context.

El siglo xx ante el feminismo (The Twentieth Century in the Face of Feminism) is a compilation of articles by the Mexican Positivist thinker Horacio Barreda (1863–1914) from 1909. Published in the respected and influential *Revista Positiva* (Positivist Journal), the articles use "scientific" logic to disprove the viability of feminism as a social theory. That is, the articles consider what Barreda conceives as women's biological and psychological makeup (drawing on anthropological material of the Aztec and Spanish family structures, among other "facts" of science and human nature), and then determines social factors that act upon them to influence their behavior (Barreda 1991, 124–26).

Barreda's study follows closely the tenets of Positivist womanhood that the originator of Positivism, Auguste Comte (France 1798–1857), expresses in *Système de politique positive* (*System of Positive Polity,* 1851–54) in the section titled "The Feminine Influence of Positivism."[15] Comte, like Barreda, posits ideal republican women as fundamentally maternal and loving and champions their superiority in domestic, moral, and spiritual matters, while stressing their essential intellectual inferiority (Landes 1988, 170–89).

The result of Barreda's applying Positivist philosophy to women is that his essays support roughly the same oppressive and traditional roles for women as they previously had in Hispanic and European culture, but his writings are packaged in the Positivist prose that is specifically in dialogue with the new threat of feminism. Whereas earlier writings about women's place in society tended to romantically extol the spiritual and virtuous beauty of women's place with their children by the hearth, Barreda's sentences, each often occupying all of ten lines in a standard eight-inch page, are a compilation of clauses into logical sequences, replete with scientific-sounding vocabulary. This style lends authority to the words, even though Barreda

---

15. For an analysis of Comte's Positivist view of women, see Landes 1988, 173–200.

lacks hard evidence, namely, statistics from any sort of organized scientific experiment or study.

Feminism, in the context of Barreda's articles, was a potential danger to the existing socioeconomic structures (Alvarado 1991, 9). Thus Barreda's study is an effort to give a Positivist examination of women's roles with the goal of maintaining their traditional domestic placement and subservient position to men; his ideas were an expression of the general male consensus of the time (9). Tuñón Pablos notes that "discourse on women focused on two basic aspects of their supposed nature: their biology and their affective temperament" and indeed these are the bases of Barreda's arguments (1999, 74).

Looking at Barreda's rhetorical approach, it is interesting to note that he puts in much effort to appear completely objective by avoiding an early dismissal of feminism. Barreda makes a point of seeming to seriously consider feminism as a viable option for women:

> La importancia del feminismo en México la examinaremos de preferencia, desde el punto de vista teórico; pero antes se hace indispensable tratar la cuestión en abstracto, con el fin de averiguar cuál es el valor real de la solución feminista, examinando en relación con las conclusions de la biología y con los principios fundamentales de la sociología positivista; esto es . . . a las condiciones *estáticas* o de existencia social. (38)

> [We will examine the importance of feminism, preferably from a theoretical perspective; but first it is indispensable to approach the question in the abstract, with the goal of determining the real value of the feminist solution, examining it in relation with biological conclusions and with the fundamental principles of Positivist sociology; that is . . . with the *static* conditions or those of social existence.]

It is not a surprise that Barreda's theoretical consideration of feminism will arrive at the conclusion that women's best route, for them and for the nation, is to serve the development of society as well-mannered and cultivated keepers of the home; feminism is not the solution to anything, but rather an obstacle to women's immutable natural condition. What is noteworthy is that feminism, this imported idea that bolstered Mexican bourgeois women's frustration with Porfirian sexual oppression in the midst of progress, is enough of a threat to Barreda (and, we may assume, to the *científicos*) to merit a lengthy, detailed analysis in one of Mexico's most prestigious journals of that era. From this fact, and from early feminist efforts in Mexico that I have discussed, it seems very likely that a number of Mexican women were familiar with foreign women's freedoms and struggles for equality and were articulating their own feminist agendas.

It is useful to look at Barreda's definitions of words, such as *progreso, libertad,* and *igualdad* (progress, liberty, and equality), that were commonly used in Positivist rhetoric, as they were applied to women. The text I analyze in this section is titled "Planteo positivo del problema social de la mujer" (A Positivist Consideration of the Social Problem of Woman). First, Barreda redefines *progress* as *development,* which implies advancement within an existing model (that is, perfecting women's traditional roles). The idea seems to be that development is good for women because it does not drastically change their current status, while progress implies evolution and moving beyond one's current situation—which seems to be too extreme a transformation for women. After a long sequence of sentences filled with vocabulary taken from the social and natural sciences to speak about this particular interpretation of progress, Barreda concludes that

> el progreso individual no podrá consistir jamás en alterar o invertir el orden fundamental de desarrollo, pero ni aun siquiera en trastornarlo, salvando algunos de sus eslabones importantes. De todo esto resulta, que el progreso en su marcha sería impotente para desarrollar bruscamente en el niño, facultades que fueran propias del hombre maduro. (43–44)

> [individual progress will never be able to consist in altering or inverting the fundamental order of development, or even disturbing it, except some of its important links. The outcome of all this is that progress, in its course, would be impotent to develop, all at once, in children, faculties typical of a mature adult.]

The message is the following: women, like infants, may not budge from their traditional roles and must remain obedient, regardless of how much society advances in terms of wealth and opportunity. Barreda compares women to children in other sections as well as in this one, where he likens the natural growth of a child with the "natural" social growth of women; just as radical progress applied to children would be pushing the natural pace of development, so it is for women. He makes it clear that progress, for women, does not mean altering their roles as domestic wives and mothers.

The next word Barreda defines for us is *libertad*. He explains that although it seems to suggest the meaning "apartar todos aquellos obstáculos que pudieran impedirnos el ejercicio de nuestra actividad en tal o cual sentido" (46) [to do away with all those obstacles that could impede the accomplishment of our activity in one sense or another]—that is, freedom is mistakenly interpreted to mean fulfilling "selfish" desires as individuals—this is not the case in the context of social laws. He corrects the misconception by explaining that "la libertad verdadera a que debe aspirar el hombre y la mujer digna, habrá de consistir en el libre ejercicio de las facultades superiores que sean características de uno y otro sexo" (49) [the true liberty to which men and worthy women should aspire should consist of the free exercise of the different mental faculties that are characteristic of each sex]. *True* freedom, for Barreda (and, we may assume, the architects of progress in Mexico), is liberty to act within a model dictated by the state. Before moving on to what these sexually particular characteristics are, so that we may see in what ways women are "free," it is important to note that the same Positivist ideas that Barreda applies to women in this essay were applied to the (largely indigenous) working classes in order to dissuade them from attempting to gain power that was destined for the bourgeoisie and elite.

In the following section, "La organización física, intelectual y moral que es característica de la mujer" (The Physical, Intellectual, and Moral Makeup that Characterizes Women), we learn that these female mental qualities are not actually mental qualities at all, but rather, emotional faculties, because "en la mujer . . . predomina la vida afectiva sobre la intelectual" (61) [in women . . . affective dominates over intellectual life]. The sections of Barreda's essay that follow, and that are quoted from in the Introduction of the present study, are worth citing at length, because it is here that he specifies women's inherent intellectual limitations, according to "scientific" Positivist thinking:

> Ahora bien, la marcada repugnancia que inspira a la mujer toda observación abstracta, profunda y prolongada, a causa de la invencible fatiga que a poco le sobreviene, pone bien de manifiesto la debilidad relativa de sus órganos cerebrales que corresponden a las funciones de abstracción. En cambio, la meditación concreta, la observación sintética de las cosas reales, admite en ella un ejercicio mucho más

sostenido; lo cual indica una aptitud cerebral mayor para ese género de observaciones. . . . La poca energía y vigor de sus facultades abstractas y analíticas ocasiona que la inteligencia femenina aprecie mejor las diferencias de los objetos que sus semejanzas. (59)

[Now then, the marked repugnance that any type of abstract, profound, and prolonged observation inspires in women, owing to the invincible fatigue that sets in shortly afterward, is an obvious manifestation of the relative weakness of their cerebral organs that control the functions of abstraction. Conversely, concrete thought, the synthetic observation of real things, allows them a more sustained activity; this indicates a greater cerebral aptitude for this kind of observations. . . . The abstract and analytical faculties' meager energy and vigor cause feminine intelligence to better appreciate the differences between objects, rather than their similarities.]

Barreda goes on to elaborate the differences between female and male intelligence, which basically amount to men's excelling at coming to universal conclusions or generalizations and synthesizing information, while women excel at "rapid" concrete observation; at focusing on details; and at negative comparisons, or how one thing differs from another (60). So, based on Barreda's "biological" assessment, abstract or analytical intellectual functions such as interpreting or modifying laws, critical thinking, and decision making would be masculine intellectual duties, while the thought process for picking out items for the house, choosing between fabrics for the sofa or clothing, and distinguishing right from wrong on a superficial level (as long as it did not entail prolonged or profound contemplation) are mental tasks appropriate to the female brain. From our current perspective, it is clear that Barreda was making a strong case by using loaded rhetoric and pseudoscientific facts in order to convince women and men that the former were incapable of holding any kind of power beyond the execution of very mundane domestic duties.

The section concludes by summarizing all of women's strengths and weaknesses, which biologically determine their static place in society, regardless of how much society itself may advance:

Así, la naturaleza física del sexo femenino, su debilidad muscular, su viva sensibilidad, la movilidad de su imaginación, la rápida sucesión de sus sensaciones, sus tendencies a la observación minuciosa de detalle, la preponderancia de sus sentimientos de amor, de adhesion, de bondad, de abnegación y sacrificio, son atributos que se hallan en consonancia con los rasgos característicos que presenta el carácter de la mujer.

Ni el valor, ni la firmeza ni la verdadera energía, son cualidades que puedan distinguir a la mujer; y en ella lo que se nota es la timidez, la indecision, la variabilidad y la debilidad en sus actos. . . . Su admirable aptitud espontánea para poder subordinar el egoísmo al altruismo, la sociabilidad a la personalidad, la eleva muy por encima del [hombre]. La mujer será siempre, biológicamente considerada, *el tipo moral* de la especie humana. . . . En cambio, la inferioridad de su inteligencia y de su carácter la colocará por necesidad, en una posición subalterna respecto del sexo masculino. (61)

[So, the physical nature of the feminine sex, her muscular weakness, her heightened sensitivity, the mobility of her imagination, the rapid succession of her sensations, her tendencies toward the observation of minute detail, the preponderance of her feelings of love and bonding, of goodness, of abnegation and sacrifice, are attributes that one finds in harmony with the characteristic traits that woman's character presents.

Neither valor, nor strength, nor real energy are qualities that can be distinguished in woman; and in her what one notes is timidity, indecision, fickleness, and weakness in her acts. . . . Her admirable spontaneous ability to be able to subordinate egotism to altruism, the sociability of her personality, elevate her far above men. Woman will always be, biologically speaking, *the moral type* of the human species. . . . On the other hand, the inferiority of her intelligence and her character will necessarily place her in a subaltern position with respect to the masculine sex.]

In Barreda's estimation of women's place in society, as in Comte's, there is no social learning that can liberate them in an age of progress in which such emphasis is placed on society's ability to move forward into international markets, and advance into an industrial stage.

Liberty, for the weaker sex, then, means the freedom to cultivate and participate in *all activities that pertain to an Angel of the House,* and remain subordinate to men in all other arenas, on the basis of their physical constitutions. Women, in addition, are granted the *freedom* to maintain their weak physical constitutions in a "safe" environment by remaining at home and fulfilling their natural function: bearing and raising children.

The section on defining *equality* in a Positivist context is fairly short, as it basically builds upon the base that Barreda has already established in the previous sections: that individuals are biologically diverse and have differing weak and strong points, and therefore the idea of equality cannot realistically be applied in the concrete world, outside theory. He admits that the slogans of liberty and equality worked well for revolutionary purposes, but that with the development of culture and society, "natural" differences between individuals became apparent. Equality is thus not only unfeasible but "opresiva" (oppressive), because it would not be fair to put the same demands on men, women, children, and the developmentally disabled, as all have very "different" levels of intelligence and development (50–51):

> Salvo el conjunto de garantías individuales que la legislación debe asegurar por igual a los diversos miembros de una sociedad cualquiera, es evidente, que no naciendo iguales los hombres, *orgánicamente* considerados, y produciendo la libre actividad de cada uno de ellos, aptitudes, capacidades y resultados muy diversos, las posiciones, prerrogativas y consideraciones sociales, tienen que ser por necesidad también desiguales. (51)

> [With the exception of the set of individual rights that legislation must provide equally to all the diverse members of a given society, it is evident that men not being born equal, *organically* speaking, and given that the free activity of each one of them produces very diverse aptitudes, capacities, and results, the social positions, prerogatives, and considerations have to be, necessarily, also unequal.]

Barreda repeatedly makes unambiguous essentialist claims that women are intellectually and physically inferior to men. From the passage above we can see that Positivist society subordinates certain men, whom we may assume to be men of the lower classes and of non-white races, as well as women.

Barreda abandons his high scholarly prose at the end of his essay to emphatically address feminism's threat to society. He concludes with this vehement admonition, which I present in an abbreviated version of the original diatribe, nineteen lines long:

> Si vuestras teorías ¡oh feministas! alcanzasen el triunfo social que ambicionáis, si la mujer llegase a ser virilizada en el grado que pretendéis . . . vuestra obra será el baldón de la civilización, podéis estar seguros de ello, y la posteridad os pediría severas cuentas de semejante labor revolucionaria. . . . Al contemplar el hogar desierto y frío . . . os gritarían con voz llena de dolor e indignación: ¡feministas! ¡feministas! ¿qué habéis hecho de la mujer? (151)

> [If your theories, oh feminists! achieve the social triumph you seek, if women become masculinized to the extent that you wish . . . your work will be the disgrace of civilization, you may be sure of it, and posterity will have much to reproach you for such revolutionary labor. . . . Upon contemplating the cold and deserted hearth, they will scream to you with voices filled with indignation: Feminists! Feminists! What have you done to women?]

Barreda's final rhetoric rings of that of the conservative Mexican thinker Ignacio Gamboa, who published the book-length essay *La mujer moderna* (The Modern Woman [1904]), in which he condemned feminism, separation of spouses, and lesbianism for causing the prospective downfall of womanhood and the end of reproduction (Macías 1982, 16). Masculinist rhetoric of the period, whether hailing from the conservative sector, the Catholic Church, or those in favor of Positivist progress, generally prescribed strictly domestic roles for women, despite their increasing presence in the workforce. Feminism, "outside theories," and, we may assume, any challenges to the angelic model were adamantly opposed in hegemonic conceptualizations of female identity. Women were ideologically tied to the home and systematically denied public voice.

While in real life this oppressive social propaganda was the code by which women were expected to lead their lives, in Barragán's fiction readers were encouraged to think beyond this mold by reading about a female character who single-handedly took control of and reversed her father's criminal affairs and traveled the countryside independently. In the following chapter, I will further discuss how Barragán's protagonist was a symbolic contestation to this real-life silencing and seclusion.

2

COMING OF AGE(NCY):
REFUGIO BARRAGÁN DE TOSCANO'S *LA HIJA DEL BANDIDO*

LA HIJA DEL BANDIDO (The Bandit's Daughter [1887]) by the Mexican writer Refugio Barragán de Toscano is an adventure novel, set in the transitional period between the twilight of Spanish colonial Mexico and the dawn of the struggle for independence.[1] The story is the fictionalized retelling of a rural legend about a cave-dwelling gang of bandits who operated in the mountainous regions of the province of Jalisco. At the time of this writing, Barragán is the earliest known woman novelist of nineteenth-century Mexico; *La hija* was her most successful work. The novel has gone through fifteen printings in Mexico, although it is virtually unknown to many scholars both within and outside Mexico today. It is part adventure novel, part document of local customs, and part historical novel. In terms of female subject formation, it is multilayered and lends itself to readings from the perspectives of psychoanalysis and women's history and culture. The protagonist, as the title suggests, is the head outlaw's daughter, whose *quinceañera* (a Mexican girl's fifteenth birthday and coming-of-age celebration) commences and frames the narrative.

In *La hija* this rite of passage to womanhood, the *quinceañera,* is a medium for psychoanalytic identity formation because of the transitional nature of coming-of-age as a social fissure and the subsequent social "lawlessness" or transgression allowed by this gap. The role of transitional and marginal spaces will be of particular importance in this analysis, because Barragán situates the heroine's agency *between* life stages, genres, historical settings, societies, geographies—and even genders—to introduce in the preadolescent girl's bond with her father a rupture that drives the plot. It is this conflict that allows the protagonist to break many of the tenets of the Angel of the House; when María, the bandit's daughter, discovers her father's deceptions, she rebels against him and becomes the heroine of the novel.

---

1. The narrator cites the current Spanish governor, Don Miguel de la Grúa Talamanca, marquis of Branciforte, who was the unpopular viceroy of New Spain from 1794 to 1798.

Barragán and Her Novel: Disruptions of Power and Marginal Perspective

Barragán's preference for balancing her narrative in the precarious political position between colonial Mexico and the early republic likely reflects her conception of the symbolic order in transition, since she witnessed the mutability of political regimes from her early childhood in the 1850s to the late 1880s, when she wrote *La hija*.[2] During these years Mexico endured the rule of Santa Ana and the French monarchy of Maximilian and enjoyed the respite of Juárez's reform.[3] In Barragán's Mexico, focusing on the moment that a regime crumbles and shifts must have been like looking through a doorway to opportunity, because it is at this moment that one may view the political structure (which, to a significant degree, dictates the social) in its most vulnerable and tentative phase.

In Barragán's Jalisco (a province just northwest of Mexico City), provincial life responded to the ebb and flow of political changes in the capital and to international concerns, such as conflicts with France and the United States. For example, in nineteenth-century Jalisco the "social structure was in constant flux as the expansion of the railroad (under Lerdo de Tejada, González, and Díaz) in Mexico closely linked the national market with that of the United States" (Zalduondo 2001, 46). French occupation meant that more than thirty thousand troops "overran central Mexico" and were stationed in provincial towns during Maximilian's rule (Meyer and Sherman 1991, 390–97). Provincial life, then, did not isolate Barragán from the instability that was more keenly experienced in the capital.

On a personal level, much like the unpredictable changes in politics, Barragán's destiny transitioned by chance—instead of leading her to the

---

2. The information in this chapter comes from the literary scholar María Zalduondo's (2001) useful research on Barragán's biography, in which she pieces together the scant sources available on the author's life.

3. The shifts in power in Mexico were extreme until Díaz's relative constancy starting in 1876. The 1850s saw postcolonial instability and the near-dozen stints of leadership under the slippery and corrupt, but talented, military leader Antonio López de Santa Anna (1794–1876) from the 1830s to the 1850s. During this time, Mexico endured the loss of Texas in 1836, and the subsequent Mexican-American War, or Guerra de Estados Unidos a México, and an extensive loss of territory to the United States (1846–48). Later, the 1860s brought the respite, for the most part, of enlightened secular liberal reform under Benito Juárez. Juárez's rule was interrupted by a French invasion, facilitated through the efforts of Mexican conservatives. Napoleon III installed the emperor Ferdinand Maximilian Joseph (1832–67, archduke of Austria) in a monarchy from 1864 to 1867. Although Juárez's republican forces defeated the French and Juárez had Maximilian executed in 1867, his presidency was cut short by his death in 1872.

common domestic life of a uneducated Mexican woman, her circumstances provided her with enough education to become a schoolteacher and, later, a noted author. She was born into a family of modest means in the town of Tonila, Jalisco, in 1846.[4] Her father was a schoolteacher and was saving a portion of the family's already small income for the education of Barragán's older brother. It was through the misfortune of both of her two siblings' deaths that she had access to education; the money intended for the eldest was used to send her to normal school in Colima, and she then moved with her family to Ciudad Guzmán and worked as a teacher there. A fissure had opened up that freed Barragán from the prescribed domestic existence.

In 1869 she married Estéban Toscano Arreola, a professor, and moved to Guadalajara. Barragán continued teaching and writing even while raising her two children—an uncommon practice for nineteenth-century Mexican wives and mothers, who were generally forced to quit once they had a man to support them. After her husband's death in 1879, Barragán remained employed as an educator and added to her significant oeuvre, which included poetry, drama, and narrative. As a widow, she faced the financial burden of being the sole provider and supported her family by publishing and teaching. However, her widowed status granted her the highest degree of legal freedom possible for a woman in the 1880s (Macías 1982, 13). Although in a much less adventurous form than her fictional female heroine, Barragán was sure to have recognized, in comparison with married women around her, the greater agency and freedom she could enjoy as a widow. She put her potential to good use: she is credited with having opened an elementary school and with collaborating with her son, who played a large role in the advent of the film industry in Mexico, to open and manage an early cinema in Puebla (Zalduondo 2001, 73, 87).

Both on a personal level and at the national one, the particular lessons of mid-nineteenth-century Mexico may well have taught the author of *La hija* that political power (with its inevitable effects on social norms) was a precarious and ephemeral force. Her numerous opportunities to experience the losses and gains of power during various moments of historical and experiential shift may explain why she chose to peer into the interstices of power to rewrite the feminine ideal.

---

4. For biographical information on Barragán, see Zalduondo 2001, 70–76. For an overview of Barragán's literary production and summaries of her works, including her novelette *Premio del bien y castigo del mal* (1884), see 76–87. Barragán also wrote poetry (*Celajes*, 1880), a drama (*Diadema de perlas*, 1873), and several children's books.

Paralleling the slippery evasions of category and stability in Barragán's political context and personal life, *La hija* is a novel that does not fit into a single genre. While some of the more poetic moments in its narrative may show some minor influence of *modernismo,* it is mainly a novel of adventure and intrigue written in the Romantic and realist styles, without any hint of decadence or the more voluptuous landscapes and personages common in *modernista* prose.[5] The author of the foreword calls *La hija del bandido* "un libro '*costumbrista*'" (Ruiz Cabañas 1934, i) [a book depicting local customs, dress, and social types]; however, this categorization is problematic, because of the prominence of the action-packed plot, which overshadows the few passages describing local customs, landscapes, and festivals.[6]

The story is based on a local legend that was told to the author as a child by her aunt (Barragán 1934, 2–3). The structure of the novel is complex, with the main plot interrupted by tangential intrigues and the nonlinear storytelling including flashbacks to keep the reader up to speed with simultaneous action that takes place in different geographical locations involving various secondary characters. For the purpose of this analysis we will recount the main action concerning the heroine and relevant subplots.

The protagonist, María Colombo, is the daughter of Vicente Colombo, the notorious chief of a gang of bandits. She has grown up in the thieves' hideout in the caves of the Nevado de Colima, a mountain in the state of Jalisco, believing that her father is hiding there for political reasons. On her fifteenth birthday, she is given a letter from her deceased mother that reveals the truth about her father's criminal activity. At that moment, her filial devotion largely vanishes and she embarks on a quest to find her maternal grandfather in the city of Zapotlán (today called Ciudad Guzmán), about sixty kilometers from the caves.

---

5. The literary movement *modernismo* differs from Anglo literary modernism. Both movements are reactions against Enlightenment and bourgeois ideals. However, first-generation Spanish American *modernismo* came about in the late 1880s and has a closer tie to Romanticism and influence from Parnassianism and the French fin de siècle decadent writers; *modernismo* innovates these tendencies with American characters and themes.

6. Localism (*costumbrismo*) was a valued characteristic of cultural production in Colima in the 1800s (Zalduondo 2001, 66–67). Barragán's descriptions of provincial Mexico inspired national pride, as evidenced by Ruiz Cabañas's foreword to the 1934 edition. His first words are "La aparición de un libro 'costumbrista,' que pinte con justeza nuestro medio—rico en el color y singular en la emoción—debe ser saludada con simpatía por lectores y bibliófilos" (i) [The publication of a book depicting local color, that paints precisely our surroundings—richly colorful and uniquely exciting—should be welcomed warmly by readers and bibliophiles]. For more on the importance of local journals and novelists, see the section titled "Rural Ties" in Zalduondo 2001.

Gaining her father's permission and the means to travel requires ability on the part of the young lady to lie, cajole, persuade, and even employ powers of seduction. Although her primary goal is originally to reunite with her maternal grandfather, in a gesture of loyalty to her dead mother, her adventures multiply when she discovers several kidnappings of her father's doing. She thus becomes the heroine who travels to Guadalajara; returns to Nevado; drugs the band of criminals, including her own father; and rescues the victims. Zapotlán is about 125 kilometers south of Guadalajara in the state of Jalisco, and the Nevado de Colima is about 60 kilometers southwest of Zapotlán. I have estimated from the travels listed in the novel that the protagonist journeys about 400 kilometers independently.

In this process of tricking evildoers and saving the day, María falls in love with a handsome young suitor, Rafael. She must, however, reject him on the basis that he would someday discover and resent her shady origins. Rafael has given evidence that this is true when he seems to recognize María as the beautiful damsel who rescues him from the bandits' cave—and questions her involvement there. Prideful and unyielding to her grandfather's and Rafael's pleas for her to wed, María instead decides to enter a convent. Her choice allows her to avoid becoming an Angel of the House and also positions her in a tradition of Hispanic women of letters who joined religious orders.

Denying the Name of the Father: María Granados's New Self

In Barragán's novel, Vicente Colombo is the symbolic father, because he is the leader of the group of bandits and has complete power over that domain, as well as being María's genetic father. Further, his name is reminiscent of Cristóbol Colón (Christopher Columbus), the first conquistador, exploiter, and symbolic father of the *mestizo* (mixed race) and *criollo* (of Spanish lineage) populations of Latin America. Colombo thus performs the "socially regulatory function of the name-of-the-father" (Grosz 1990, 51), to use Lacan's phrase, on abstract levels.[7] Recognizing that Colombo is both father and law makes María's power over him especially significant from a

---

7. Lacan's idea of the Name-of-the-Father originates in Freud. In Freud's onset of "normal" adult sexuality (which justifies phallic/social power) the liminal is the transitional space in which this resolution of the conflict with the father occurs. In *Totem and Taboo* (1912–13), Freud links the change of state from the infantile autoerotic to the discovery of a sexual object (the mother), and later resolution of the incestuous desire, to symbolism and ritual in tribal societies. Freud bases his theory of the Oedipal complex on the Darwinian imagining of a "primal horde" (a group of jealous sons

feminist perspective. The vicious criminal himself says, "Delante de María soy un cordero, un niño, un maniquí a su voluntad y sin fuerza propia" (41) [Before María I am a lamb, a child, a puppet to her will, without strength of my own]. Thus, embedded in an action-packed adventure novel, in which the reader's attention is drawn into the multiple story lines, there is always the underlying transgression of María's rebellion against her father and the patriarchal law that his name represents.

The symbolic nature of the Name-of-the-Father is relevant to a feminist reading of the novel because it is Colombo's *name* that is his handicap in his ability to monitor his daughter's actions; the same name that means *law* in the hideout marks him as a wanted man in society. Thus he cannot circulate in public unless he disguises himself. María, then, must deny the name of the father and assume a legitimate one in order to stay in Zapotlán. Here, she coaches her servant Juana in the art of assimilating the newfound false identity—the identity that will be her ticket to liberty and public agency:

> Juana murmuró con cariño, dando a sus ideas otro sesgo:
> —Yo temo no saber desempeñar bien mi papel en esta comedia. Y si no, ¿Qué diremos ahora?
> [—] Simplemente que venimos desde México a cambiar temperatura, buscando aires más puros, porque me hallo enferma del

---

who kill and eat their father in order to gain access to the women of the tribe [Freud 1995, 883]). Freud adds to this myth the idea of the sons' *remorse*, which is the basis for social taboos (thus law): "[Tribal societies] created two fundamental taboos of totemism out of the *sense of guilt of the son*, and for this very reason these had to correspond with the two repressed wishes of the Oedipal complex [desiring the mother, killing the father]" (885; emphasis in the original). The rite of passage is resolved, then, with the sons' love for and identification with the dead father, and their pact not to desire the mother. In Freud's European application of the primal horde, the Oedipal complex, the son's guilt (and subsequent renunciation of the desire for the mother) marks the transition from boy to man and an implicit pact/alignment with the father that determines social structure: "Society is now based on complicity in the common crime, religion on the sense of guilt and the consequent remorse, while morality is based partly on the necessities of society and partly on the expiation which this sense of guilt demands" (887). This pact between father and son, which has not gone unnoticed among feminist scholars such as Irigaray and Kristeva, "founds patriarchy anew for each generation, guaranteeing the son a position as heir to the father's position" (Grosz 1989, 68).

Although in Freud the correlations between father, law, and society are clearly present, Lacan presents them in terms of abstract law. Citing the fact that a father figure need not be genetically related, and drawing on the God the Father metaphor in religion, Lacan comes to the conclusion that "the attribution of procreation to the father can only be the effect of a pure signifier, of a recognition, not of a real father, but of what religion has taught us to refer to as the Name-of-the-Father" (1977). In this sense he takes Freud's theory of the primal horde and the dead father from *Totem and Taboo* and posits it as a master signifier of the symbolic order.

corazón. Además, por lo que pueda ofrecerse, no olvides que mi padre se llama Laurencio Granados; mi madre Gabriela Alvarado, y que soy huérfana. (46)

[Juana murmured affectionately, giving her ideas another slant:
"I fear I will not know how to play my role well in this comedy. And if not, what will we say then?"
(María replies) "Simply that we come from Mexico City to change climates, searching for cleaner air, because I have a heart condition. Moreover, in case anything comes up, do not forget that my father is named Laurencio Granados, my mother Gabriela Alvarado, and that I am an orphan.]

So, in the context of nineteenth-century Mexican society, where women were almost exclusively defined in relation to their male relatives, María's assumption of her own, original identity—intentionally detached from that of Vicente's—is a heavily loaded symbolic act. It inserts into the symbolic order an example of a woman who finds her developing sense of self and worth through her own words and deeds.

Apart from the focus on María's relationship with her father, there is a phenomenon of the elimination of paternal figures in the novel in a more general sense.[8] Two of the female characters are stolen from their fathers and must fare for themselves: Colombo had abducted María's mother, Paula, and, by Colombo's orders, the bandits capture Cecilia, María's friend and surrogate sister, as well. Women are not the only fatherless young people in the novel. María's suitor, Rafael, is an orphan, and this term is applied to the gang of bandits. While in nineteenth-century novels in the Hispanic world, Europe, and the United States orphans and orphan-bandits are plot staples that lend themselves to adventures and intrigues (as in novels by Ignacio Manuel Altamirano and Manuel Payno of Mexico, Gertrudis Gómez de Avellaneda of Cuba, Charles Dickens of Britain, and Victor Hugo of France), these writers do not simultaneously draw attention to the triangular relationship of mother-father-child, as Barragán does in *La hija,* to then

---

8. Paula, María's mother, writes of her life prior to her capture by Colombo in her letter to María: "No tenía madre ni hermanos; pero tenía a mi padre que me amaba por todos ellos" (23) [I didn't have a mother nor siblings, but I had my father, whose love for me made up for all of them]. In the case of Rafael, the narrator informs us that "Carecía de padres y hermanos" (62) [He lacked parents and siblings].

rupture it. The symbolic father's role of "instilling in the child the sense of lawfulness and willing submission to the social customs," then, gives way to agency (Grosz 1990, 68). This is one way that the author breaks down the stability or perceived invincibility of her imagined symbolic social structure: by creating a fatherless society in which individuals act independently of this particular restriction.

At the same time that the protagonist rebels against the patriarchal figure, she valorizes the maternal impulses of her mother, who had died soon after María's birth. María's postmortem discovery of the mother's voice via a written document is her impetus for leaving the bandits' cave. By valorizing the mother as the voice of "truth," Barragán's discursive gesture is similar to those of Kristeva, Irigaray, Lacan, and others who have given importance to the mother's role in identity formation.

Barragán's Strategic Liminality

La hija del bandido is a tale set on the threshold of hegemonic society—it is close enough so that the reader is mindful of the dominant social structure's proximity and influence, yet the novel's historical, social, and geographical settings, as well as its protagonist, are slippery enough to fall into an imaginary space just out of mainstream nineteenth-century Mexico's delineations between civilization and barbarism, law and order, and urban and rural. In particular, it breaks the dichotomy of the association of *criollo* men with public participation and agency on the one hand, and the linking of women to private domestic space and passivity on the other. While ruling-class power in historical Mexico grants agency to men almost exclusively and is concentrated in the urban centers, the novel focuses on rural and provincial spaces and marginal bandit society. The author chooses these marginal spaces to present the counterhegemonic notion of feminine agency. The action of the novel takes place about five years before the Wars of Independence, when antiroyalist sentiment was circulating. The positioning of an unorthodox female character at a time when the undercurrents of rebellion were in place is a way of putting a chisel into a crack that is already present in order to open up a space for change.

María's transitional stage between girlhood and womanhood is the most important liminal experiment in the novel. In Hispanic culture the *quinceañera* is generally acknowledged to be a religious and social event that marks a young woman's transition to adulthood. It is "a performance of budding womanhood on at least two levels ... religious and social," complete with "symbols of sexual awakening," such as the donning of adult formalwear and high-heeled shoes (Cantú 2000, 27–29). This coming-of-age celebration is thought to have stemmed from Aztec and Mayan rites of passage that were assimilated into Catholic religious and social culture in colonial Mexico. Early ecclesiastic documents support this hypothesis, as does the absence of celebrations of its kind in Spain, although there is no conclusive evidence to its origins (3–8).[9] Important for the focus at hand is the fact that a girl's fifteenth birthday meant that she was a woman rather than a child and thus marriageable.[10] The date of the fifteenth birthday roughly coincides with menarche and childbearing. It is a date repeatedly mentioned in *La hija*, it marks the pivotal point in the narrative that begins the main action of the story, and it is also the threshold between girlhood and the commencement of a woman's role as an Angel of the House within marriage.

Because the *quinceañera* is such a poignant moment in a woman's formation and is profoundly embedded in the fabric of Spanish American society and its gender power hierarchies, I will draw on Victor Turner's theory of the liminal and liminoid to interpret this rite of passage as a key aspect of the story of *La hija*. Turner uses derivations of *limen* (Latin for "threshold") to refer to the conditions and persons who "slip through the network of classifications that normally locate states and positions in cultural space" (1969, 94). The limen, then, can be thought of as marginal space where the laws and rules of a dominant culture are temporarily frozen or neutralized, allowing alternative modes of being to happen, as the liminar transitions from one social role to his or her next.

While in Turner's earlier work liminality refers to a specific ritual stage in tribal cultures, his later development of the idea of the *liminoid* (liminal-like phenomena) in industrial or post-tribal societies amplifies significantly the applicability of liminality. In brief, liminal personae are participants in a rite of passage who are cut off from their hierarchical societies and lose all social markers, such as class and rank. Normally, in this status-less condition, the members form a "generalized social bond," which Turner refers to as *communitas*; in the liminoid, however, the marginal state can be achieved

---

9. The *quinceañera* is still widely celebrated today in many Spanish American countries (most notably in Mexico, Central America, and the Caribbean) and by Latinos in the United States.

10. In Mexico in the 1930s a girl could get married at the age of fourteen (Cantú 2000, 5). In recent times the *quinceañera* does not mean a young woman is marriageable, but, according to one scholar's surveys of girls and their families, it often means that she is given more privileges, is allowed to date, and is allowed to wear heels and makeup (28).

by an individual, rather than within a social group, as is the case of María in *La hija*. Turner's definition of the liminoid is worth noting because he describes how it relates to art and literature: "We have seen how tribesmen *play* with the factors of liminality, with masks and monsters, symbolic inversions, parodies of the profane reality, and so forth. So also do the genres of industrial leisure: . . . the novel, poetry, . . . and so on, pulling the elements of culture apart, putting them together again in often random, grotesque, improbable, surprising, shocking, sometimes deliberately experimental combinations" (1977, 43). In liminality "the underling comes uppermost" (1969, 102). That is, there is a carnavalesque reversal of authority in which the leader loses all power and the weak exert authority over him or her. Turner identifies the court jester who is allowed to criticize the king as liminal in this sense, a reversal of power that brings to mind María's influence over Colombo.

Several aspects of the liminal (in tribal rituals) and liminoid (in post-tribal societies) can be applied as a way of thinking about how the author positions the protagonist María into a fictional space ripe for symbolic social change. Liminal personae are "necessarily ambiguous, since this condition and these persons elude or slip through the network of classifications that normally locate states and positions in cultural space" (Turner 1969, 95). Like María, they are often "neophytes in initiation or puberty rites" (95).[11] Liminal entities, Turner explains, "are neither here nor there; they are betwixt and between the positions assigned and arrayed by law, custom, convention, and ceremonial" (95). The quality of existing between positions applies to María, as she embarks on adventures upon her fifteenth birthday that bear little resemblance to preparing her for marriage and children, yet she is no longer a child: she is, in fact "betwixt and between" social categories.

---

11. The main criterion is that the liminar is in fact in transition. Turner, drawing on Arnold Van Gennep's 1960 study, recognizes the rite-of-passage transition stages as separation, margin (or limen), and aggregation:

> The first phase (of separation) comprises symbolic behavior signifying the detachment of the individual or group either from an earlier fixed point in the social structure, from a set of cultural conditions (a "state"), or from both. During the intervening "liminal" period, the characteristics of the ritual subject (the "passenger") are ambiguous; he passes through a cultural realm that has few or none of the attributes of the past or coming state. In the third phase (reaggregation or reincorporation), the passage is consummated. The ritual subject . . . is in a relatively stable state once more and, by virtue of this, has rights and obligations vis-à-vis others of a clearly defined "structural" type; he is expected to behave in accordance with certain customary norms and ethical standards binding on incumbents of social position in a system of such positions. (1969, 94–95)

Although she is pursued by suitors, the protagonist's mind is on doing everything in her power to free her father's kidnapping victims and making her world a better place.

The liminal is important in terms of social power structures (for example, that of patriarchal oppression) because "[we] are presented, in such rites, with a 'moment in and out of time,' and in and out of secular social structure, which reveals, however fleetingly, some recognition (in symbol if not always in language) of a generalized social bond that has ceased to be and has simultaneously yet to be fragmented into a multiplicity of structural ties" (Turner 1969, 96). This threshold space of social structure is a place outside the usual social law and the hegemonic symbolic order, where individuals may experiment with the rules of conduct and acceptability: in liminality "new ways of acting, new combinations of symbols, are tried out, to be discarded or accepted" (Turner 1977, 40). It is indeed a space of "creative potentials," "great flexibility," and "radical novelty" (40).

So, the liminoid in *La hija* is this ritualistic space between girlhood and womanhood, between civilization (Ciudad Guzmán) and barbarism (the bandits' caves), and between viceroyalty and independence, where it is perfectly acceptable that the protagonist does not abide by laws of seclusion and angelic obedience to father or husband—bearing little resemblance to the social and legal restrictions placed on women in nineteenth-century Mexico, as we saw them in Chapter 1 of this study. To give one brief example of María's unrealistic independence (living alone in Zapotlán and doing as she pleases), her suitor, Rafael, questions her: "¿No vives aquí sola, no eres la dueña de tus acciones?" (60) [Do you not live here alone, are you not the master of your actions?]. As noted in Chapter 1, enclosure, chaperoning, and teaching women to internalize appropriate norms of conduct were the three primary safety guards that men used to protect women's honor and ensure their sexual and social conduct (Carner 1987, 97)—measures that are discounted in María's symbolic world.

The Liminoid and the Reconnection with the Mother

In the pre-liminal state, the novel's protagonist is a guileless child and the bandit's hideout cave is the only home she knows. The pre-liminal setting is one of false appearances and lies; María believes that her father is a Mexican freedom fighter hiding out from the Spanish authorities. Because she believes that he is a defender of justice, she shows him due respect and follows his orders with "alegría infantil" (Barragán 1934, 20) [infantile joy]. When Colombo tells her to enjoy her birthday, for example, she responds in a way that is almost exaggeratedly subservient: "Haré todo lo que me ordenes, y voy a divertirme leyendo este libro" (21) [I will do everything that you say, and I am going to entertain myself reading this book]. The book to which she refers is a prayer book and she has just finished making an altar to the Virgin Mary (her namesake). The semiotics of willing obedience and religious devotion reflect the prescribed comportment for a young woman from a respectable middle-class family.

Before her fifteenth birthday, María believes that she and her father must hide in the cave because he is part of the independence forces and therefore wanted by the Spanish government: "Hija mía, yo estoy aquí porque así conviene a la cooperación de esa grande obra con que los mexicanos soñamos tanto tiempo hace; la obra de la Independencia" (32) [My daughter, I am here because this is what is most convenient to my participation in this great feat about which we Mexicans have dreamt for so long: achieving Independence]. As long as María believes this lie, she remains childlike and obedient to her father. The irony of Colombo's story is rich: María believes that he represents freedom, yet he is one who imprisons others. In fact, María will be the heroic representative of freedom in the chapters to come, as it is she who both frees herself from Colombo's clutches and liberates his victims.

Through a revelation upon her fifteenth birthday, she discovers that the safe "home" to which she is confined is based on deceit. María is soon to be undeceived about her father's artificially constructed home life—and this marks the moment that she enters the quasi-magical liminoid, and the liberty from social bonds it implies. The pivotal moment of transformation in María's life is when her servant and maternal replacement, Juana, gives the girl a letter from her deceased mother, Paula. The letter, which is among the most poetically written passages in the novel, makes reference to a girl's fifteenth birthday three times, a common number used in rituals: "Mi juventud se encontraba en la fuerza de su vida . . . [como el espíritu] de los 15 años . . ." / "Quince soles han brillado sobre tu tierna frente . . ." / "Cuando hayas leido este manuscrito, tendrás quince años; ésta es mi voluntad" (28) [My youth was in full force . . . [like the spirit] of the fifteenth year of life / Fifteen suns have shone upon your tender brow / When you have read this manuscript you will be fifteen years old; this is my will]. The magical three-time repetition, which recalls the chanting of a spell, marks the daughter's passage into the liminal.

The reconnection with the mother presents Paula as the source of truth and liberation (in effect, she takes the place that María's father previously occupied). In a gesture that presents the mother as savior, Paula's voice emerges from the grave and comes to María to release her from her metaphorical prison: the bandits' cave—María's domestic sphere, repeatedly referred to as a "tomb":

> [El] alma [de María] entera estaba suspendida entre dos tumbas. La tumba silenciosa, desde cuyo fondo se levantaba la voz de su madre suplicante y llorosa; y la tumba agitada y llena de peligros, en que su padre aguardaría su vuelta; la tumba en que vivían, pues no podría darles otro nombre a aquella extraña morada, sepultada entre las rocas. (35)
>
> [(María's) entire soul was suspended between two tombs. The silent tomb from whose depths rose the voice of her crying and imploring mother; and the rough one full of danger, in which her father would await her return—the tomb in which they lived, as she could not give another name to that strange dwelling, interred among the rocks.]

Within the confining, suffocating enclosure, María feels her mother's *chora* (Kristeva's term for pre-linguistic drives and rhythms that originate in the womb) through the letter, the maternal kiss and emotions: "Sentía [los] besos [de su madre], le parecía escuchar sus palabras ahogadas por el llanto; y luego de aquellos besos y aquellas palabras, no quedaba ante sus ojos más que la soledad espantosa de una tumba" (33) [She felt her [mother's] kisses and she thought she heard her words drowned out by the sobs; and after those kisses and those words, nothing was left before her eyes except the frightening loneliness of a tomb].[12] These maternal impulses, which seem to radiate through the rocks, set off María's agency and propel her into the public sphere to vindicate her mother by reuniting with her maternal grandfather and deserting Vicente.

The idea of the discovery of truth within the shadows of the cave resonates with Plato's cave as a metaphor for the awakening of human

---

12. Kristeva's *chora* is part of the semiotic realm, a complement to the realm of the symbolic. These pre-linguistic impulses are similar to the rhythm one may sense in music and poetry (1947b, 93–97).

consciousness. Although the cave is a literary commonplace that goes back further than Cervantes' seventeenth-century cave of Montesinos in *Don Quijote* and is prevalent in nineteenth-century Romanticism, here its links to ignorance and discovery suggest a Platonic reading. In *The Speculum of the Other Woman* (1974), Luce Irigaray posits that Plato's cave is the black hole of ignorance and is analogous to the female *hystera,* or womb, while the light that shines from within the cave from the location of the forms represents masculine enlightenment. (We see another clear example of the cave metaphor as the site of ignorance and the light as enlightenment in Zeno Gandía's novel, which I discuss in Chapter 5.) In Barragán's novel the gender associations with primitiveness and enlightenment in relation to the cave are reversed. Here the dark cave, the site of ignorance and shadows, is the *paternal* space, while the resurrected mother is the source of light and of knowledge.[13] Paula's maternal words awaken María's consciousness as a subject, activate her agency, and launch her into the public sphere. To do so María must reject the name of the father, a symbol of patriarchal law, as his name carries with it the stain of his crimes. As we have seen, she rechristens herself María Granados.

Following the dramatic scene of the maternal epiphany, the reader is given some light comic relief. The narrator parodies the coming-of-age spectacle of a girl's first grown-up toilette, which here characterizes María's transformation from adolescent ignorance to liminal consciousness:

> ¡Pobre María! Enjugó sus ojos; arregló sus cabellos, y procuró serenar su semblante, otros días tan festivo. Después fue a mirarse a un espejo; ensayó una sonrisa, y aguardó con cierta coquetería a que entrase su padre a saludarla. Como se ve, la niña comenzaba a ser mujer, y se ataviaba para desempeñar la primera escena. Pronto sería cómica. Había tomado una resolución, ya sabremos cuál era. Para llevarla a cabo, necesitaba fingir, engañar a su padre con una alegría aparente; con una tranquilidad que estaba muy lejos de sentir. . . . Más claro aún, si ella engaña, si ella finge, es porque

---

13. This Platonic "darkness," the black cave, for Irigaray, is the maternal womb (*hystera*), so that the black space is a metaphor for feminine ignorance and bodily primitiveness, while light is analogous to masculine enlightenment (1985, 243–46). In Plato's metaphor, a line of prisoners faces the interior wall of a cave with a light source behind them. They are able to see only the shadows cast upon the wall of objects that are projected from behind them; they cannot see the actual objects (what Plato calls the *forms*).

aquél munca le habló verdad. María engañada por su padre, ... se preparaba también a engañarle. (33)

[Poor María! She dried her eyes, arranged her hair, and tried to calm her countenance, which on other days held such a festive expression. Afterward she went to look at herself in a mirror; she practiced a smile and waited with a certain coquetry for her father to enter and greet her. As we can see, the girl was becoming a woman and she was dressing herself to play the first scene. Soon it would become comic. She had made a resolution and now we will find out what it was. In order to see it through, she needed to feign and deceive her father with artificial happiness, with a serenity that she was very far from feeling. ... And clearly, if she deceived, if she feigned, it was because that man never spoke the truth to her. María, deceived by her father, ... prepared herself to deceive him in return.][14]

In this passage there is an ironic twist in the boudoir scene of the *quinceañera*; normally the young damsel would don womanly and seductive attire for the first time in a performance of subservient femininity in preparation for marriage. Here, however, María is beautifying herself to more easily trick or "seduce" her father into allowing her to go to Zapotlán—venture out on her own in the world and, later, to shun her hegemonically prescribed betrothal. The narration is unambiguous about María's conscious decision to resist paternal authority and forge her own path in life. The Freudian rebellion against the father for the love of the mother is the impetus for the story from here on. However, María does not come to identify fully with the mother, as this stage would mean crossing the line from girlhood to womanhood (that is, leaving the liminal and entering the stage of marriage and motherhood).

María perpetuates her liminality by running away from the symbolic domestic space of the cave and moving constantly between social modes and geographical spaces. During her adventures, she neither takes full part in the society of Zapotlán nor completely loses her connection to the bandits in the caves. For example, when the villain of the story, a bandit named Andrés Patiño, reveals the outlaws' hideout, placing them in danger in exchange

---

14. I have altered the short-paragraph formatting of the original text to save space.

for a valid passport, María shows solidarity with her former "family" by exclaiming, "¡Desgraciado . . . !" (199) [The wretch . . . !]. She also insists on wearing mourning for her father after he dies, putting herself in jeopardy by implicating herself with the bandits (199). She is between girlhood and womanhood, in between the purely marginal bandit culture of the caves and the mainstream cultures of Guadalajara and Zapotlán, just as she is, to some extent, loyal to the mother yet still bound to her father in a sentimental, if not an obedient, way. Within this fictional transitional mode in which social structure is softened and claims to power are more easily laid, Barragán takes full advantage of liminal spaces to allow her fictional protagonist to fulfill her desires as an individual, rather than within the marriageable ideal.

Feminine Agency for an Era of Progress: The Carriage and the Opium Vial

In terms of her transition from girlhood through the onset of her *quinceañera*, the pre-liminoid in the narrative is associated with the seclusion within the cave-home, while the liminoid is characterized by ambulatory freedom to roam. Before María's *quinceañera*, her father recognizes that "la pobre niña vive siempre guardada, si no por espesas rejas de hierro; si, por rocas impenetrables, donde solo el águila anida, y donde habrán de estrellarse siempre, todas las pesquisas de la policía" (7) [the poor girl lives constantly enclosed, if not by thick steel bars, by impenetrable rock where only the eagles nest, and where all the police investigations might some day be launched]. Descriptions of the cave, a metaphor for the home and domestic life, are filled with language denoting darkness, graves, death, crime, and seclusion (11–13). This space is associated with María as the obedient daughter; her "burial" deep in the bowels of the cave is analogous to the *recogimiento*, the domestic seclusion of the home, that I discuss in Chapter one.

While María is in the liminoid mode (post-*quinceañera*), feminine agency challenges patriarchal power, engaging her in active, extradomestic activity that lays claim to public power. In an ironic twist of roles, Vicente's movement is restricted to the domestic cave—he can only go to Zapotlán in disguise and at great risk of being caught by the authorities (103).

María navigates power in the city surprisingly well for a girl who has never ventured out from a subterranean bandits' lair. She uses her charms to win over the loyalty of the count of Tunerada (a man of power and her "protector" in Zapotlán), to then arrange with him to help her free her father's kidnapping victims. Her energy and decisiveness are reflected in the narrator's remarks on Tunerada's admiration of María: "Jamás se había imaginado que aquella joven, arrullada por las brisas de la montaña, fuese capaz de tanta energía como la que acababa de revelarle sus últimas palabras" (113) [Never had he imagined that that young girl, lulled to sleep by the mountain breeze, was capable of as much energy as her words had just revealed].

After directing the count on what to tell her father in order to free the prisoners (113), she shows that she is aware of how power works and how to put it to her own use: "Mi padre es algo supersticioso tratándose de mí, y creo que accederá; de lo contrario apelaremos a la franqueza, y . . . quizá al ruego para conseguirlo; pero de todos modos lo haré; apoyada en el prestigio de Ud." (114) [My father is somewhat superstitious when it comes to me and I believe he will give in; if not, we will call upon frankness, and . . . perhaps begging to achieve our goal; but no matter what, I will do it, supported by your prestige]. We see this same determination repeated throughout the plot: when she gets her father to establish her in Zapotlán, when she throws an opium-laced dinner party for the bandits to carry out her plan (which later leads to their demise), and when she frees the prisoners—including her own suitor—in the caves. This is, perhaps, one of the most noteworthy single acts in the story: the damsel navigating the subterranean hideout to release her distraught, imprisoned suitor, the young, handsome law student Rafael.

In addition to being street smart and unabashedly moving in political circles to reach her goals (like Cabello's Blanca Sol, as we shall see), María displays another important element of agency, in her penchant for travel. Travel, except in the case of relocating with one's husband or family, was not acceptable for a Mexican woman who considered herself honorable (chaste and marriageable). Not even in the rare cases of their working as physicians in Mexico City did women venture out to attend an emergency call for a patient; "a respectable woman could not go out alone or at all hours" (Macías 1982, 12). Foreign women's travel accounts of real women in Mexican society are in line with this image of Mexican women as sheltered and immobile. In 1884, Helen Sanborn (a U.S. citizen living in Mexico) writes: "It is contrary to custom and all rules of etiquette for a lady to go on the street alone, even in the daytime . . . it is improper for ladies, even in groups of two or three, to be out after dark unattended by a servant. . . . An American girl does not half appreciate her freedom and independence until she goes to one of these countries" (quoted in Agosín 1999, 210). Thus the narrative inscribes a vehement desire for freedom to travel (expressed by the narrator, as we will discover) that was strictly forbidden in actual society.

The reader catches a glimpse of real-life Mexico's disapproval of women's travel in Barragán's symbolic experiment: María's nanny, Juana, unsuccessfully tries to stop her charge's solo travel. The young heroine shrugs off Juana's fears, issuing her the following mandate before embarking on her quest: "You will remain here until I order your departure or come back for you" (95). María's words are emblematic of her decisiveness in acting on her will and driving the action throughout the plot. Reminding the reader of the real-life Argentine writer and traveler Juana Manuela Gorriti and the fearless French Peruvian Flora Tristán, the novel's dynamic heroine moves freely between the private and public spheres; receives male visitors at her home unchaperoned; and, without anyone getting in her way, travels independently on "dangerous" roads (95). Thus, Barragán's heroine differs from characters in nation-building texts such as those described by the twenty-first-century Hispanist and critical theorist Mary Louise Pratt, in which women are models of republican motherhood: "[Women] are imagined as dependent rather than sovereign; they are practically forbidden to be limited and finite, being obsessively defined by their reproductive capacity" (1992, 30). This is clearly not the case in *La hija del bandido*, as María is an individual who acts according to the dictates of her mind and heart.

Yet counteracting policies of enclosure is only the tip of the iceberg in this feminist altering of the symbolic order of Porfirian Mexico; travel is a metaphor for discursive freedom and the voyage of the intellect. To give an idea of the narrator's conception of travel, freedom, and its link to imagining and writing fiction, let us examine a passage in which the narrator defends her right to make a temporal leap in the plot by comparing her pen to a magic wand:

> Cuando yo era niña, solían referirme algunos cuentos de encantadoras, en los que varitas mágicas encendían en mí deseos irrealizables . . .
>
> Hoy, gracias a Dios, he llegado a alcanzar una varita de aquellas, por la que puedo a mi antojo, cruzar en un segundo los mares, visitar el Viejo Continente y el Nuevo y el Austral: en una palabra, entrar y salir a donde quiero, sin pedir licencia: andar tan de prisa que dejo atrás a los que iban delante; y oigo y observo, sin que nadie me observe a su vez. (197)

[When I was a little girl, they used to tell me tales of enchantresses, from which the idea of the magic wand ignited in me impossible desires. . . .

Today, thanks to God, I have come to obtain one of those wands, by which I can, at my whim, cross the seas in a second to visit the old world, the new, and the south pole: in a word, to come and go wherever I want, without asking permission: to walk so fast I leave behind those who were ahead of me; and I hear and I observe, without anyone observing me in turn.]

The magic wand is the writer's pen and the landscape is only limited by the writer's imagination. The idea of freedom is closely linked to the imaginary journey and writing. Here the narrator (who, by her own references to herself as the author, is conflated with the female writer) expresses autonomy in terms of physical movement of one's body through space and the uncensored liberty to observe. Both these themes are reflected in the novel: the fictional María travels and the narrator comments, giving voice to what the heroine sees. Here, again, the narrator's lack of (and desire for) agency and freedom are overt:

¡No hay momentos . . . en que se piense más; en que la imaginación remonte, con más ahinco, su vuelo por los espacios intelectuales y morales . . . que cuando se camina a caballo . . . nos damos cuenta de todas las bellezas agrestes de la soledad. . . .

Pero dejémonos de viajes; pocos o ninguno de mis lectores leerán mi libro viajando; y yo, al escribirlo, no emprendo más viaje que el de la imaginación que inventa, el corazón que siente, y la mano que escribe. (79)

[There are no moments . . . when one thinks more; when the imagination elevates its flight through the intellectual and moral realms with more zeal. . . . Only by riding on horseback . . . do we become aware of the rustic beauty in solitude. . . .

But let us leave the theme of voyages; few or none of my readers will read my book while traveling; and I, upon writing it, do not set forth on any journey, other than that of the imagination that invents, the heart that feels, and the hand that writes.]

The narrator's tone of yearning is apparent in this passage and it is one of the moments of slippage, in which (similar to the novel's riding the edge of fantasy and history in terms of its roots in local legend) nonfictional desires momentarily creep into social commentary by pointing to the almost nonexistent opportunities for women to explore public space without repercussions.

Barragán's expression of early feminism in the topics of freedom, space, and gender politics is a literary gesture not unlike those of later feminist theorists. For both nineteenth- and twentieth-century feminist thinkers, women's space and writing are intimately linked. Latin American women writers during Barragán's era, such as Gorriti, Matto de Turner, and Wright de Kleinhans, were opening up symbolic and real-world spaces by founding their own periodicals and literary organizations.[15] On a concrete level, Virginia Woolf is perhaps the first feminist to write at length, in *A Room of One's Own* (1929), of the important material link between writing and the need for women writers to lay claim to their own private space—signaling the fact that even in the domestic sphere, women did not have control over their environment. The twentieth-century Mexican feminist thinker, writer, and diplomat Rosario Castellanos explores with satire and humor the intricate and, at times, sinister implications of the myths of femininity perpetuated in and by typically feminine spaces, such as the home, the beauty salon, and the secretary's desk, in her 1975 dark comedy *El eterno femenino* (The Eternal Feminine).

Other twentieth-century theorists associate feminine space and writing in more abstract ways. Cixous, for example, believes that women's transgressive writing is the way to break free from the masculine creation of "harem" space (1981, 251), thus creating an abstract space of their own, but also a concrete one, because they could move within their physical space with a feeling of ownership. Irigaray theorizes all space, even the domestic, as masculine, and thus women never truly own it. For Irigaray, the mother is the "space by and in which man can find a position and locate himself" (Irigaray quoted in Grosz 1989, 174) In this view, woman cannot occupy a space of her own because she *is* space, and she later exchanges her possibility for space for his: his home (174). For Claudine Herrmann, *space* refers to both the physical areas around us (the home as well as nations and territories) and the mental arena; each is vulnerable to masculine domination (cited in

---

15. For a discussion of women's periodicals and literary salons in the late 1880s, see the Introduction in this study.

Grosz 1989, 168). Herrmann draws a parallel between men's control over physical spaces and their domination of a language that is awkward and foreign (literally as well as figuratively) in the mouth of a woman (169). If for Hermann the way that men oppress women is by aggressively taking possession of mental and physical space, it seems that the gesture in women's writing of revalorizing women's space is one vehicle for repossessing it for themselves by being agents within it. The theories outlined above that offer an abstract concept of space should be taken into consideration for the analysis at hand to remind us that women writers repossess not only imagined "physical" space in writing, but abstract and mental space as well. These views offer interesting alternatives to viewing women's space in terms of the dichotomies private-space-for-women and public-space-for-men. In her novel Barragán appears to change the symbolic ownership of space by envisioning a woman who dominates various social orbs and an author/narrator who is an agent within her own creative and imaginative space—and who occupies, temporarily, the imagination of her reader as well.

By writing the theme of travel into her novel as I have described it here, Barragán is pointing to the independence and self-realization that one scholar has found in women's travel writing of the nineteenth century: "Traveling embodies a journey of the imagination and the possibility of creating a world of experiences, allowing women to tell of their own adventures instead of being mere receptacles for their male counterparts' stories. Traveling also allows women to witness life first-hand, to become accountable for their own histories, their own destinies" (Agosín 1999, 13). The self-invented María Granados dominates the spaces of the criminal's lair, the city, and the open road in her quest to correct wrongdoing. Her aggressive attitude toward the spaces she inhabits makes her one of the most dynamic heroines of the nineteenth century.

The Other Side of Agency: Equalizing Standards

By focusing on María's agency, I do not mean to imply that she escapes a superficial classification as an *ángel* on numerous occasions in the narrative. Despite the many heroic acts that María performs (her travel, dexterity at handling both known and unknown dangers, and so on), she is still described, at times, with images that conjure up the angelic ideal—although her actions contradict such characterizations, and at times, on the contrary, she is referred to as a "fallen angel" for her ties to the lugubrious bandits' cave (Barragán 1934, 170). At other times, the narrator makes generalizations about women and motherhood that seem to advocate the Angel of the House, for example: "La que cría y nutre con el alimento de su cariño y la abnegación de su ternura es madre" (63) [A mother is she who raises and feeds [her young] with the nutrients of her affection and her tender abnegation]. Nonetheless, we see the main female protagonist engaging in none of these maternal activities. It is true that she saves the kidnapping victims (which denotes a self-abnegating altruism); however, this is a feat that the (male) authorities would have performed, and one that wins the hero (or heroine, in this case) praise and recognition, unlike the day-to-day nurturing required of a wife and mother that goes largely unnoticed and unrewarded.

The narrative, however, seems to impose angelic standards on the male characters; Rafael (María's suitor) and his confidant, Adolfo, are held to ideals normally reserved for women. While storming the bandits' cave to look for one of the kidnapping victims (whom they do not find), they witness, but ignore, a scene of a woman being taken away on a horse, causing the narrator to comment on their "egoísmo" [selfishness] and lack of "abnegación," "compasión," and "buenos sentimientos" (83) [abnegation, compassion, and good sentiments]. In another section, the narrator exclaims, "¡Oh! Si el hombre tuviera dominio sobre sus pasiones, ese clavo de la virtud" (209) [Oh! If men could only dominate their passions, this urge that impales virtue]. The message is that it is just as important for men to be self-abnegating and restrained in their passions as it is for women.

Barragán also includes an equalizing gesture about morality and gender when she comments upon the wife of one of her father's kidnapping victims. The pair has been separated for a significant period of time (unspecified, but long enough for his wife to suffer in poverty from the absence of his earnings). Rather than present a romanticized view of the reunion between husband and wife, the narrator points out the unjust blame that the wife is likely to face, because their daughter has also disappeared:

> Doña Mercedes fue preparada por sus amigos, para recibir no sé si la alegría o el pesar por la vuelta de su esposo, pues en sus tristes circunstancias todo podía caber. Además, en el matrimonio la mujer lleva la peor parte en todo lo que a él atañe; ni mis lindas lectoras dejarán de afirmarlo. Sucede un acontecimiento fatal en la familia, y el hombre culpa a la mujer, aunque ella no tenga culpa. (196)

[Doña Mercedes was prepared by her friends to receive (I do not know which) either joy or sorrow in regard to her husband's return, as in her sad circumstances anything was possible. Moreover, in matrimony the woman bears the heaviest burden in everything related to it; neither will my lovely women readers fail to affirm it. Some fatal event occurs in the family, and the man blames the woman, even if she is not culpable.]

So, just as Barragán equalizes agency in the plot of her novel, she also points to the discrepancy in moral standards set for women versus those set for men. The critique of marriage that the narrator levels above sets the stage for María's refusal to marry and sets up her continuance in the liminal mode.

At the end of the novel, María successfully rescues her father's victims, he dies in a shoot-out with the police, and she is left in the charge of her maternal grandfather, who longs to see her wed and thus protected. He urges: "Un buen esposo a tu lado sería la paz de mi muerte" [A good husband at your side would grant me a peaceful death]. Barragán describes María's reaction: "Pero . . . balbuceó la joven" (220) [But . . . stammered the young woman]. María's hesitancy belies a fear of entering an institution that would deny her the personal autonomy to which she has become accustomed.

Conclusions: The Perpetuation of Liminality

Like all temporary reversals of authority, María's too, must come to an end— or, it *almost* comes to an end. Whereas Turner has found that rites of passage often end in a "return to society as a structure of statuses," María's liminality is never quite resolved, as the convent is another marginal space where society's rules do not apply (1969, 104). Normally in a coming-of-age ritual such as the *quinceañera,* the return to status is marked by a resumption or commencement of sexual relations (marriage); María shuns the marital vow her grandfather wishes to see her take in order to enter the Capuchin order.

By refusing to marry, María refuses, both literally and figuratively, to reproduce the patriarchal model. Opting for convent life means choosing a matriarchal society, one that boasted a history of respected Hispanic poets who were nuns. The best-known examples are the sixteenth-century Spanish mystic Santa Teresa de Avila (real name Teresa de Cepeda y Ahumada, 1515–1582), a Carmelite, and the seventeenth-century Mexican baroque poet Sor Juana Inés de la Cruz (real name Juana Inés de Asbaje, 1648?–1695), a Geronomite, whose early feminist messages are the topics of many studies.[16] Although she was not a writer, Catalina de Erauso (1592–1650), known as "la monja alférez" (the nun lieutenant), lived her life in a convent but ran away before taking her vows. Risking charges of heresy, she disguised herself as a man, took the false name Francisco de Loyola, and, as a soldier and later lieutenant in the Spanish army, traveled through South America, leading a life full of drama that included duels, battles, and love intrigues. Barragán's María is imagined into this tradition of spunky sisters who reject marriage and follow their own agendas inside and outside the convent.

There are several moments in the narrative when Barragán seems to restate Sor Juana's famous *redondilla,* which begins with "Hombres necios" (Foolish men). In Sor Juana's verses the poetic voice accuses men of placing blame on women for lapses that the men themselves provoke: "Hombres necios que acusáis / a la mujer sin razón, / sin ver que sois la occasion / de lo mismo que culpáis" (Cruz 1985, 109) [Foolish men who accuse / women unjustly / not seeing that you are the reason / behind the sins for which you blame them]. María hurls the same accusation at Rafael, just before vowing to become a nun: "¡Así sois los hombres todos . . . juzgáis, aborrecéis y despreciáis, sin examinar primero la causa" (Barragán 1934, 201) [Such are all men . . . you judge, you despise and disdain, without first examining the cause]. In another passage, in speaking of how men fail to see that women trick them out of necessity, the narrator restates the same message: "Para alcanzar a conocer [a las mujeres], deberían los hombres hacer un estudio minucioso de sí mismos. Porque la mujer ha sido, y será siempre lo que el hombre quiere que sea" (33) [In order to know women, men should conduct a detailed study of themselves. Because women have always been and will always be what men want them to be]. There is a very close connection, then, between these messages and the famous poem by Sor Juana, which Barragán's readers might have known, and more important, with which Barragán appears to have been familiar.[17]

16. For further reading on the early feminist messages in the oeuvre of Sor Juana, see Cruz 2005; Dill 2001; González Boixo 1995; Kirk 1998; Merrim 1999.

17. According to the early twentieth-century Mexican writer and scholar Ermilo Abreu Gómez (1938) in his book chapter on the history of criticism on the writing of Sor Juana Inés de la Cruz, well-known nineteenth-century critics such as the Mexican scholar Ignacio Montes de Oca y Obregón (1840–1921) read and wrote about the work of Sor Juana, albeit without the depth that came with twentieth-century criticism. It is likely that a well-read woman such as Barragán would gravitate to the work of an intellectual Mexican foremother; the allusions to Sor Juana's poetry in *La hija* are evidence of this.

It is, therefore, more feasible to interpret María's entry into the convent as a rebellious act than a domestic-like enclosure.

To conclude, the fifteenth birthday, anthropologically and psychoanalytically significant as a celebration of womanhood, would normally entail the expectation of marriage and a life limited to home, church, and family. In Barragán's novel, however, it is the catalyst for a plot that focuses on the young woman's heroic agency. Barragán's narrative is significant as an early feminist work—not only because it features a dynamic female character, but also because it employs in its narrative strategy dominant (masculine) culture's fissures, gaps, and marginal spaces to create an ambiance in which to subvert the basic tenets of the Angel of the House. Within this space, the author grants the female protagonist freedom to travel, perform the public authorities' job of solving crime, and reject the prospect of a marriage to a man who unjustly questions her morality. Barragán's fantastic liminal agent, María, speaks to the frustrations of women in the Porfirian era (as outlined in Chapter 1) when, surrounded by discourses of progress and scientific advances, they were sheltered, secluded within the home, kept uneducated, and had legal rights only minimally greater than those of minors (Ramos Escandón 1987b, 147).

3

WOMEN IN PERU:
NATIONAL AND PRIVATE STRUGGLES FOR INDEPENDENCE

IF ONE WERE TO LOOK at a graph charting women's participation in public life in Peru through the nineteenth century, it would consist of a peak in activity in the first two decades, followed by a sharp decline in the new republic at midcentury, and then a gradual rise through the 1870s and 1880s, when women began seeking education reform and publishing their own essays, fiction, poetry, and journal articles.

As in the case of Mexico, Peru's wars of independence with Spain (1817–1825) brought social disruption that allowed women a chance to break free from their limited social roles and experience a broader range of activities and personal autonomy than in peacetime. Women's participation in the history of Spanish America became somewhat accepted and even necessary during the struggle for independence. As the historian Renán Jaramillo Flores puts it, this cause finally gave women the chance to leave their roles as "decorative elements" in the household and enter the symbolic order as agents in society and politics (1977, 21).

Although this study focuses on historical and fictional women of the bourgeoisie (as these are the women Cabello represents in *Blanca Sol,* which we will discuss in the following chapter), the symbolic reconstruction of womanhood during the independence period happened at all social levels. A well-known example is found in the pre-independence rebellion initiated by the Incan leader Tupac Amaru and his wife, Micaela Bastidas, in 1777. Bastidas participated in the rebellion in military, political, and administrative capacities. Her intelligence, dedication, and ruthlessness in battle inspired an anonymous author in the 1796 chronicles written by the royalist functionary Melchor de Paz to proclaim of Micaela that "dicha Cacica es de un genio más intrépido y sangriento que el marido" (Paz quoted in Guardia 1985, 42) [the woman Indian chief they spoke of is of a bloodier and more intrepid nature than that of her husband].

The Peruvian women whose participation is most often mentioned in historical accounts are the indigenous *campesinas,* called *rabonas,* who, as camp followers, were the most visible women agents in the war effort. The *rabonas* traveled with their husbands and lovers from battle to battle gathering food, cooking, rationing water, managing supplies, and participating in direct combat when necessary. These women were so important to the soldiers that when there was talk of excluding them from the camps, the soldiers protested because they feared they would suffer if the women's tasks were left to the military. As virtual parts of the army, *rabonas* were not spared the consequences when the pro-independence forces were defeated in battle; they were the victims of rape, murder, and imprisonment. Historical accounts praise them for their heartiness and bravery.

It is perhaps because of the *rabonas*' dramatic role on the battlefield that historians favor their inclusion in twentieth-century historical accounts of independence, while the roles of women of the bourgeoisie seem to have been largely overlooked.

Bourgeois Women's Agency in the Independence Era

The educator and historian Elvira García y García's 1924 study is one of the few sources dedicated to women's history in Lima (the bustling city center and setting for *Blanca Sol*). Her work shows that women of Mercedes Cabello de Carbonera's social class were a vital part of the independence movement in Lima, as was true throughout Spanish America. The desire for power by Lima's upper crust and growing bourgeoisie drove the fight against the Spaniards, so it was often within these rising-class households that much of the conspiring took place and women were actively included (Jaramillo Flores 1977, 22). Although Jaramillo Flores provides few examples from Lima in particular, he claims that in general Latin American women were involved in activities of the pro-independence leaders as hosts for their meetings and that they also had a role in decision making (22). He mentions that some women in Buenos Aires took part in the distribution and purchase of arms and that ladies of means sold their jewels and valuables to contribute to the constant costs associated with the war effort.

Rosita Campuzano, Jaramillo reveals, was a wealthy *limeña* of the elite who contributed financially and politically. It is possible that the historian mentions her because of the racy tidbit of rumors of her romantic involvement with Argentine freedom fighter General José de San Martín (28). While her amorous liaison may have made her seem unique to this particular historian, her participation in the revolution was not uncommon. In the name of independence, women in Lima performed jobs that they would not have dreamed of under the strict social restrictions of the colonial period: they acted as spies, messengers, financial contributors, hosts for pro-independence affairs, and writers of propaganda.

García y García's history offers the most detailed catalog of the activities of *criolla* women (women born in Peru of Spanish lineage) in Lima during independence. The study, despite being written in a Romantic style in which all women are repeatedly praised for their "unparalleled bravery" and "supreme dedication," is nonetheless valuable for its extensive listing of the names of individuals and the specific tasks they performed during independence.[1] García y García's main sources are the official records of the Peruvian Ladies' Society (Sociedad Peruana de Damas), an organization created by San Martín in 1821 to honor women's wartime assistance. The study gives short descriptions of about 50 of these women and identifies 136.

García y García's research on the Sociedad Peruana de Damas archives reveals that women from Cabello's social class left the domestic sphere and their responsibilities to children and hearth to take part in worldly activities that were normally strictly taboo for women: war and politics. For example, two sisters named Juana and Candelaria García donated all their wealth to help the pro-independence forces, carried messages from pro-independence prisoners to their troops, and informed troops of the whereabouts of the Spanish. Both were caught by royalist forces, bravely withstood torture without revealing any information, and were finally released when the Spaniards departed Lima. Other women who were honored for their participation were Josefa Carrillo, the marquise of Castellón; Rosa Merino, a famous vocalist who delivered the first public performance of the national anthem at the postindependence victory gala; and Angélica Zevallos, who provided the army with weapons. Petronila Ferreyros is mentioned for serving as messenger and also for writing the pro-independence propaganda that

---

1. An interesting side note to this history of women is that its author, the well-known educator and director of el Liceo Fanning (a school in Lima) Elvira García y García (1862–1951), did not agree with Cabello's untraditional views on girls' education. Upon hearing the novelist's criticism of religion and the clergy and her suggestion that girls learn about their bodies, García y García responds that "en su colegio se respeta mucho la religión, que no se tomó examen de fisiología sino de zoología" (in her school religion is well respected and physiological exams are not given, but rather those on zoology [quoted in Glave 1999, 103]). This may explain the more traditional, romanticized, and, by extension, Angel of the House–style prose used to talk about historical women here.

was distributed throughout the country. Although partaking in war-related activities was less comfortable at times than tending the home, these women were engaging in a struggle for power on a large scale, likely for the first time in their lives.

This era of increased and diversified agency necessarily altered women's day-to-day activities. Social roles were more fluid than they had been under colonial rule. For example, Ferreyros, a woman of means, served in the hospitals "en el mismo rol que las sirvientas" (García y García 1924, 211) [in the same role as the servants]. Previously sheltered women were leading more varied lives with more mobility. Freedom fighters needed nurses, messengers, and others helpers, and this gave women the opportunity to transgress social norms (for example, by traveling freely without a chaperone), thereby gaining a broader understanding of the world outside the family and hearth. Women embarking on these adventures were sure to have viewed themselves and their contributions to society in a new light. Wartime experiences likely made them cognizant of their ability to engage in society and politics; they were aware that their intervention contributed to a grand cause. It is likely that, upon interacting with women and men of various social backgrounds united in civic duty, these women discovered facets of themselves they never knew existed and were able to develop a sense of self with more complexity than women whose existences did not extend beyond the usual domestic concerns.

This newfound individuality had its consequences for the angelic standard, by which women were expected to forgo their own desires for those of male heads of the household. For example, in Colombia a woman named Genoveva Ricaurte went against the wishes of her husband, a royalist Spaniard, by aiding her fellow freedom fighters who had been taken prisoner (Jaramillo Flores 1977, 28). Similarly, the well-known Manuela Sáenz of Ecuador, daughter of a wealthy and powerful Spaniard, abandoned her husband and privileged position to become independence leader Simón Bolívar's lover for seven years, traveling with him and advising him as he led battles across Spanish America. This is perhaps the first time in the history of *criolla* women's history in Latin America that larger numbers of women were publicly actualizing their own desires and beliefs, against those of their parents and spouses.

From a gender-conservative pro-independence perspective, women's participation in independence was a double-edged sword: it was necessary for success and also represented a threat to the ruling class's hold on power.

If women were taking on responsibilities outside the home and were needed beyond the domestic sphere, they were gaining power in these new realms that, under normal circumstances, were exclusively occupied by men.

The self-conscious wording of García y García's biography of Brígida Silva de Ochoa, honored for her services in 1822, seems to reveal this fear of women's venturing into the political realm. Silva was a bourgeois woman noted for helping her two freedom-fighter brothers, Remigio Silva, a colonel in the armed forces, and Mateo Silva, a lawyer. Reflecting what must have been the opinion of the era, García y García first carefully praises Silva's role as wife and mother of *seven children* (1924, 211). Only after this emphasis on "la augusta misión de madre de familia" (her august mission as mother) does the historian introduce her role in the independence process. García y García then takes a gendered perspective in her praise of Silva: "Doña Brígida Silva se reveló siempre como la mujer toda corazón, que no se convierte en ningún marimacho, ser híbrido, que carece de las delicadezas propias de la mujer" (212) [Doña Brígida Silva always behaved as a woman full of heart, who never turned into a butch [*marimacha*], a hybrid being who lacks the delicacy common to women]. The historian's emphasizing Silva's motherhood and femininity, while defensively reviling the notion of any contamination of this femininity, reveals her desire to counter women's agency with elements of the Angel of the House, symbolically angling women back into that role. Although written in 1924, this account reveals the element of discomfort a traditional ruling-class person likely felt toward women's level of freedom in wartime Peru. It also demonstrates the slow pace at which expectations for women have changed.

After independence, the fate of many women of the privileged class who had lent their services to the war was poverty: they had donated much or all of their property and the new republic did not offer compensation for their contributions. Some were taken prisoner by the Spaniards and even tortured or killed; many were widowed. Their overall condition would worsen when the stability of colonial rule gave way to chaos and economic decline. For those who survived, the level and scope of their activities returned to the domestic sphere. Rather than acting upon their high-minded beliefs for a lasting cause, they likely went back to preparing meals that would simply disappear and have to be prepared again the next day. While their war efforts and suffering must have brought them some glory, caring for children was merely the expected minimum. Women who had experienced some thrill of democratic participation and power were now to serve as models of morality and self-sacrifice. That is, they were now the mothers of the new nation.

Republicanism and the Tightening of the Moral Noose: The Mid-1800s

After the South American freedom fighter Simón Bolívar's permanent departure in August 1826, Peru experienced two decades of political instability. Between 1826 and 1845, less than twenty years, the new nation suffered the inconsistencies in policy and rule of thirty different chief executives, the majority of them *caudillos* (military strongmen). Debate and strife over the independence of Bolivia added to the general turmoil, under which social reform and rebuilding after the battles of independence were impossible. The once prosperous colonial city of Lima was in a state of disrepair and the previously thriving mining economy was stagnant.

During this postindependence period, there appeared to be a campaign to limit women's rights and freedoms. It is possible that keeping women at home in their traditional role was one way for the ruling class to add an element of control over the political and social turbulence. Lima's growing population and the increase in the numbers of urban masses and rural workers also motivated policies to restrict women's activities (Hunefeldt 2000, 149). While bourgeois *limeñas* did not experience the mobility that comes with entering the market economy in the capacity of vendors or artisans, as the historian of women's culture of the Andean region Christine Hunefeldt points out, they had, as we have seen, enjoyed increased freedom and participation during the independence period. The experience of leaving the domestic sphere, coupled with the efforts of liberal politicians to implement education for girls, was sure to have provoked counterreactions aimed at keeping women from gaining power in the emerging nation. Unofficial regulation of women's activities came in the form of greater emphasis on the Angel of the House standard. As I discussed in the Introduction of this study, two tenets of the angelic ideal of womanhood were self-abnegation and seclusion or chaperoning to ensure virginity and properly monitored behavior. We have seen that special institutions, such as *beaterios* and *recogimientos* (reform homes run by nuns for women who were temporarily separated from their husbands pending an ecclesiastic conjugal trials or who were prostitutes), were created in an attempt to uphold high moral standards for women.

Although records show there were ample opportunities for women to slip out of such refuges or receive visitors (Hunefeldt 2000), the practical function of *beaterios* and *recogimientos* was to control the whereabouts and movement of women who were not under the protection of a husband or father. The late eighteenth-century Spanish-born bureaucrat José Ignacio de Lequanda, member of the Sociedad de Amantes del País of Lima (Society of Friends of the Country, an organization from the pre-independence era), in an article in the Lima newspaper *El Mercurio Peruano* voices his approval of the policy of enclosure that was brought back in the early republican era: "Nadie duda que la reclusión de las mujeres contribuye a conservar las buenas costumbres" (quoted in Rosas Lauro 1999, 143) [Nobody doubts that the women's seclusion helps to maintain good behavior]. Thus, the church, together with the bourgeois society in power, exerted efforts to restrain women's movement and, therefore, limited the scope of women's experience and kept them in the role of the Angel of the House. In these ways, women were kept from participating in public affairs. Perhaps there was some fear on the part of the men of the ruling class that women's essential roles as camp followers, spies, financial supporters, and organizers of meetings, among other things, would warrant demands for political voice in the new nation.

Pressure for women to suppress complaints about their domestic situations coincided with the social policies of seclusion and domesticity mentioned above. Christine Hunefeldt's study of 1,070 conjugal suits in the archbishopric of Lima between 1800–1910 reveals an increased emphasis on suffering in silence for women who endured domestic problems at mid-century. During these years, women could not argue their case plainly in court as they had done in the years following independence: "Between 1840 and 1860, fewer women resorted to lawsuits; and women filing suit had to find the 'right' mix of arguments—for example, demonstrating poverty and suffering coupled with her own virtuous behavior—or present dramatic evidence of extreme abuse. Short-term personal suffering no longer constituted a sufficient reason to win a judge's compassion" (Hunefeldt 2000, 325). This observation shows that it behooved women to articulate their arguments within a discourse of the long-suffering Angel if they wanted positive results from the judicial system. A woman had to prove that her virtue had hitherto prevented her from speaking out, and that she finally did so out of concern for her family, rather than for "selfish" motives.[2] Speaking of women from the lower classes, Hunefeldt notes that, with the threat of women's participation in the urban economy, "decency and correct moral behavior became mechanisms to separate women from men and women from each other to maintain class boundaries and political exclusion" (57).

---

2. An example of this type of court case argument is that of the upper-class *limeña* Fermina Godoy (Hunefeldt 2000, 326).

Some women seeking legal separation, however, found a loophole in the Angel of the House's emphasis on maternity.[3] As the scholar of nineteenth-century literature Doris Sommer (1991) notes, the health of the national family was a major concern of policy makers at a time when it was believed that to govern meant populating the large expanses of territory in new Latin American countries. Thus at around midcentury in Peru, women began using the excuse of "sexual incompatibility" for ecclesiastic separation (Hunefeldt 2000, 140).[4] The church considered this a valid argument because it prevented procreation—the main goal of marriage. Women could not, however, legally remarry and start families with other men; if the courts allowed separation because of sexual incompatibility, wives were allowed to return to their parents' homes and live apart from their husbands (141).

Historical records of upper- and middle-class women's activities in public life show a sharp decline in the first decades of the republic. Although García y García manages to write about sixteen women who were significant during this time period, the short biographies read more like the socialite pages of a gossip magazine than a study noting the feats of women worthy of inclusion in the annals of history. Most of the women are mentioned because they are the wives of presidents or generals and have found their way into the pages of the study for being supportive, loyal spouses—a sharp contrast with the spies, writers of propaganda, and weapons dealers of the independence period! Most are praised for their excellent manners, beauty, and conversational skills. Some are noted for writing verses—that were never published, so far as we know. (The act of publishing one's intimate thoughts would be considered too public to be modest or virtuous.)

---

3. Hunefeldt explains that divorce in nineteenth-century Peru meant "a temporal separation of the spouses with ecclesiastical court approval and not the dissolution of the marriage" (13). Despite debate in the 1850s over whether marriage should be considered a sacrament (thus indissoluble) or a civil contract, the latter view did not prevail until 1930, when dissolution by divorce was legalized (Hunefeldt 2000, 83–85).

4. Arguments of sexual incompatibility took various forms and usually entailed medical examinations of the genitals. In one case a woman argued that genital size made intercourse impossible; another complained that she did not receive pleasure from intercourse with her husband *and claimed this as her right* (Hunefeldt 2000, 142; my emphasis). The sexual incompatibility argument was later expanded to include character incompatibility. It is of particular importance that these women were focusing on their own desires and happiness, even as they were insisting on the official standard. It is also noteworthy that they were voicing their concerns in quasi-medical terms by speaking of intercourse as a purely biological, reproductive function, thus taking a Positivist approach, which I will discuss shortly. Such attempts at circumlocution around an unhappy marriage indicate that women were finding ways to challenge the system even before the greater early feminist movements of the 1870s.

Two exceptions in the first half of the century are Flora Tristán, whom I will discuss shortly, and the extraordinary Francisca Zubiaga de Gamarra ("la Mariscala"), who commanded her own troop under her husband, General Agustín Gamarra. It is clear from this general decline in women's agency during the postrevolutionary period that women were once again confined to the domestic sphere and restrictive roles they endured under colonial rule.

Flora Tristán, a Frenchwoman of Peruvian descent who traveled to Peru in 1833–34 in a frustrated attempt to claim her inheritance, wrote a detailed account of bourgeois Lima society in the early republic.[5] In her travel narrative, *Les pérégrinations d'une paria* (*Peregrinations of a Pariah*, 1834), Tristán describes women's condition in the nation at the time. Although she initially states that women in Lima are freer than in any other place in the world because the traditional dress of *manta y saya* (a shawl, which was worn partially covering the face, and a skirt) allows them to leave home and move outside the domestic sphere without being recognized, her later accounts do not uphold this view (329–30). Her psychological portraits of specific women in her family paint a bleak picture of the hardships women were forced to endure within marriage and in convents.

One example is that of Tristán's cousin Carmen, who must choose between the two options for women at that time: to enter a convent or marry. Carmen opts for the latter and is the victim of an abusive husband who marries her for the dowry, parades mistresses in front of her blatantly, abandons her, and only returns when he has wasted her fortune on gambling and debauchery (Tristán 1983, 131). When Carmen dares to complain about her spouse to friends and family, they silence her by saying that she should be happy to have a good-looking husband, since she herself is ugly. Carmen's voicing of her unhappiness and desire to work against the system, rather than within it, go against two main principles of the Angel of the House: silent suffering and self-abnegation. The female self does not exist in this economy, except as a tool for the well-being of others. Tristán laments the apparent lack of recourse for an unhappy marriage and women's entrapment in marital "hell" (132, 143).

---

5. Although Tristán was born and raised in France and her mother was French, her father was a Peruvian from a wealthy family in Lima. After the death of Tristán's father, her relatives in Lima offered her a stipend but refused to grant her the inheritance because of lack of ecclesiastic proof of her parents' marriage. This disappointment probably instigated her subsequent antibourgeois, pre-Marxist activism; she dedicated her life to fighting injustices against men and women of the working classes, with whom she most likely identified.

Tristán's narrative offers a view of how women were oppressed: they had very few options and were perceived to hold a superior position only in regard to morality, but were left ignorant despite a promising natural intelligence (335, 141). *Pérégrinations* nonetheless offers insight into the meager or nonexistent education for women that Cabello overtly criticizes in *Blanca Sol*. Tristán's observations confirm Hunefeldt's research findings that "in the absence of efficient mechanisms of social control, morality was *the* weapon to maintain order. This control was acted out in the realms of family and marriage" (2000, 76).

Although I have highlighted the negative side of the Angel of the House, it is important to note that exceptional virtue and adherence to the angelic model could also provide social mobility. That is, conforming to patriarchal ideals had its rewards. A woman who was raised "properly" and was sheltered or constantly chaperoned (and who, hence, would have been assumed by society to be a virgin) could be offered in marriage to a better-off man.[6] This appears to be the case of the secondary character Josefina in Cabello's novel, whose hard work and self-sacrifice in raising her siblings and supporting her grandmother wins her a husband from a higher social class (although, as we will discover, even in this case Cabello's angelic facade is just that—a false and unrealistic front). Significantly, Cabello chooses to situate this benefit of female virtue within the secondary plot. The novelist focuses rather on the main character as a means of condemning stereotypes and critiquing the meager career options for women. Nonetheless, it is worth mentioning that meeting unrealistic standards of virtue promised financial and romantic benefits, which explains why the Angel of the House standard was often appropriated and perpetuated by women themselves.

It was not until 1845, under President Ramón Castilla, that the government stabilized and began to perform its basic duties. This consistency in leadership, coupled with the discovery of guano (natural fertilizer) for export, gave Peru the peace and funds required for desperately needed reform. Under liberal leadership, women would benefit to some degree through qualified inclusion in public education reform. But eventually they would have to engage in a kind of struggle different from the battles of independence, one toward personal liberty, in which women would use language to defend

---

6. I emphasize the idea of social perception of chastity here because if a woman did not have a protector or someone to chaperone her (to give the appearance of living a sheltered life), she might not have been considered chaste by society, regardless of her moral caliber. Likewise, a woman who was not a virgin but who was very discreet might have been perceived as virtuous by society.

their interests. This battle would necessarily have to entail an attack upon the angel standard through the elimination of virtue as the sole saving grace for their sex (an ambitious goal for that era), or at least an expansion of what it meant for a woman to be virtuous. In addition, women would have to privilege their own intelligence and skills outside the home.

Challenges to the Angel of the House: Liberal Reform and Women's Education

The political situation during the first part of the nineteenth century was generally characterized by fluctuations between liberal and conservative tendencies, with no formal political party coalescing until the later part of the nineteenth century, with the appearance of the Civilianist Party (*civilistas*).[7] Many of the politicians who welcomed education for female citizens did so because of women's role as the guardians and caretakers of the future generations of Peruvians—but these supporters wanted women's education to be limited to subjects that would improve child-rearing and homemaking skills. These politicians favored women's education as a means of distinguishing their (more enlightened) nation from that of Spain, where little effort was being made toward public education for women.[8] Although some liberal politicians believed the new nation could benefit from educating its female population, women took it upon themselves to voice concern for a thorough reform in the 1870s.

Liberal and conservative tendencies in the late 1800s meant that women intellectuals and activists such as Cabello and her early feminist friends

---

7. The label *liberal,* in the context of the first half of the nineteenth century in Peru, roughly implied a faith in the innate goodness and ultimate perfectibility of man, characteristic of the Enlightenment. Liberals believed in Peru's capacity for self-government and sought to protect the individual from the abuses of those in power. They favored nearly universal manhood suffrage and relatively unrestricted access to government office. While women were not directly incorporated in this democratic vision, there were advances in education for women under liberal governments. Conservatives feared rule by the masses and subscribed to literacy and property qualifications for voting and election to public office. They were often frustrated royalists adapting to independence by favoring an aristocratic republic with a strong president (Peru had been, after all, one of the most loyal territories of the Spanish Crown and among the last to rebel). Conservatives believed that society was composed of inferiors and superiors and that the latter group should ensure its control over the state (Werlich 1978, 67–68).

8. As Bridget Aldaraca has found, Spain was a major emissary of the angelic standard: "[From the 1850s on] the growing public of Spanish middle-class women were instructed in minute detail on how to be and act, what to do and think, and, especially, what they as superior beings might never aspire to" (1982, 63).

Clorinda Matto de Turner and Juana Manuela Gorriti would fashion their pro-woman arguments in dialogue with liberal discourses of progress.[9] As the literary critic Oswaldo Voysest has pointed out, Peru's national literature grew to become an integral part of Positivism, as the novel was "supposed to render a service to the nation since . . . [writers such as Matto and Cabello] viewed it as an essential endeavor that offered a critical spirit to all social processes" (1998, 195). In their essays Cabello and Matto criticized the conservative faction while using the language of Positivism to court the liberals who were flexible regarding fixing higher standards for women's education, while Gorriti critiqued conservatives as well as Positivist views of history and society that excluded women and racial minorities, as we will see in a moment.

After the initial declaration of Peru's independence in 1821, as noted, a special effort had been made to initiate the education of the "bello sexo"; this was, in part, the vehicle that politicians used to articulate Peru's national identity as distinct from the mother country of Spain, where no effort was made to create public schools for women (Villavicencio 1992, 37). However, this education would be significantly inferior to the formation available to boys. The education women received was clearly geared to prepare them to be better housewives and mothers, with some very basic knowledge of geography, history, composition, and penmanship. A closer look at girls' education is particularly relevant to our study of *Blanca Sol,* as the protagonist's poor education and role models are important underlying causes of the action of the plot.

A curriculum from a Peruvian girls' school from 1822 shows that girls' education was heavily geared toward piety and homemaking: religion, spelling, calligraphy, and arithmetic (Tauzin Castellanos 1988, 99). The curriculum for the Colegio del Espíritu Santo in Lima, a school for girls of wealthy families, added French grammar, history, geography, and mythology (99). An 1826 curriculum from the Escuela Normal de Mujeres, established to prepare women to teach primary school for girls, is indicative of the very basic education that would continue to be made available to girls: it included spelling, grammar, arithmetic, catechism, and sewing (98). It is noteworthy that the listing of arithmetic in the girls' curriculum provoked heated dialogue, published in local newspapers; arithmetic was later removed in 1840 (99). Religious and domestic instruction, as well as classes on social graces, would continue to be the foundation for curricula in girls' schools. In 1826

---

9. For an overview of Juana Manuela Gorriti's literary gatherings in Lima and women's intellectual culture across Latin America, see the Introduction in this study.

under President Santa Cruz, fully state-subsidized (although not mandatory) primary education was made available to girls, and in 1836 Santa Cruz issued a decree to create equal numbers of learning institutions for both sexes, at the primary level (Villavicencio 1992, 38). It is clear that girls' preparation was grooming them to be authorities in domestic chores, morality, and spirituality. In other words, these educational programs were never intended to change women's role in the symbolic order or broaden their horizons, but rather to make them better Angels of the House.

Although liberals and conservatives clashed frequently over the years, the former enjoyed almost two decades of rule at midcentury. The economic success in the 1840s to 1870s from the export of guano (the historical setting for the novel *Blanca Sol*) provided income to fund infrastructure, social programs, and public education. In her late adolescence, Cabello witnessed both the reforms and the shortcomings of reform efforts that surely shaped her own social and political views. This experience would manifest itself in her later essays on women's place in society and the importance of education for women. Weak secular and ecclesiastic educational options for girls is also a central theme in *Blanca Sol*.

In 1845, the year Cabello was born, Ramón Castilla's presidential inauguration marked the beginning of an age of liberal politics.[10] From about 1845 to 1862, during Cabello's formative years, the young author witnessed Castilla's abolition of slavery as well as his elimination of the tribute tax indigenous groups had been forced to pay, earning him the title of "the Liberator." The constitution of 1856 called for the direct popular election of the chief executive and limited presidential power. Despite the increased wealth of the national economy, governmental efforts for women's education waned from the 1830s through the 1850s as enrollment dropped and the quality of the girls' schools significantly diminished. Nonetheless, there was a Ruling for General Instruction in 1850 that fixed curricula for girls' education and improved it somewhat from the earlier years. The ruling added classes such as drawing, French, English, geography, and basic history, but continued to concentrate heavily on domestic arts and religion (Tauzin Castellanos 1988, 101). In 1855 the primary school Los Sagrados Corazones

---

10. There are two book-length biographies published on Cabello: Augusto Tamayo Vargas 1940 and Pinto Vargas 2003, the latter an exhaustive study. Luis Miguel Glave's (1999) biographical article is another useful source on the suffering the author endured at the end of her life and on her alleged insanity; it also highlights the harsh criticism she suffered for voicing her ideas on girls' education and women's role in society. All biographical information on Cabello in this section is from Tamayo Vargas's work unless otherwise indicated.

was founded and later expanded into two schools when education for girls was made obligatory (Guardia 1985, 51).

It was not until the 1860s (when Cabello was fifteen to twenty-five years old) that the campaign for women's education was revived by Mariano Amézaga, who published articles lobbying for this cause and condemning the tradition of keeping half of society ignorant (Villavicencio 1992, 42). In the 1870s, for the first time in Peru's history, a group of women engaged in the struggle for the enlightenment of their sex. In 1874 a woman named María Trinidad Enríquez was allowed, with special permission, to enter the University of San Antonio Abad in Cuzco. She later founded a girls' school with a truly academic curriculum, which included mathematics, law, philosophy, and logic (Guardia 1985, 52). Later María Aragón de Rodo, Luisa Rausejour, and Magdalena Chávez were to follow her lead and start more schools of this type (52). Cabello was also at the vanguard of this battle, and the repeated message in *Blanca Sol* of the necessity of education for women is proof of her passion for this cause.

Cabello's own education is exemplary of the inconsistency in public education for girls. Because there was no regularly functioning school in her hometown of Moquegua, Cabello received lessons from private tutors (Tauzin Castellanos 1988, 105). Cabello's education seems to reflect the failure of public schooling for women, as sources show that beyond some basic lessons in subjects considered appropriate for young ladies of the bourgeoisie, she was primarily self-taught. Biographer Tamayo Vargas describes her education in history as coming from both formal lessons and tales told in the home (1940, 14).

We also know that Cabello preferred reading and studying music, two areas in which she was very skillful, to practicing more domestic hobbies, such as sewing:

> Ella no cose a las caídas de la tarde, ni pasa rozando con sus manos las teclas del clavicordio. Hace estudio intensivo de música, y su gozo es dominio absoluto de técnica, apreciación de un metódico superarse diario. Y si la cultura del colegio no era usual en las mujeres, ella tiene cultura de mesa de noche y de rincón de la huerta. (16)

> [She does not sew when afternoon falls, nor does she spend the time passing her fingers idly over the keys of the clavichord. She studies

music intensively, and her joy is absolute mastery of technique, the cumulative value of improving her skills methodically, day by day. And while classroom culture was not common to women, she had [her own brand of] night-stand and garden-niche culture.]

The end of the quotation alludes to Cabello's desire to study on her own, whenever and wherever she could. From available sources we may assume that most of her education came from her voracious appetite for books; she was very well read for a woman of her time.

Cabello's intellectual development and self-education were facilitated through her marriage to a prestigious doctor who did not hinder her intellectual development. The couple did not have any children; Cabello was widowed young and never remarried. She was a single, independent woman of means at a young age. It is significant that all these factors seem to have had to be in place to allow Cabello to be as prolific as she was in her writing career. Nonetheless, she was likely aware that this type of independence was not possible for the general female public and that if women were to enjoy a degree of independence and development of their own identities, they had to challenge oppressive ideals of virtue.

The political situation, however, did not facilitate such modification of women's roles. In the midst of the focus on education and building up the new nation's infrastructure, Peru's disputes over borders with the more stable and better-equipped Chile intensified, erupting in war. The disastrous and expensive War of the Pacific (1879–1884) drained much of the wealth that Peru had acquired from guano and mining. The country suffered a humiliating occupation in 1881 during which Chilean troops pillaged Lima as well as towns in the interior. In the process of losing the war, Peru was forced to turn over the rich mining region of Tarapacá.

Regarding women's roles in the War of the Pacific, it seems that the ruling class of the Peruvian republic had significantly less interest in involving "el bello sexo" in the struggle than did the pro-independence forces during the revolution. The *rabonas* followed soldiers into battle and performed the same duties as they had during the war of independence. This was not the case, however, for women of the bourgeoisie, who were involved in the distribution of charity and worked with the Red Cross rather than as spies and conspirators as they had done during independence.

A comparison of the language that García y García employs in her introduction to the wars of independence versus that of the War of the

Pacific is indicative of the less active role women played in the latter. For the independence era, the historian speaks of women's "courage," "loyalty," "accomplishment of their designs," and "irrepressible fire" in their desire to battle and that patriotism had awakened in them in "a lively and violent way" (García y García 1924, 207). In contrast, the vocabulary in the introduction to the War of the Pacific shows the marks of the Angel of the House: phrases such as "limitless abnegation," "tenderness," and "proverbial charity" characterize this section (351). For example, the historian characterizes Magdalena Ugarteche de Prado, a woman who organized the distribution of charity, by focusing on "su conducta de esposa solícita y ejemplar y de madre amorosa y abnegada" (351) [her solicitous and exemplary wifely conduct and her loving and selfless [role as mother]. Clearly, during this national crisis women were extending their services in capacities compatible with the Angel of the House ideal.

Tamayo Vargas does not mention whether the literary salons started in 1876 by the Argentinean writer and longtime Lima resident Juana Manuela Gorriti (1818–1892) continue during the war, but he does tell us that Cabello was still publishing articles under the pseudonym Enriqueta Pradel in the periodical *El Album* (The Album) and *El Recreo* (The Re-creation) (Tamayo Vargas 1940, 35). Cabello also managed to publish her novel *Las consecuencias* (The Consequences) in Lima in 1880 during the war. However, she would write the rest of her novels in the aftermath of this national disaster: *Sacrificio y recompensa* (Sacrifice and Recompense [1887]), *Blanca Sol* (1888), and *El conspirador* (The Conspirator [1892]). Naturalism and Positivism were the cultural movements that influenced her literary production during these years.

The Roles of Naturalism and Positivism in the New Generation of Women Writers in Peru

If Romanticism was Spain's legacy to the colonies, then Naturalism and Positivism (also European in origin) were the first literary and philosophical movements adapted to a Peruvian context by the writers of the new republic.[11] As Voysest has pointed out, these schools of thought facilitated the new

---

11. For introductory reading on Romanticism, Naturalism, and Positivism in Spanish America, I recommend the following texts: Carilla 1975; Zea 1949, 1963; Pérez Petit 1943; Foster and Altamiranda 1997.

nation's articulations of a national literature distinct from any expression that prevailed in the colonial years (1998, 195). As such, they could be tools of power for those writers who could wield them effectively, and Cabello was one of these early few.

Naturalism entered Latin America at the end of the century through the novels that Émile Zola (France 1840–1902) published in the 1870s and his 1880 manifesto, *The Experimental Novel,* in which he describes his application of the experimental method of French scientist Claude Bernard (1813–1878) to the process of writing a novel. Naturalism is a product of Positivist philosophy of 1800s Europe and its profound faith in science. In the Naturalist method, the writer approaches the problems of society and the individual (which form the subject matter for Naturalist literature) in an empirical manner, through direct and detailed observations of human behavior and environment, which are then objectively relayed to the reader. Zola thought the function of the novel should be to present an objective diagnostic photograph of society's ills for politicians to then "treat." Naturalist novels create an experimental space in which to diagnose and examine social problems. Observation and deductive logic take center stage, in place of emotions, exoticism, or patriotism. The settings for the Naturalist novel do not showcase the beauty of nature or the grandeur of civilization, but rather the breeding grounds for society's problems: the brothel, the congested coal mine, the opium den, and urban slums. An important feature of Naturalism (one that was sure to have inspired the writers who followed it) is that it most directly links the novel with the power to change society.

Latin American writers who incorporated Naturalist techniques have tended to modify Zola's model, often mixing it with a more subjective and somewhat Romantic tone (Voysest 1998; Epple 1980). Few come close to representing society's ills in such grim detail as the French originator (of the Hispanic Naturalists, the Puerto Rican novelist, doctor, and politician Manuel Zeno Gandía arguably follows Zola's model most faithfully). The Argentinean novelist Eugenio Cambaceres (1843–1889), for example, follows Zola's Naturalism in terms of the influence of the environment on the individual, but his writing mixes Naturalism with Romantic elements. The emotional and dramatic ending of his novel *Sin rumbo* (1885), in which the protagonist disembowels himself by carving a cross into his gut, is one example, as the literary critic George Schade has noted. This is true of Cabello, who employs Zola's method and structure while swapping the urban alleys and coal mines for the elegant ambiance of Lima's high society.

While Zola's view does not admit belief in any metaphysical force that cannot be empirically proved, writers such as the Spanish novelist Emilia Pardo Bazán (1852–1921) maintain their Catholic faith. In the controversial essay "La cuestión palpitante" (1883), Pardo Bazán offers her own Catholic version of Naturalism. Cabello's adaptation of Naturalism to a Peruvian context is similar; Cabello critiques some superficial practices of Catholicism, such as the way women in Lima's high society used religious festivals to show off their latest fashion; however, she never denies belief in the Catholic God (nor was it in the writer's best interest to do so, as the mere suspicion that Matto disrespected the figure of Christ by publishing a controversial story while editor of *El Perú Ilustrado* led to her persecution). While Cabello opposes clerical policy in her belief that religion should play only a minor role in education (Zalduondo 2001, 162), she is quick to include characters' formulaic invocations to the heavens and the hope that a higher power will save the day in certain scenes of her novel. Notably, this rhetoric is most commonly associated with Josefina's elderly grandmother, a representative of an outdated Peruvian elite in economic decline.

Although Cabello has been generally viewed as a Naturalist writer, it is important to note that there has been lengthy critical debate over the years regarding whether or to what degree her novels are Naturalist and, based on this conclusion, whether they should be considered "modern" and progressive.[12] In fact, as several critics in this debate point out, Cabello herself does not purport to follow Naturalism, but rather a mix of Romanticism, Realism,

---

12. Tamayo Vargas's 1940 evaluation of Cabello's novels contains praise of the writer as an early innovator of the Peruvian novel for her foray into the genre of Naturalism. Lucía Guerra's "Mercedes Cabello de Carbonera" (1987a) focuses on the Positivism and Naturalism of Cabello as elements of her total view on morality and art. Guerra reads the writer's philosophy of art as "una trayectoria de permanente perfectibilidad" (trajectory of permanent perfectability) based on the Comtean ideals of progress and on the aim of art to present human beings as they are and as they should be (27–28).

Juan Armando Epple's 1987 article "Mercedes Cabello de Carbonera y el problema de la 'novela moderna' en el Perú" differs from the aforementioned studies in that he aims to show that *Blanca Sol* is not progressive, but rather retrograde. Epple considers Cabello's views of society conservative and backward looking because of Cabello's spiritual, moralizing discourse aimed at finding a "conciliatory" relationship between the newly rich Peruvians and the old ruling classes, as well as her reluctance to grapple with the racial issues that Peruvian Positivists such as Manuel González Prada were bringing to the fore. If one is to define "modern novel" by the degree to which a work is Naturalist, as the early twentieth-century critics Ventura García Calderón and Tamayo Vargas have done, then Epple correctly notes that the novel is not fully Naturalist—it is, in fact, a combination of genres, as Cabello intended. While I agree with Epple's findings in regard to Cabello's reluctance to take up the cause of Peru's racial diversity, it should be pointed out that his assessment of the novel ignores gender politics to explain her use of spiritually loaded discourse (namely, that

and Naturalism that she calls American Realism (*el realismo americano*). For the purposes of the study at hand, the degree to which Cabello's Naturalism follows that of Zola is not as important as the fact that her incorporation of the newest literary current of the 1880s sparked controversy and interest in her work that continues into today; she is the best-known writer of the three women whose work is featured here and many of the critical studies on Cabello concern her use of Naturalism.

In her 1892 essay "La novela moderna," Cabello criticizes Romanticism for representing an overly idealized perfection of humankind and Naturalism for focusing disproportionately on its base and animal aspects. She therefore proposes her own genre, namely, American Realism, which is a mixture of the two. To construct her American Realism, Cabello draws on Zola's approach for the narrative structure of *Blanca Sol*, while the characters of the

---

women novelists taking on risqué topics could elude critique more effectively if they included some traditionally feminine rhetoric in their prose) and does not consider an interpretation of *Blanca Sol* as a novel about women's education and social options, a progressive project for her era, even if her particular view of women's advancement did not fit within today's notions of progress.

Later studies reevaluate and valorize Cabello's creation of a hybrid literary genre that was not meant to follow Naturalism to the letter. Voysest is perhaps the contemporary critic who has focused most closely on Cabello's Naturalism. He points out, along with Henri Mitterand, a French specialist on Zola, that Zola himself did not follow his own theory of the novel as he outlines it in *The Experimental Novel* and that the French writer's theory includes a paradoxical mix of objective science and artistic individualism (1998, 196). Voysest reads two lines levels of discourse in the novels of both Cabello and Matto: one mode of discourse is representative (which goes along with the objectivity of Zola's style) and the other is evaluative (which is subjective and can be seen as a remnant of Realism). Voysest coined the phrase "spiritual Naturalism" to describe Cabello's approach: "*Naturalismo espiritual*—una tendencia a aunar ideas o movimientos a menudo opuestos como una respuesta a un momento histórico de ambivalencias, contradicciones y prejuicios que pedía soluciones urgentes" (2005, n.p.) (Spiritual Naturalism—a tendency to link movements considered opposite as a response to an historical moment of ambivalence, contradictions and prejudices that required urgent solutions).

Peluffo's "Las trampas del naturalismo" is a response to claims that Cabello's writing is too sentimental to be Naturalist. Peluffo points out that to Gorriti's 1880s ear Cabello's stark Naturalism was scandalous; in fact, Gorriti criticizes Cabello's 1889 novel *Las consecuencias*, claiming that the Peruvian writes more boldly than Zola ("con más valor aún que Zola" [quoted in Peluffo 2002, 38]) because she attacks not only the lower classes, but the elite as well. Supporting what Voysest has affirmed in his studies regarding the Latin American preference for the Naturalist novel as an *étude sociale* (1998, 197), Peluffo aptly demonstrates that Cabello follows the experimental method outlined by Zola by pointing out the many environmental and educational influences in the title character Blanca Sol's formative years that shaped who she would become as a young woman. Joan Torres-Pou seeks to counter claims by early critics such as García Calderón and John Brushwood that Cabello's novels were weak examples of Naturalism. In Cabello's defense, Torres-Pou correctly points out that the novelist never intended to follow Zola's Naturalism to the letter. Torres-Pou supports this argument with pertinent quotes from Cabello's essay "La novela moderna" (1892) in which she advocates a hybrid genre of Romanticism, Naturalism, and Realism (Torres-Pou 1998, 252).

novel are mostly from the nouveau riche of the guano boom. As Voysest points out (1998), Cabello's work, unlike Zola's Naturalism, includes subjective, moralizing discourses in the narrative. Her writing is Naturalist in its lengthy descriptions of the protagonist's psychological background and society's influence on her development, which account for her frivolous behavior. In *Blanca Sol* the experimental space is Lima, with its detrimental symbolic representations of womanhood. Within this controlled environment, the author shows how a potentially upright person can be capable of reprehensible behavior. The main character's misguided education teaches her to value money, glamour, and social position above virtue, love, and family life. While championing these characteristics seems to support the angelic norm, many elements of the plot structure significantly complicate the unattainable ideal of the Angel of the House.

Taking this scientific approach to literature into consideration is important in examining Cabello's agenda, specifically because of the degree to which this method authorizes the novelist to pass informed judgment on the symbolic order. Zola's conceptualization of the novel grants the author a tremendous amount of power, placing him or her in the role of both "authoritative" observer and social activist. The goal of the experimental novel's author is to "possess knowledge of the man, scientific knowledge of him, in both his individual and social relations," rendering the novelists "examining magistrates of men and their passions" (Zola 1880; 1964, 9–10). No behavior is mysterious; conduct is dictated by specific genetic or environmental conditions. The experimental novel has the purpose of aiding in the reversal of this determinism (although to a lesser degree in the case of hereditarily determined illnesses): hence the role of author as social scientist whose work is meant to influence political decisions. Cabello's use of aspects of Naturalism reveals her quest for textual power in the intellectual milieu. She uses Naturalist techniques as a means of authorizing herself to critique the debilitating roles society imposes upon women.

Positivism also plays an important role in the early feminist thought of Cabello, as well as in that of the fellow women intellectuals living in Peru Matto and Gorriti (although Gorriti's stance is more critical of the rationalist approach to progress than that of her younger contemporaries). Whereas Naturalism is a form of aesthetic expression as well as a social consciousness-raising literary movement, Positivism is a political and philosophical school of thought that Cabello and Matto drew on to express their views on women's role in the nation's progress. As I mention in Chapter 1, Positivism is based on the ideas of the French philosopher Auguste Comte (1798–1857) and followers such as the English philosopher Herbert Spencer (1820–1920). The origins of Positivism in Peru can be traced to 1850; however, the philosophy did not become popular until the end of the century (Trazegnies Granda 1987, 16). Cabello's contact with Positivism was most likely through the noted Peruvian poet and essayist Manuel González Prada (1844–1918), whose literary circle Cabello joined in 1887 (Denegri cited in Zalduondo 2001, 154). The scientific approach to social reform would prove invaluable to the author in her agenda for helping society to restructure the way people thought about women, and it is most apparent in the scientific language of her essays.

We can see an example of Cabello's use of Positivist language in her "Influencia de la mujer en la civilización" (Woman's Influence on Civilization [1874]):

> La instrucción y la moralidad de las mujeres ha sido en todo tiempo el termómetro que ha marcado los progresos, y el grado de civilización y virilidad de las naciones . . . Educad a la mujer, ilustrad su inteligencia, y tendréis en ella un motor poderoso y universal, para el progreso y la civilización del mundo; y una columna fuerte e inamovible en qué cimentar la moral y las virtudes de las generaciones venideras. (quoted in Villavivencio 1992, 65)
>
> [Women's education and morality has always been a thermometer to mark progress, the quality of civilization, and virility of nations. . . . Educate Woman, bring her intelligence to light, and you will have in her a universal and powerful motor for progress and world civilization, and a strong and sturdy column onto which to build the morality and virtue of upcoming generations.]

Cabello's discursive strategy here is pointed: she uses the charged lexicon of the nationalist discourses ("civilization," "morality," "virtue," "strength," "power," and "virility")—and goes beyond them by updating this rhetoric with technical language ("progress," "thermometer," "motor").[13] As we saw

---

13. The nation-building lexicon to which I refer can be found throughout the writings of revolutionary leader Simón Bolívar (Venezuela, 1783–1830) and the noted Argentine essayist and politician Domingo Faustino Sarmiento (1811–88). The essay *Ariel* (1900) by José Enrique Rodó (Uruguay, 1872–1917) also transcribes the fear of moral weakness and vulnerability to neo-imperialism that was circulating among the ruling classes in the second half of the nineteenth century.

in Chapter 1, Barreda's antifeminist essay (which draws heavily on Comte) used Positivism to prove women biologically incapable of analytical thought. Cabello, conversely, uses a Positivist discourse to lobby for women's opportunities. In addition, the essay contains several digressions on advances in the sciences that are aimed at linking women's education to progress and modernity. Cabello's incorporation of nation-building language plays on the ruling class's fears; she formulates her agenda so that it becomes the answer to one of the most important political concerns of her day. She posits that educating women, the mothers of future leaders and citizens, will prevent society from falling into the "barbaric" lifestyle that her fictional character Blanca Sol is forced to endure.[14]

The adoption of Positivist principles that advocated an empirical and scientific approach to social problems allowed Cabello and Matto to position women's advancement as essential to the nation's desire for progress. As Berg notes, Matto's 1882 essay "La industria nacional" (National Industry) allowed the reader to envision women's advancement as compatible with and necessary to the future of the nation: "[Matto's] essays deplore national chaos and sloth and suggest following the model of French postwar recovery, with emphasis on industrialization and education" (Berg 1995, 81). Matto's essay "La mujer y la ciencia" (Woman and Science, published in Matto's periodical *El Búcaro Americano* in January 1898) "points out that women cannot hide behind sentimental notions of motherhood, because 60 percent of women are in fact not actively engaged in the roles of wife or mother" (Berg 1995, 85). Although Matto's female characters exhibit characteristics of the Angel of the House, Matto viewed as an obstacle to women's rights the Romantic, sentimental, traditional definition of woman as *exclusively* mother and wife. Her later essays further undermine the dependent model of womanhood by advocating women's career advancement and their development as self-sustaining individuals as a way of furthering the progress of women *and the nation*.[15]

Rather than incorporate Positivist discourse to tout women's advancement, Gorriti's writing, as Denegri points out, deconstructed rationalist approaches to social problems while highlighting the suffering of marginalized groups

---

14. I use the term *barbaric* in reference to the book-length biographical essay *Civilización i barbarie: La vida de Juan Facundo Quiroga* (1845) by the Argentinean essayist and politician Domingo Faustino Sarmiento (1811–88). Like Sarmiento, Cabello juxtaposes civilization and barbarism, but for the latter the aim is to promote women's education.

15. Berg's essay refers to several of Matto's articles in *El Búcaro Americano* that advocate women's self sufficiency and condemn viewing women as objects (1995, 85–86).

under such policies. Employing a tactic that she would use into the early twentieth century, Gorriti's collection of short writings *Sueños y realidades* (1865), for example, rewrites the official history of the Argentine Federalist Juan Manuel de Rosas's dictatorship (1829–52) in order to highlight the suffering of orphans and women in the conflicts between Unitarians and Federalists. Rather than downplay sentimentality, Gorriti evokes strong emotion and the pain of the female characters to make her point: that neither side wins in such a bloody conflict. Denegri's observations aptly characterize Gorriti's strategy: "Desarrolló su propia escritura precisamente a partir de las diferencias que existían entre su discurso intuitivo y centrado en la mujer, y el de la razón erudita masculina" (112) [She developed her own writing precisely based on the differences that existed between her intuitive discourse centered on woman, and that of the erudite masculine reason]. In sum, whether intellectual women were critical of Positivism or whether they embraced it for new causes, they had to negotiate it, as Positivism was part of the language of the new nations in the second half of the century.

Cabello's Intellectual and Literary Strategies

One can hypothesize that Cabello saw in certain techniques of Naturalism and Positivism new and highly desirable means of voicing her concerns for women's condition. Why so? First, I have already mentioned the empowering nature of Naturalism. Second, from the perspective of the Peruvian intellectual, Naturalism and Positivism were established and relatively respected (if not undisputed) modes of thought. Finally, there was clearly a preference by the ruling class during the postcolonial era to emulate and appropriate European culture as a means of "civilizing" the nation and helping it earn international respect. The visual dominance of French-inspired architecture in many of Latin America's capital cities and nineteenth-century efforts to attract European immigration confirm this. By voicing her concerns in the language and symbols of the new Peruvian republic, Cabello was helping her nation distinguish itself from the mother country of Spain. She was a forerunner in the development of the Peruvian novel and was using it as a vehicle for her early feminist beliefs. She was ambitiously taking the initiative and using her position as a pioneer novelist (among the first to experiment with Naturalist techniques) to advance a social agenda that placed women's plight at dead center. That is to say, she was consciously placing the nation one step closer to its "own" literature, which it so desperately desired, but with the implication that it must consider women's education, social options, and development as individuals as a central concern.

However, Cabello's outspokenness did not go without harsh repercussions, despite the subversive strategies she used in her narrative to include and appear to support some aspects of angelic virtue. Her unconventional vision of girls' education and the feminist ideas in her writing inspired negative criticism from many Peruvian intellectuals of her day, including the poet José Santos Chocano (1867–1935), the author of short prose narratives (*tradiciones*) Ricardo Palma (1833–1919), and the well-known educator Elvira García y García (1862–1951) (Glave 1999, 102–3).[16] Besides insults and harsh criticism being published about her in the most important newspaper of Lima, *El Comercio,* the novelist was declared insane toward the end of her life and institutionalized in horrible conditions, as Glave's research has confirmed. Glave convincingly argues that Cabello was unjustly confined.

Cabello's choice of expression and literary techniques, nonetheless, were popular with readers, and *Blanca Sol* went through three early editions. The novel interests us for early feminist writings of the self because it was a widely circulated story that focused on a subversive and active female heroine. The novel made enough of an impression on its readers to earn it a comparison with one of the most popular French novels of its day—it was praised as the *Madame Bovary* of Lima (Torres-Pou 1998, 251). According to Torres-Pou, the work's brief but certain success among its audience, the Peruvian elite, had to do with the supposition that the protagonist was loosely based on an actual figure in Lima's society (251), although Cabello herself denies any such parallel in her foreword to the text. It is probable that the Naturalist techniques aided in sparking interest in readers, who likely found it fresh and innovative. Whatever the reasons for its success, the novel seems to have accomplished part of its author's aim: she had the ruling class's attention.

---

16. For a detailed discussion of the denigration Cabello suffered, see Zalduondo 2001, chap. 4.

4

NEW MODELS FOR NEW WOMEN: RETHINKING CINDERELLA'S VIRTUES AND HUMANIZING THE STEPMOTHER IN MERCEDES CABELLO DE CARBONERA'S *BLANCA SOL*

Del infantil grupo se levanta leve
Argentada y pura una vocecilla
que comienza: "Entonces se fueron al baile
y dejaron sola a Cenicentilla.

Se quedó la pobre triste en la cocina,
de llanto, de penas nublados los ojos,
mirando los juegos extraños que hacían
en las sombras negras los carbones rojos.

Pero vino el hada, que era su madrina,
le trajo un vestido de encaje y crespones,
le hizo un coche de oro de una calabaza,
convirtió en caballos unos seis ratones,
. . . .
¡Cuentos que nacisteis en ignotos tiempos
y que vais volando por entre lo oscuro,
desde los potentes arios primitivos,
hasta las enclenques razas del futuro!

[From the group of children softly rises
the clear and pure voice
that begins: "Then they went to the ball
and they left Cinderella alone

the poor thing was left behind in the kitchen,
her eyes, clouded with tears and sorrow,
gazed upon the strange play
of the red coals in the dark shadows

But then came the fairy, her godmother,
who brought her a dress of lace and crepe,
she made her a coach of gold from a pumpkin,
she turned six mice into horses,
. . . .
Oh, Stories, born in times past
and carried through the dark of ages

> from the powerful and primitive Aryans
> to the debilitated races of the future!]
>
> —José Asunción Silva, "Crepúsculo"

The epigraph is a fragment of a poem from 1895 by the well-known Colombian *modernista* writer José Asunción Silva (1865–1896) that depicts a group of fascinated children listening to a musical voice telling the time-honored tale of the unfortunate Cinderella, whose unparalleled self-sacrifice and virtue attract the love of a prince who transforms her existence from a dreary inferno into dreamy happiness.[1] At the turn of the century, when psychoanalysis opened up the subconscious mind to intellectuals and artists, writers such as Silva—and Mercedes Cabello de Carbonera—became aware of the profound influence of fairy tales. Foreshadowing twentieth-century studies on the psychological and social impact of fairy tales, Silva explains in "Crepúsculo" that these fanciful legends are "más durables que las convicciones [sic] de graves filósofos y sabias escuelas" (40) [longer lasting than the convictions of serious philosophers and wise schools of thought]. Rich in imagery, these magical stories delve deeply into the human psyche and therefore provide ideal material for rewriting social fictions of female subjectivity.

The Cinderella fairy tale embedded in *Blanca Sol,* the story of the courtship and marriage of two secondary characters, is a patch of the symbolic social fabric that Cabello reconfigures, but which has been overlooked by critics to date.[2] Cabello rewrites womanhood by taking pieces of social signifiers, such as gender stereotypes, and recoding them in ways that critique and undermine tenets of the Angel of the House.

Cultural Myths and Social Critique

Possibly a reaction against women's auxiliary roles in the struggle for independence, representations of bourgeois women in the early republic placed them

---

1. *Modernismo,* a nascent literary movement in the 1880s, was known for its sensual and piquant subject matter and its exquisitely wrought language. Silva's interest in the Cinderella fairy tale fits the basic ideas associated with Latin American *modernismo* because it provides a perfect opportunity to indulge a love of escapist and fantastical settings.

2. *Blanca Sol* has received more critical attention in the past twenty years than have the novels of Barragán and Roqué. Many scholars debate Cabello's use of Naturalism (see the overview of criticism on Cabello's Naturalism in Chapter 3), while others consider the role of gossip, Cabello's early feminism, and the role of beneficent activities in the novel. In addition to the critical works in Chapter 3 and in note 12 of that chapter, one can find articles on Cabello's essays and other novels

squarely back in the home and couched narratives about women in terms of how serviceable they could be to the men and children in their lives. Although small groups of pioneering women worked toward reforms, women's education was viewed as impractical, and single women's professional options were few and their work poorly remunerated. In short, Cinderella provided a tempting fantasy for women in desolate conditions who were encouraged to believe that, if they were sufficiently virtuous and dutiful, their fortune might change through an introduction to a man who would save them.[3]

Cabello, like other well-educated women of her day, was a firm advocate for improvements in women's academic formation. She passionately lobbied for women to be educated beyond the basic reading and writing skills and cursory knowledge in the humanities, as evidenced by her use of Positivist discourse to support women's access to higher education in her 1874 essay "Influencia de la mujer en la civilización," as I discuss in Chapter 3. In *Blanca Sol* we find that her interest in reforming notions of womanhood includes expanding restrictive definitions of femininity to accommodate a more human and less ethereal standard for her sex. This broadening of the definition of womanhood acknowledges women's desires and needs and portrays those needs as human, healthy impulses, rather than as evidence of an egotism that endangered the sanctity of domestic life.

Perhaps Cabello learned from history how preexisting images in the myths and symbolic beliefs of a culture or nation can be manipulated by a dominant class to achieve some social, political, or religious goal within that culture. For instance, the Spaniards colonizing the New World in the sixteenth century took advantage of the presence of cults of female deities, such as the Andean fertility goddess Pachamama, and replaced them

---

as well as on her participation in the *veladas literarias* of Gorriti (see the Introduction in this study for more information). John Miller's 1977 article is an early attempt to place two Peruvian women writers into their national literary history. Miller reads the novels of Matto and Cabello as literary discourses in dialogue with the social problems of corruption, clerical abuse, racism, and poor education after the War of the Pacific. Masiello's 1996 study of turn-of-the-century melodrama includes a short analysis of *Blanca Sol* in the critic's discussion of gossip and the press. Masiello observes how Cabello links gossip with the deformation of reality to question the process of the cataloging of knowledge (277). Ana Peluffo's studies from the early 2000s add new angles to the body of criticism on Cabello. In "Bajo las alas del ángel" (2004) she examines women characters' beneficent activities as a means to take on a position of power outside the home in a society that otherwise did not allow its women to lead public lives. Peluffo points out that the opportunities for participation in public life that charitable activities offered are exploited and satirized in *Blanca Sol*.

3. The Cinderella fantasy persists today, not only in new animated versions of the tale, but also in the form of soap operas such as the internationally popular 1986 Venezuelan telenovela *Cristal* and its 1998 Mexican remake, *El privilegio de amar*.

with a cult of the Virgin Mary, thus facilitating the spread of Christianity. Sometimes this displacement occurred unwittingly, as when the Aztecs associated the arrival of Hernán Cortés from the West with the return of the bearded Aztec deity Quetzalcoatl. As another particularly relevant example, the biblical story of Eve the temptress (a female figure analogous to the chaos-inducing Pandora of Greek mythology), has been read as a justification for confining women to domestic spaces and keeping them out of positions of power.[4] In each of these examples the power of widely consumed and accepted stories facilitated the imposition of a new cultural order.[5] In *Blanca Sol*, Cabello takes advantage of the power of the Cinderella fairy tale to blur the neatly constructed lines between "virtue" and "evil," thereby rewriting the standards of morality and legitimacy for women of her era.

The most famous version of Cinderella, the one reflected in Cabello's *Blanca Sol*, was published by the French writer Charles Perrault (1628–1703) in 1697 and was extremely popular in Spain by 1810. (This is the story of Cinderella "much concerned with social detail" that Walt Disney has made famous worldwide [Tosi 2001, 94].) A Spanish translation of the opera *Cendrillon* (*La Cenicienta* [Cinderella]) by the French composer Nicholas Isouard (1774–1818) and the dramatist Charles-Guillaume Étienne (1778–1845) was staged fifty times in Madrid between 1810 and 1818, making the production one of the two most frequently performed musicals of this eight-year period of the nineteenth century (Lorenz 1941, 380). Folklore specialists have found early Spanish versions of the Cinderella story in Spain, Chile, the Philippines (Gardner and Newell 1906, 273), and Puerto Rico (Boggs 1929; Espinosa and Mason 1925), while the existence of Silva's "Crepúsculo" indicates that it was known in turn-of-the-century Colombia. Cabello was probably familiar with these versions. Her principal biographer, Ismael Pinto Vargas, confirms that children of prominent families from Cabello's hometown of Moquegua, including several of the writer's relatives (2003, 64–74), often traveled to Europe to be educated. Cabello herself spent formative years of her life in the bustling cosmopolitan city of Lima. There can be little doubt that well-to-do Peruvians such as Cabello, with their exposure to European literature, were familiar with Perrault's version of Cinderella.

4. See the feminist studies on the biblical myth of Eve by Elizabeth Menon (2006) and Manelon Sprengnether (1989).
5. Many prominent scholars of fairy tales, including Jack Zipes (1987), Bruce Bettelheim (1976), and Maria Tatar (1987), have convincingly shown that fairy tales are cultural myths that ensure that certain values are ingrained in the social consciousness.

In Cabello's own version, rather than eliding the circumstances under which the "evil" and "virtuous" characters came to be immoral (in the case of the stepmother character) or poverty stricken (in the case of the Cinderella character), Cabello consciously traces these outcomes to specific causes in the social structure and through the character development of the social-climbing protagonist Blanca and her alter ego, the humble seamstress Josefina (two superficially opposite, yet inextricably linked, characters), Cabello critiques the harmful fantasies instilled in young girls that derail their transition to self-reliant adulthood. She places blame squarely on the social and political systems of mid-1800s Lima for providing a paltry education and few economic options for single women and widows. Unlike the Cinderella fairy tale, the narrative Cabello offers emphasizes the limited educational infrastructure of nineteenth-century Lima that produces girl-women who are forced to rely on a paternal figure and their attractiveness to the opposite sex for survival. Cabello dismantles the tenets of the Angel of the House, a model mirrored in the virtues of the humble, self-sacrificing Cinderella, to write female characters who have agency and voice, but who run into the aforementioned roadblocks to self-realization because of their environments.[6]

Elements of the Cinderella Fairy Tale in *Blanca Sol*

Blanca Sol was one of the first best sellers of the nineteenth century in Peru, given its three editions in the short span of 1889, 1890, and 1894 (Peluffo 2002, 39).[7] In keeping with the author's opening statement about her philosophy of narrative (that it should include a mixture of Romanticism, Realism, and Naturalism), the story opens with a discussion of the protagonist and title character's childhood to give the reader an idea of her upbringing and environment. The narrator makes it clear that Blanca Sol is a young woman who is naturally gifted in intelligence and charisma, but whose faulty upbringing leads her astray. Blanca's mother is a society

---

6. Marcia Lieberman has noted that tales such as Cinderella present a picture of sexual roles, behavior, and psychology, in such a way that good temperament, meekness, and beauty are rewarded, while ill temper and ugliness are punished. Intelligence for women simply does not play a part in the Cinderella economy (Lieberman 1987, 187–89).

7. Peluffo notes the competitiveness that Cabello's sales figures likely inspired on the part of her male contemporaries in Peru such as Ricardo Palma and Manuel González Prada, as well as Pedro Paz Soldán (penname Juan de Arona), who mocked Cabello and Clorinda Matto de Turner with scatological and dehumanizing nicknames (Peluffo 2002, 39).

woman who has lost her fortune but is skilled at using credit and her good taste to present the appearance of opulence. Although naturally bright, Blanca attends a school where such superficial qualities as wealth, beauty, and social status are valued and cultivated, while intelligence and diligence go unrewarded. She falls in love with an attractive and well-born young man but she does not marry him, because he lacks an adequate fortune. Instead, Blanca's mother and others of her social class convince her to marry the unattractive and dull—but fabulously wealthy—Don Serafín Rubio. The optimistic Blanca compares her Serafín to a shrimp: he is pink and ugly but *rico* (which in Spanish means both "wealthy" and "tasty").

Blanca marries Serafín (who pays off her mother's exorbitant debts) and the young woman becomes a high-society personage. She is content to be admired and envied by women and pursued by men of elevated social positions, whom she universally disdains. She endures the duties of married life and produces several children over the course of her marriage.

Although society has taught Blanca to be selfish and materialistic, her underlying compassionate nature shines through at times. One day, her heart is softened at the sight of a poor orphaned seamstress named Josefina who is struggling to support her grandmother and siblings. Blanca takes Josefina under her protection and provides for the orphaned young woman's siblings and grandmother in exchange for the flowers the seamstress sews for Blanca's social and beneficent events. When Blanca's attractive and successful suitor Alcides Lescanti (with whom she has an extramarital flirtation but nothing more) falls in love with the humble and virtuous Josefina, Blanca suddenly becomes aware of her feelings for him. This epiphany comes too late. Scorned once too often by the capricious Blanca, Alcides rejects the coquette in favor of the simple seamstress. Blanca is devastated by Alcides's rejection. Moreover, she discovers that her extravagant whims have consumed Don Serafín's fortune and they are financially ruined.[8] To make matters worse, Alcides purchases all of Blanca's debts so that she is not only

---

8. The commonplace of the vain lover or wife who financially ruins the man in her life because of her expensive tastes in clothing and other luxuries is prevalent in novels of the era. Gustave Flaubert's *Madame Bovary* (1857)—with which *Blanca Sol* has been compared—Zola's *Nana* (1880), and the Spanish writer Benito Pérez Galdós's *La de Bringas* (1884) are three examples featuring this sort of woman. A lesser-known example of this story line is revealed through the protagonist Rosario in the Puerto Rican writer Carmela Eulate Sanjurjo's novel *La muñeca* (1895). As the analysis in this chapter demonstrates, Cabello's early feminist novel is far more sympathetic toward the lead character than the three novels noted above, as Blanca's faults are clearly linked to the poor examples and weak education provided by Lima society.

rejected by her beloved, but also financially indebted to him. Don Serafín loses his mind and is committed to an asylum. Bitter and enraged at her poverty and left to support her six children alone, Blanca turns her home into a brothel for the wealthy men of Lima as her last means of survival. Her voice echoes in the last lines of the text, swearing to corrupt in turn the society responsible for her misery. Blanca's tremendous potential is short-changed by her upbringing, and when her own socially scripted fairy tale dissolves into the grim social realities of patriarchal Peruvian society, the greatness of her being is reduced to her sexual allure.

Blanca's fate highlights society's moral double standards and hypocrisy, while Josefina is similarly shown to be a normal woman (morally flawed, and not always angelic) who seeks survival, as her lack of education and vocational skills impede full self-sufficiency. The Josefina subplot is a tricky, subtle one to read, as Cabello simultaneously presents Josefina's good fortune as an unrealistic tale (Peluffo [2002] points out the noticeable Romantic tone used in the narration of the subplot, whereas Naturalism and Realism prevail in the sections focusing on Blanca), and also slips in hints that *no one is completely* virtuous . . . not even Josefina. Josefina's superficial virtue represents the mainstream ideal of domestic perfection, that is, that of the Angel of the House—one that Cabello masterfully and subtly disassembles.

The embedded Cinderella subplot, therefore, is that of the rise of Josefina from a poverty-stricken waif to one of the wealthiest women in Lima through her marriage to the Italian magnate Alcides.[9] While critics have not explored the Cinderella allusions, the scholar of nineteenth-century women's writing Ana Peluffo hints at the parallel when she describes Josefina's social ascent as one in which the destitute young woman "emerge de la cenizas," (2002, 45) [rises from the ashes], while the critic Lucía Guerra compares Josefina to Cinderella in passing (1987a, 38). The general reading of the Josefina-Alcides subplot is that it offers up to the reader, in didactic fashion, an example of woman's ideal virtue. I propose that there is significant early feminist depth to this subplot: Cabello employs allusions to the Cinderella tale in order to deconstruct the ideal of the Angel of the House.

---

9. The fictional character of Lescanti represents a real wave of immigration of Italians to Lima in the 1840s. Giovanni Bonfiglio (1994) has studied Italian immigration in Lima in depth, finding that it was spontaneous and that many Italians came from the city of Liguria and were merchants and sailors. They came during the Guano Age in the mid-1800s to amass fortunes and return home to Italy, but many remained to make up an influential economic and cultural segment of Lima society.

The parallels between the Alcides-Josefina story and Cinderella are fairly clear: the indigent and modest Josefina is Cinderella; Blanca embodies the would-be villain from the privileged class, a stepmother figure; and Alcides is the handsome Prince Charming who saves Josefina-Cinderella through marriage and permits an unrealistically steep ascension up the social ladder for the beautiful and "morally perfect" girl.

Apart from this central structure, there are several details that provide clues to decipher the allusion. Cinderella and Josefina are both fallen aristocrats; because of unfortunate circumstances, they must work for others for meager compensation. In both stories the Cinderella figure runs away from the prince, and he must undertake a tedious search for her (in Alcides' case, he does not know Josefina's new address when she flees from Blanca's home). In Cabello's novel, Alcides himself searches for his love, but he also hires spies to help him (136), just as the prince has his footmen help in the search for Cinderella.[10] In both the fairy tale and the novel, the Cinderella character is destined to prevail because of her virtue. The narrator specifies the expectation that the Romanticized ideal of virtue win when she reveals Josefina's grandmother's thoughts on Josefina's union with Alcides: "No le causaba á ella novedad, pues bien segura estaba de que, la virtud de su nieta, había de recibir el justo premio, que Dios depara á los buenos" (147) ["It was not a surprise to her, because she was sure that her granddaughter's virtue had to receive the just reward that God provides to good people"]. Complementing the importance of moral decency is the insignificance of luxurious attire to winning the prince: Blanca, like the Cinderella stepmother and the stepsisters, is finely dressed, while both Josefina and Cinderella are in ragged garb when finally rescued and embraced by their princes. Both Alcides and Prince Charming recognize their brides-to-be by an unparalleled extremity: for Cinderella it is the tiny foot that fits the slipper among a slew of large-footed hopefuls, and for Josefina it is the delicate white hand that clearly stands out in a racially mixed crowd (136–38).[11] Last, the ornate carriage from the Cinderella tale in which the royal couple departs is present in Cabello's novel, carrying Alcides and his new bride in elegance (176). The overall structure and the supporting

---

10. All quotes are from the 1889 edition of *Blanca Sol*.

11. The significance of the white hand is an interesting topic whose analysis does not fit into this study. However, an in-depth look at the lower class's comments about Josefina and Alcides is worthwhile for their equalizing value: the crowd's message seems to be that white people are guilty of the same moral lapses of which they accuse other races.

details of the stories make the similarities strong enough to render the allusion recognizable.

A New Moral Code for a Progressive Era: Debunking Ideal Virtue

In Cabello's literary-theoretical essay "La novela moderna" (1892), she passes judgment about traditional notions of morality:

> En el orden moral, las ideas muertas pasan a servir de base a otras escuelas y a otros principios. . . . Los que se llaman conservadores no son más que insensatos que pretenden hacer vivir cadáveres. (63)
>
> [In the category of morality, dead ideas pass on to serve as the basis for other schools and other principles. . . . Those who call themselves conservatives are nothing more than fools who attempt to revive cadavers.]

Although Cabello does not explicitly mention it, among the "dead ideas" in the category of morality she likely includes the suffocating moral standard of the Angel of the House. Enveloping her ideas in the progressive Positivist discourse of the new republic, she rhetorically equates restrictive moral policy with "dead ideas"—to be read as backward-looking ideas from the colonial era under imperial Spain.

We find a similar disdain for close-minded morality as it regards the idealized notions of women's virtue in Cabello's rewriting of the Cinderella story. While the fairy tale centers on Cinderella, Cabello is far more interested in the stepmother figure, Blanca Sol. Josefina is not the protagonist but rather a secondary character who is not fully developed, an alter ego of Blanca herself:

> Blanca halló en Josefina un nuevo motivo de simpatía: parecíale estar mirando en un espejo tal era el parecido que notó entre ella y la joven florista, pero enflaquecida, pálida y casi demacrada, Josefina era la representación de las privaciones y la pobreza, Blanca la de la fortuna y la vida regalada. (89)

[Blanca found in Josefina a new motive for her affection: it seemed as if she were looking into a mirror, such was the similarity in appearance that she noted between her and the young florist. But Josefina, scrawny, pale, almost emaciated, was the representation of deprivation and poverty, while Blanca was that of fortune and the easy life.]

For Cabello, this subplot is a case study in patriarchal oppression, particularly concerning women's poor education and lack of preparation or opportunity in the workforce:

> Josefina . . . pertenecía al número de esas desgraciadas familias [aristocráticas], que con harta frecuencia, vemos víctimas del cruel destino. . . . Entre los muchos adornos con que sus orgullosos padres, quisieron embellecer su educación, la enseñaron á trabajar flores de papel y de trapo, y á esta habilidad, poco productiva . . . recurrió Josefina en su pobreza. (88)

> [Josefina . . . belonged to the number of unfortunate [aristocratic] families, that so often we see become victims of a cruel destiny. . . . Among the many adornments with which her proud parents tried to embellish her education, they taught her to make flowers out of paper and cloth, and it was on this ability, so poorly remunerated . . . that Josefina had to rely in her poverty.]

Josefina's paltry earnings must support herself, her grandmother Alva, and her two younger siblings. She exhibits "la virtud y trabajo de la mujer" (89) [virtue and work of woman], yet even the best Angel of the House cannot better her conditions without a living wage, to use a fitting anachronism.

Cabello's rewriting shifts the focus onto the "villainous" Blanca Sol by granting her the dominant voice in the narrative. Blanca Sol speaks approximately 257 times in the text—almost two and a half times more than any other single character.[12] She speaks more than seven times more than Josefina, the Romantically idealized woman. The narrative ascribes actions to Blanca as a subject who claims actions as systematic parts of her identity, as conscious desires leading to identified social agency. Despite the fact that Cabello is

---

12. I have counted both characters' thoughts and dialogue as speech.

careful to preserve proprieties by following up Blanca's overtly transgressive acts with punishments for her and others, these destructive outcomes can be explained by revisiting the primary Naturalist goal of the novel: to show how an insufficient education for naturally intelligent women ultimately leads to further corruption of the system and the people in it. Rather than judge Blanca to be an immoral person, the narrator blames her poor education and society's materialistic examples of womanhood. The skill that Blanca demonstrates in gaining power, albeit deleterious, is worth attention.

The protagonist's acquisition of the post of minister for her husband, a dull man with no experience, is arguably the most profound public gesture the character enacts. Blanca wishes to rid herself of something that irritates her substantially: "la pequeñez de su esposo" (35) [her husband's insignificance]. As the literary scholar Lucía Fox-Lockert and others have pointed out, Blanca and Don Serafín represent two social classes of the time: Blanca is part of the fallen aristocracy and Don Serafín is emblematic of the new bourgeoisie.[13] Since Blanca holds an established family name and Don Serafín does not, she wishes to procure a title for both of them, so that her husband will not be a *"don nadie"* (35) [*Mr. Nobody*].

Blanca's desire for a title points to an insecurity inherent in the condition of being part of the newly wealthy class as defined at the time. Serafín's father was a lowly soldier who made his fortune as a merchant. Blanca wants some official designation in order to claim a place as near to the established elite class as possible. To achieve this goal, she uses her powerful influence as a well-connected socialite to cause several figures of the existing political structure to fall in order to procure the post of minister for Serafín. Blanca's resolve in this matter is unstoppable: "Blanca sin desistir un momento de su idea, prometióse á sí misma, que su esposo sería Ministro . . . con, ó sin su gusto (36) [Blanca, without abandoning her project for a moment, promised herself that her husband would be minister . . . whether he liked it or not]. Cabello's representation of Peru's political structure as a corrupt, fragile one is a theme that she repeats in *El conspirador,* as the literary critic Cristina Mathews points out (2005, 468). On a subversive level, this act of political manipulation proffers Blanca Sol as a female agent who would have great

---

13. Fox-Lockert cites an uneasiness and discontent with the economic situation in late nineteenth-century Lima. She explains these socioeconomic circumstances as follows: "While this [uneasiness] is only an opinion, it is confirmed by economical data of the period wherein landowners lost out to foreign investments, business came to depend almost entirely on *guano* and social upheaval was caused by complicated governmental and political systems which sought to control dwindling urban resources" (1979, 149–50).

public potential if her desires were well guided. Since her actions reflect the public role models of Lima, she manages, instead, to indulge her desire for status and put an unintelligent, unprepared, and uninterested man in a position of power.

We can take two things from Blanca's social agency. The first is that women's mental and social aptitude and agency are not to be underestimated (indeed, one may argue that Blanca would make a far better public official than Serafín) and the second is that how women are educated not only is important on a domestic level, but also will affect the fortitude of the social system. Using a covert strategy to express her views by putting them into the words of a friend of Alcides', a representative for the upper-class male citizenry of Lima, Cabello intimates to the reader that "las mujeres pueden mucho cuando quieren" (59) [women are able to accomplish a great deal when they so wish]. His words, in the context of the story, sound like they could be an admonition of doom or a promise of hope—the interpretation seems to depend on what steps society takes to empower women with the education and opportunities to realize their potential.

Returning to the Cinderella fairy tale allusion, we see that Cabello deconstructs hegemonically prescribed ideals of virtue, as Blanca displays a much more intricate morality than that of the original stepmother.[14] In her article on *Blanca Sol* Guerra explores the "desvíos no-disyuntivos de la virtud" (the nondisjunctive detours of virtue). She reads the complex representation of morality in the novel as a sign of disconnect between Romantic ideals of virtue and the difficulty of fulfilling them in a corrupt, materialistic society. In this complex system, Blanca Sol is "un signo oximorónico en el cual la confluencia simultánea de dos significados primarios pone en evidencia una tensión no resuelta" (an oxymoron-like sign in which the simultaneous confluence of two primary meanings points to an unresolved tension" 1987a, 41). While for Guerra this "unresolved tension" means that the coincidence of good and bad in Blanca does not have a specific purpose, but rather is a sign of "las contradicciones ideológicas de la autora" (41) [the ideological contradictions of the author]—possibly referring to Cabello's adherence to both Catholicism and Positivism—I read it as a conscious effort to muddy the waters of established gender-biased categories of morality.

---

14. Arambel-Aguiñazú (2004) points out the moral complexity of Blanca Sol's character, while other critics have portrayed this figure as a villain. Several critics read the lack of moral clarity of Blanca Sol's character as a manifestation of Cabello's ideological confusion or ambiguity (Guerra 1987a; Nagy-Zekmi 1999).

The Cinderella allusion in the novel helps to clarify how Cabello complicates traditional dichotomous categories of virtue and vice. While indisputably vain and superficial, Blanca never indulges in the harsh punishments that the stepmother administers to Cinderella. In fact, when Blanca sees the desperation of Josefina's living conditions, she employs her, lodges her, dresses her, and arranges accommodations for her grandmother and siblings:

> Con su natural sensibilidad, Blanca habíase compadecido de Josefina y la dió su decidida protección.—Desde hoy—habíale dicho—no trabajará U. sino para mí sola, y la abuela de U. recibirá una mesada con la cual podrá llenar las necesidades de los dos hermanos de U. (91)
>
> [With her natural sensitivity, Blanca pitied Josefina and she gave her her resolute protection. "From today forward," she had told her, "you will only work for me, and your grandmother will receive a monthly allowance with which to support your two siblings."]

The narrator further specifies that Josefina regains her health and beauty, as she thrives under Blanca's protective care (91). Cabello's rewriting places Blanca on a much higher moral ground than that of the stepmother, and yet the protagonist is punished far more ruthlessly than the evil women in the fairy tale. While, in the most famous version of the tale, the stepmother is invited to the court of the newly married Cinderella, Blanca is humiliated and soiled by a cloud of dust from Alcides' and Josefina's stately carriage as she walks on the side of the road, descending later to a life of degradation (176).

Similarly, the rescripted Cinderella story offers a humanized Josefina in place of the idealized model as a means of diluting the long-suffering standard to one in which the Cinderella character is treated humanely, rather than abusively, by the stepmother; Josefina does not have to prove that she has suffered sufficiently in order to be rescued by the prince. Josefina, unlike Cinderella, is not materially disinterested; rather she is shrewd in recognizing that she must focus on making a favorable marriage to elevate her position. Before the Cinderella allusion is introduced, we have a subtle passage, cleverly slipped into a dialogue between anonymous characters, that voices the criticism of the angelic standard for contradictorily demanding that women be self-sacrificing and virtuous, while also putting disproportionate emphasis on social status and beauty for the establishment of their identity.

In the scene in question, two men are speculating over the immoral means by which a woman may have obtained her elegant gown: "Amigo mío, nosotros rendimos homenaje más que á las virtudes, al lujo de las mujeres, y luego queremos que no sacrifiquen la virtud para alcanzar el lujo" (48) [My friend, we praise women's luxurious attire more than their virtue, and then we expect them not to sacrifice their virtue for luxury].[15] It is an announcement of upcoming messages in the text that invite the reader to reevaluate the ideals of virtue in light of the social realities of 1870s Lima as they concern Blanca and Josefina.

Josefina's perfectly human, yet imperfectly angelic, nature is apparent in certain moments when we glimpse the seamstress's competitive side: "Josefina se sonrió pensando cuan súbitamente podría ese pobre y raído vestido, trocarse por el elegante y lujoso que llevaría, si por acaso llegaba el día, que ella fuera una gran señora, la señora de Lescanti" (148) [Josefina smiled thinking how soon she could exchange that poor, threadbare dress for the elegant and luxurious one she would wear, if by chance the day came, when she would be a great lady, the wife of Lescanti]. Her words show that she is thinking of her intended's fortune and the prizes it will bring, voicing it in the same terms as Blanca had before marriage, with dreams of being a "gran señora." Josefina even takes great pleasure in having won her mistress's lover: "Nunca se había atrevido á considerarse superior á una gran señora, á la señora de Rubio; pero hoy sí, hoy que era amada y respetada imaginaba estar á incomensurable altura, más arriba aún que la señora de Rubio" (144) [Never had she dared consider herself superior to a great lady, to Señora de Rubio, but today she did, today, as she was loved and respected, she was imagining being at an unreachable

---

15. This quotation brings to mind famous *redondillas*, cited in Chapter 2 of this study, of the baroque poet Sor Juana Inés de la Cruz (Mexico 1648?–1695). In her verses that begin with "Hombres necios" (Foolish men) the poetic voice accuses men of placing blame on women for lapses that the men themselves provoke, from the patriarchal ideal of chastity:

> Hombres necios que acusáis
> a la mujer sin razón,
> sin ver que sois la ocasión
> de lo mismo que culpáis
> (Cruz 2005, 109)

> [Foolish men who accuse
> women unjustly
> not seeing that you are the reason
> behind the sins for which you blame them]

height, even higher than Señora de Rubio]. Josefina is relatively virtuous because she works long hours to support her grandmother and siblings. However, the interested, envious emotions that the seamstress experiences offer a Naturalist-Realist view of human nature rather than the stepmother and Cinderella roles in which simplified images of good and evil are pitted against one another.

Cabello was aware of the concept and dangers of stereotyping, as she uses this exact term as a verb, *esteriotipar* in the novel (128). The narrator employs the term in defense of Don Serafín, whom Blanca seems to be stereotyping as the apathetic and weak husband.[16] The term appears italicized to draw attention to it, probably because it was still new at the end of the nineteenth century. This use of *esteriotipar* draws attention to the negative consequences of making quick and superficial judgments and implies a reproach of society; the author stimulates new awareness of the concept that leads the reader to recognize that stereotyping women or men is oppressive.[17] For example, when the narrator criticizes society's harsh judgments of men such as Don Serafín who do not prevent their wives from flirting, the narrator is quick to point out that women frequently suffer from this type of gender prejudice: "La sociedad que con tanta frecuencia es injusta para juzgar á la mujer, lo es también en un sólo caso para juzgar al hombre" (99) [Society, that is so frequently unjust when judging women, is also unjust in only one case when judging men]. Critiquing stereotyping is one way the author encourages society to broaden its definition of gender roles and to rewrite its symbolic order in new ways to accommodate a new republic striving toward modernity. Repeatedly, we

---

16. The exact phrase in the novel is "tiene el alma atravezada," which does not translate in current Spanish usage, but it appears to imply that Don Serafín was apathetic or did not care about Blanca (128). Regarding the term *stereotype*, according to the *Oxford English Dictionary* (online), it was first used in 1804 to describe the means of reproducing a print.

17. Cabello had her own personal experience with being stereotyped because of her intelligence. Her unusual knowledge earned her praise as well as gender-biased scorn for being a writer and an intellectual. Such scorn was not uncommon:

> La figura de la marisabidilla o "mujer que escribe" se convirtió en "diabólica" y también en sinónimo de "masculinización". La asociación que siempre se ha hecho entre "mujer fea" y "escritora", o "mujer masculina" y "escritora", la encontramos presente en todo momento. (Portugal 1987, 8)

> [The figure of the (female) know-it-all or "woman who writes" turned into the "diabolical woman" and also into a synonym of "masculinization." The association that has been made between an "ugly woman" and a "woman author," or "masculine woman" and "woman writer," was prevalent at that time.]

see the narrator defending Blanca Sol and critiquing the social factors that affect her life:

> A no haber poseído esa fuerza poderosa que da la hermosura, el donaire y la inteligencia, fuerzas suficientes para luchar con la saña envidiosa y la maledicencia cobarde, que de continuo la herían; Blanca hubiera caído desquiciada como una estátua para pasar oscurecida y triste al número de las que, con mano severa, la sociedad aleja de su seno. (8)

> [Without having possessed that powerful strength that beauty, elegance, and intelligence provide to battle invidious rage and the cowardly slander that continually hurt her, Blanca would have fallen like a statue, to pass into the dark and sad number of those who, with a cruel hand, society banishes from its bosom.]

Knowing that Cabello was the object of name-calling for being a successful woman intellectual allows us to better appreciate the narrator's pronouncement of society's denigration of Blanca Sol.[18] The author was addressing a contemporary problem for women in Peru (as well as in other Spanish American countries and beyond), one that she herself experienced: society's persecution of "powerful strength" in women. The characterization of Blanca Sol ought to be read as a biting criticism of bourgeois Lima—not

---

Cabello's biographer, Tamayo Vargas, gives further evidence of an ostracizing attitude toward the author when he writes that there was something masculine in her temperament, although she was considered physically attractive by her peers: "Presentaba en los momentos, que podríamos llamar de prueba, una actitud hostil, una altanera energía que respondía a cierta masculinidad de su temperamento, en contraste marcado con su afán de agradar y su apariencia femeninamente afable" (16) [She presented at times what we might call a hostile attitude, a lofty energy that responded to a certain masculinity in her temperament, in marked contrast with her desire to please and her femininely pleasant appearance]. This is a case when the symbolic order comes into conflict with itself; "masculine" is positive for a writer, unless that writer is female. Although it is true that a woman could sometimes be praised by saying that she thought like a man, a woman who took a step beyond this and published her work, it seems, could be deemed a bit too manly for a society in which women's primary role was domestic. The description of the author as having a "lofty energy" necessarily brings to mind the descriptions in the novel of Blanca Sol, who is called energetic, haughty, and proud throughout the work.

18. For an analysis of the persecution Cabello endured for being an early feminist intellectual and student of Positivism, see Arango-Ramos 1994, which also offers a feminist reading of Cabello's novel *El conspirador*.

only condemning women's poor and frivolous education, but also expressing discontent with the limited definition of the feminine to which women were expected to conform.

The narrator's final defense of Blanca Sol is an essential element of the early feminist strategy of the author. The idea that Blanca is undeserving of blame, and that society is at fault, is repeated five times in an emotional apology. I include it here so that the reader might get a sense of its full rhetorical effect:

> ¿Qué culpa tenía ella, si desde la infancia, desde el colegio enseñáronla á amar el dinero y á considerar el brillo del oro como el brillo más preciado de su posición social? . . .
>
> ¿Qué culpa tenía de haberse casado con el hombre ridículo; pero codiciado por sus amigas, y llamado á salvar la angustiosa situación de su familia?
>
> ¿Qué culpa tenía si, siendo una joven casi pobre, la habían educado creándole necesidades, que la vanidad aguijoneada de contínuo por el estímulo, consideraba como necesidades ineludibles, á las que era forzoso sacrificar, afectos y sentimientos generosos?
>
> ¿Qué culpa tenía, si en vez de enseñarla, la moral religiosa que corrige el carácter y modera las pasiones, sólo la enseñaron la oración inconsciente, el rezo automático y las prácticas externas de vanidosas, é impias manifestaciones?
>
> ¡La sociedad! Qué consideraciones merecía una sociedad, que ayer no más, cuando ella se presentaba como una gran cortesana . . . la adulaba . . . (181)

[How was she to blame, if from infancy, since grade school, they taught her to love money and to consider the brilliance of gold the brilliance most prized in her social position? . . .

How was she to blame, for having married a ridiculous man, but one coveted by her friends, and having been called upon to save her family's distressed situation?

How was she to blame, if, being an almost poverty-stricken young woman, they had educated her creating needs that her vanity, constantly incited by stimuli, considered unavoidable needs, and to fulfill them it was necessary to sacrifice affection and generous sentiments?

How was she to blame, if instead of teaching her religious morality that corrects the character and moderates passions, they only taught her to pray unaware of the meaning: prayer by rote and the superficial practices of vain and impious manifestations of religion?

How was she to blame if the life lesson learned in school was to view domestic virtues with scorn, and to view the extravagances of vanity with admiration and covetousness?

Society! What consideration did a society deserve that, only yesterday, when she was a great socialite, . . . adored her.]

The criticism of society here is a vindication of Blanca Sol, going a long way toward redeeming her in the eyes of the reader (a benefit that the stepmother in "Cinderella" never enjoys). However, it is worth noting that, despite the intensity achieved through reiteration, the narrator still cautiously works within the boundaries of what could be acceptably criticized by women so overtly; the passage blames society for faults in Blanca's religious, domestic, and sentimental education. All three were areas in which women were generally considered to have more experience than men and were expected to take a moral high ground to defend the standards of preparation for young women. So, the use of rhetoric here allows the author to affix a traditional filter to the narrator's words in order to avert negative criticism and, thus, enabling her to reprimand so harshly the patriarchal society that is the butt of her attack.[19]

---

19. Villavivencio points out Cabello's and other women authors' strategy of criticizing within accepted boundaries of domestic topics:

> El discurso femenino fue tibio y se cuidó de no alterar lo que consideraba el fundamento biológico y social de la mujer. De allí que constantemente las escritoras, para defender su oficio, señalaran que sus actividades no se contradecían con sus responsabilidades de madres, hijas o esposas, las cuales reconocían como principales. (1992, 59)

> [The feminine discourse was mild and it took care not to alter what was considered the biological and social foundation of woman. It was from this premise that women writers constantly pointed out, in order to defend their work, that their activities did not contradict their responsibilities as mothers, daughters, or wives, roles they recognized as fundamental.]

It should be noted, however, that despite Cabello's effort to situate her commentary within the domestic and spiritual safe zones, she nonetheless suffered harsh personal insults as a result of speaking out.

Consequences: A Valorization of and Return to the (Step)Mother

Whereas the crux of the Cinderella fairy tale depends on a stark contrast and animosity between Stepmother-Stepsisters (physically ugly, morally evil and hurtful, materialistic and wealthy) and Cinderella (physically beautiful, benevolent, spiritual and poor), Cabello consistently tempts the reader to imagine an alliance between Josefina and Blanca Sol that suggests the makings of female solidarity—one, of course, that she does not fully deliver. First there is the strong resemblance between Blanca and Josefina, which hints not only at the similarity of their natures, but also at some sort of a symbolic blood bond between them.[20] Then, we witness Blanca's affection for and protection of Josefina, which is broken when she learns of Josefina's courtship with Alcides. Finally, a betrothed Josefina, after envying Blanca, discovers Blanca's faithfulness to her dull husband and appreciates her lofty and honorable character. When Josefina learns that high-society gossip has condemned Blanca as an immoral adulteress, when this was never the case, she sympathizes with her former protector: "Cómo es posible que sucedan tales absurdos y tan estupendas injusticias" (176) [How is it possible that such absurd and such stupendous injustices are allowed to happen]. Josefina's words recognize that Blanca was never at fault; she is, as her name in Spanish indicates, "white," connoting purity of body and soul. In this case, the woman in the role of the stepmother is actually not so evil after all, a radically different take on the traditional model of blaming or killing off the mother in fairy tales, an idea that is fleshed out in contemporary studies of children's fairy tales.[21] Cabello, in the 1880s, a century before

---

20. Cabello's parallels between Josefina and Blanca could be read as a reconnection between mother and daughter figures. The scholar of fairy tales Maria Tatar has found that the Cinderella story and its many variants respond to the Electra fantasies of female children, in which the little girl's desires are projected onto the father, while her vilified mother is the rival for the father's affection (Tatar 1987, 150–53). In the traditional model the male-identified woman rejects the mother to align herself with the father—a gesture that twentieth-century women intellectuals, such as Kristeva and Irigaray, might read as a tremendous obstacle to women's ability to stake a claim for equality; for Kristeva it means a denial of *jouissance* (1974a, 156), while for Irigaray it marks the cyclical reproduction of patriarchy (1985, 41). Cabello's Cinderella subplot centralizes and vindicates the mother figure to create a symbolic bond of sympathy that radiates from Josefina toward Blanca. From a psychoanalytic perspective, Cabello's version readjusts the focus to the pre-Oedipal maternal body and its impulses, as the novel ends with the story of the fallen stepmother.

21. In her feminist analysis of fairy tales and pornography *Hating Women*, Andrea Dworkin notes that benevolent fairytale mothers are "soon dead.... When she is bad she lives, or when she lives she is bad. She has one real function, motherhood.... For a woman to be good, she must be dead [or asleep, as in the case of Sleeping Beauty and Snow White when the prince finds her in the glass

feminist critiques of *Cinderella,* was reevaluating the agency and power of the self-serving "witch," and the unfairness with which she is treated—while inviting her reader to rethink for herself the motives and consequences of acting selfishly in a society that necessitates such action. Blanca is the netherspace fairy-tale woman. She is neither good nor evil, and she is certainly not dead, asleep, or passive (metaphorically or literally), as the feminist writer Andrea Dworkin finds in the case of traditional fairy-tale women. In regard to motherhood, ironically, the reader sees Blanca become a better mother to her children the further she falls into moral decline in the eyes of society. Blanca is never in any moment primarily mother, or wife, or daughter, but rather a human individual grappling with social forces, and she herself is a force that society must reckon with, as she embodies an unapologetic critique of Lima society's superficiality and hypocrisy. While the traditional fairy-tale wicked woman is repulsive because she attempts to control others and get her way without exhibiting redeeming qualities, Blanca Sol is humanized and defended in her efforts to achieve material comforts and the power of her own volition in a world where these privileges are both highly valued and reserved for men. Like the twentieth- and twenty-first-century revisionist fairy tales written by Gregory Maguire, Jill McCorkle, and Robert Munsch, Cabello's novel presents the reader with alternative myths of feminine being.[22] It is a step toward a renewed valorization of a new type of fairy tale woman and mother, one who dominates the textual space with her words and actions, one who is permitted to have human flaws—and flaws that were learned from patriarchal society.

Conclusions

In *Blanca Sol* we are presented with an image of what a woman is capable of accomplishing through her mental aptitude and social skills. The novel

---

coffin], or as close to it as possible. Catatonia is the good woman's most winning quality (Dworkin quoted in Bennett 2002, 7; comments in brackets are Bennett's). Bennet discusses further the black-and-white nature of women's moral categories as they are presented in fairy tales: "Unless women want to be the dead mother, only two options offer themselves: beautiful but passive princess or evil step-mother/witch. Good and bad, beautiful and ugly, loved and unloved. . . . Perhaps it would be best to evaluate the witch and see . . . that being a witch isn't so bad. After all, she has the magic . . . and she has power" (11).

22. Indeed, the Cinderella myth is an obstacle to women's psychological development of self and independence in our own era, as journalist and researcher Collette Dowling roundly proves in her 1981 study *The Cinderella Complex.*

presents a strong defense of a female protagonist who is brash and intelligent, and who independently steers her life and her affairs, as far as she is allowed within a symbolic system that confines women to playing the roles of dependent and subservient children when they are married, and underpaid social servants (such as primary schoolteachers or uneducated laborers) when they are single. By reminding readers of the moral complexity of the protagonist and even of Josefina, I hope to have disproved the notion that Cabello's characters in *Blanca Sol* are "feminine stereotypes," as some critics have claimed (Mazquiarán de Rodríguez 1990, 95), that they lack psychological complexity (Torres-Pou 1998, 248), or that "the whole novel is constructed upon essentialist categories (vanity/modesty, passions/moral nobility, materialism/religiosity, etc.)" (Voysest 1998, 199). The text invites the reader to consider the unjust punishment that befalls the woman who pushes the status quo set for her sex and who tries to surge beyond the unrealistic standard of the Angel of the House in order to forge her own unique identity.

Cabello's changes to the Cinderella fairy tale serve as a way of questioning what abnegation and selfishness, spirituality and worldliness, and reward and punishment mean as far as her female characters are concerned. Cabello's rewriting of the Cinderella story challenges the reader to question the legitimacy and viability of the image of the Angel of the House as a realistic ideal for women, through the portrayal not only of Blanca, but also of Josefina. The author is working to counteract the social myth that even a poverty-stricken (connoting disinterest in material things) woman can win all the socially prescribed prizes if she is an Angel of the House.

Cabello, of course, is not interested in purely virtuous and passive women, as her society defines them. She is interested in proactive, intelligent women. *Blanca Sol* revives the image of an active female agent who has power in the symbolic order, recalling the politically engaged women of the independence era six decades earlier. Cabello writes the novel at a time when women are just beginning to rediscover their voices after years of using their agency, only to serve others during the early postcolonial period, and she seems to be encouraging them to be brave enough to break free from the most limiting gender roles for women, so that they may use their potential to become a positive force in a society ready for progress.

The novel is effective as an argument for providing women with a solid education because it plays on a principal fear of the ruling class, the argument being that Peru might decline to barbarism rather than rise toward civilization and progress.[23] The message from the novel is that educating the mothers of future leaders and citizens will prevent society from falling into the "barbaric" degradation that befell Blanca Sol. We are further invited to recognize that the hegemonic power structure will crush women's potential, as well as its own, by neglecting to cultivate its precious resource.

The veiled early feminist message in the text is an appeal for the ruling class to broaden its definition of the feminine and give women opportunities for education and personal growth. It also communicates a threat and an exploitation of hegemonic fears in its suggestion that society as a whole can be negatively affected by encouraging superficial and material desires in women. Cabello formulates and packages her views on a new, revolutionary female subject as the key to entering the twentieth century in a state of preparedness to face the challenges of new nationhood. However, these are changes that would also improve the lives of women as individuals by allowing them to focus on cultivating their intelligence and pursuing their desires, rather than focusing on others (as the self-sacrificing Angel of the House) or expending energy to live up to superficial social norms.

---

23. The opposition of civilization and barbarism was wrought into Latin American bourgeois consciousness with the publication in 1845 of Sarmiento's *Civilización i barbarie: La vida de Juan Facundo Quiroga* (*Civilization and Barbarism: The Life of Juan Facundo Quiroga*) in 1845. Although this message is implied in the novel, Cabello expresses it clearly in her essay "Influencia de la mujer en la civilización" (Woman's Influence in Civilization [1874]).

5

WOMEN AS BODY IN PUERTO RICO:
MEDICINE, MORALITY, AND INSTITUTIONALIZATIONS OF SEXUAL OPPRESSION IN THE LONG NINETEENTH CENTURY

DECADES BEFORE THE WARS of independence erupted across the continent, Puerto Rico had been struggling economically because of scarcity of gold in its mines, attacks by Caribs, sackings from various European pirates and privateers, and trouble starting its sugar industry.[1] Spanish restrictions on trade and the island's need to import many necessities created a perpetual negative trade balance. By the early nineteenth century, years of poor economic conditions were compounded. The loss in 1811 of the *situados*, a tax paid by Mexico that resulted in an important source of income for the island, augmented an economic decline that was already in progress. In an attempt to replace the loss of the *situados*, more money was printed, which led to inflation, causing widespread poverty.

The Cédula de Gracia (Royal Decree of Graces) of 1815, which increased European immigration and provided industry incentives for sugar cultivation, aided the rejuvenation of the sugar industry in the second decade of the nineteenth century. During this time, the United States became a major importer of Caribbean sugar. These changes improved the island's economy and enriched the class of sugar plantation owners. Despite Spain's agreement with Britain in 1817 to terminate the importation of slaves, the labor-intensive sugar industry demanded the import of additional human beings from Africa for unpaid work at midcentury.[2] In 1850 the introduction of

---

1. For a critical analysis of the problem of authority in the writing of Puerto Rico's history, see González-Quevedo 1996, chap. 1. Salvador Brau's *Historia de Puerto Rico* (1904) (which followed his *Puerto Rico y su historia* in 1892) was the history textbook used for many years in Puerto Rican schools and presents a paternalistic history that views U.S. occupation as a route to material progress (González-Quevedo 1996, 12–13, 23). González-Quevedo identifies Fernando Picó as the historian who first "raises questions" about Brau's view and presents the U.S. invasion as an usurpation of independence and gives significance to the nationalistic gesture of the Grito de Lares (27). González-Quevedo regards Blanca Silvestrini and María Dolores Luques Sánchez's *Historia de Puerto Rico: Trayectoria de un pueblo* (1991) as the first feminist history (16–19).

2. The importation of slaves reached its maximum in Puerto Rico between 1825 and 1835, with between sixty thousand and eighty thousand slaves brought to the island between 1815 and 1845 (Scarano 1993, 405–6).

steam-run mills increased sugar production, but also caused sugar prices to drop, contributing to a future decline in the economic viability of the industry.

When slavery was abolished, the industry could not withstand the absence of free labor; because of abolition and other factors, sugar was replaced by coffee as lead cash crop, starting roughly in the 1870s.[3] The Puerto Rican medical doctor, writer, and politician Manuel Zeno Gandía's novel *La charca* (1894) is a realistic portrait of the socioeconomic condition of the Puerto Rican highlands and is set during these years. The characters in the novel depend on coffee production for their livelihood and, paralleling the historical reality (Scarano 1993, 468), Zeno Gandía tells the story of the exploitation of small farmers by large landowners who manipulated their less technologically advanced neighbors into incurring large amounts of debt. Only a class of small- and medium-sized growers was able to resist the quasi-feudal takeover by large plantations.[4]

Despite the wealth that landowners accumulated during the coffee boom, the Puerto Rican peasants (*jíbaros*) lived in miserable poverty. They suffered from common illnesses, epidemics (malaria, yellow fever, and tuberculosis, among others), nutritional deficiencies, and lack of education. The prevalence of illness was precipitated by poor housing near swamps or other wet areas, as well as lack of medical care and hygiene education. Alcoholism, gambling, and promiscuity were ways to cope with the hardships. Women of this class were in a particularly difficult situation because they were responsible for child rearing and domestic chores and participated in agricultural labor yet did not directly receive their own pay; a male family member received a female relative's wages, which the men commonly spent on alcohol or gambling (Scarano 1993, 474). *La charca*, in which these problems are vividly depicted, evidences the intellectual elite's concern over these social problems and their effects on the future of an independent Puerto Rico.

Politically the 1800s were characterized by tension over the future of the island's governance and its contemporary need for reforms. Conservatives

---

3. While sugar was the main cash crop from roughly 1820 to 1876, coffee replaced it from 1876 to 1898 (Scarano 1993, 461).

4. These, along with small tobacco growers and cigar makers, cattle ranchers, and fishermen, made up a middle class. People of the middle classes also worked in administrative positions, commerce, shipping, and skilled services. The lowest on the social ladder worked as farm laborers and domestic servants.

(mostly Spaniards who were government officials or wealthy landowners and merchants) were staunchly faithful to the Spanish Crown, while liberals (mostly educated men of the middle class) were divided on how much autonomy the island should have and the nature and degree of reform. From a political perspective, a cause for the poor social conditions had to be found and corrected. The historian Ribes Tovar re-creates here the views of nineteenth-century liberal intellectuals who blamed Puerto Rico's problems on the moral weakness of the island's inhabitants: "Civic irresponsibility, the enervating action of the tropical climate, ignorance, indolence, vagrancy, rampant sexuality, ignorance of physical culture and the whole tone of community life on the island, which emphasized sensitivity and sensuousness at the expense of the intellect [were the causes of poverty and disease]" (1972, 85). This general idea of social illness, frequently related in discourse of the times with physical illness, was at the base of policies that attempted to correct women's contributions to Puerto Rico's problems. In this passage there is an implied dichotomy between healthy, masculine traits (the intellect, knowledge, abstraction, responsibility) versus traits that were historically attributed to femininity (ignorance, sensitivity, sensuousness, irresponsibility). As the nineteenth-century Latin American literary and cultural studies scholar Benigno Trigo has found, for liberal intellectuals, the metaphor for the literal and figurative diseases that plagued the country was the infirm female body that would give birth to a nation of enervated leaders. To cure this diseased nation, a segment of the intellectual elite focused on miscegenation, concubinage, and vagrancy in the lower classes, while bourgeois women and elite women were targeted for improving their motherhood skills and eliminating vanity (which was associated with flirtatiousness). The Catholic Church's policies to mitigate sexual promiscuity supported the goals of the liberals, despite the fact that the church's impetus was moral reform in a religious sense rather than social reform with an eye to the future of a "healthy" independent nation.

Power struggles between liberals and conservatives created a tense political climate. For almost three and a half centuries, Puerto Ricans did not have any say in choosing their local leaders, as all were appointed from Spain. The 1868 Grito de Lares (Outcry of Lares, named for the town where it originated) was a significant moment in history because it was an organized, albeit unsuccessful, insurrection against Spanish rule. The leader in the movement for Puerto Rican independence Mariana Bracetti (aka Brazo de Oro [Golden Arm]) had a central organizing role in the rebellion, and the respected Puerto Rican poet and independence activist Lola Rodríguez de Tió was sympathetic to the cause.[5] In 1870, the first liberal political party was born: the Liberal Reformista (Liberal Reformist Party). As a reaction to this, the conservatives began the Partido Incondicional Español (Spanish Unconditional Party), composed of wealthy royalist Spanish landowners, officials, and merchants who controlled economic and political affairs on the island. With the formation of these two factions, political struggle intensified and liberals and conservatives were more polarized.

The late 1880s was a time of intense economic decline on the island and much anti-Spanish sentiment. In 1887 the Puerto Rican Autonomist Party formed in support of greater Puerto Rican representation in voting and decision making, a decentralized colonial government, and less restrictive trade policies with Spain. The founding members were liberals from the upper and middle bourgeoisie who hoped to also draw smaller businesspeople and artisans to the movement.

The creation of the Autonomist Party occurred at approximately the same time that some bourgeois liberals began organizing boycotts against Spanish interests on the island. To crush the boycotts, the Spanish governor Romualdo Palacio began the *compontes,* a term that refers to "corrective" torture sessions and a period of persecution against suspected organizers of boycotts of Spanish interests. Founding members of the Autonomist Party, known as *patriots,* were tortured and persecuted for confessions and information. During this time, many patriots were exiled to New York, where women saw the greater agency and freedom of female U.S. citizens (Ribes Tovar 1972, 181).

After years of wavering commitment to allowing Puerto Rico greater self-rule, nationals earned some degree of self-government. In 1886 there was a vote for Puerto Rican representatives in the Spanish Congress and in 1897 Spain approved the Autonomic Charter, in which it conceded political and administrative autonomy to the island. This success was halted in 1898 when the United States invaded and took official possession of Puerto Rico, judging that it was unprepared for any significant self-rule.

5. Bracetti was imprisoned for her participation in the Grito de Lares. Rodríguez de Tió (Puerto Rico, 1824–Cuba, 1924), a distinguished national poet; author of Puerto Rico's national anthem, "La Borinqueña"; and fervent pro-independence activist, was twice exiled from Puerto Rico (to Venezuela in 1877 and to Cuba in 1889) for her patriotic verses and for speaking out in defense of pro-independence political prisoners. In 1892 she was exiled from Cuba for independence activism and moved to New York, where she worked with the Cuban poet and revolutionary José Martí and a group of writers and intellectuals to actualize Cuban and Puerto Rican independence. When the United States took Puerto Rico she left New York in 1902 for Cuba, which was then freed from Spanish rule, and lived there until she died. Her husband was the journalist and independence activist Bonicio Tió y Segarra.

In the generalized Western move toward modernization, liberal reforms in public health and education were planned to take place in Puerto Rico regardless of whether the island was under Spanish or U.S. control. Toward the end of the nineteenth century before the U.S. takeover, liberals succeeded in obtaining support for education from the Spanish Republic. The women of the island "sought to benefit from [liberal reforms], but the conservatives tried to keep them in a state of subjugation. In the press they carried on a subtle campaign against rights for women with poems extolling their beauty, the nobility of their life in the home, and on other topics" (Ribes Tovar 1972, 181). The late nineteenth and early twentieth centuries was a time when early feminists such as Rodríguez de Tió, Roqué, and the Puerto Rican feminist anarchist and workers' rights activist Luisa Capetillo began to voice their critiques of women's situation and demand reform. However, conservative women's magazines (generally directed by men) that concentrated almost exclusively on fashion, religion, domesticity, and feminine virtue were very popular throughout Spanish America as ways of maintaining a conservative model for women, as was the cult to the Virgin Mary, which was the epitome of the self-sacrificing standard of the Angel of the House.

When the United States took control of the territory in 1898, women were anxious to continue the development of education started in the nineteenth century and, under U.S. influence, looked toward gaining more rights (Ribes Tovar 1972, 185). The United States improved infrastructure, education, and scientific research centers, with particular emphasis on the control of epidemics and teaching proper hygiene for disease prevention (186). This is the context in which Roqué writes as she dreams up a fictional doctor who, in medical terminology, defends a woman's right to sexual pleasure as a physiological necessity, a few years before her compatriot Luisa Capetillo writes a treatise that advocates free love for women and promotes dissoluble marriages. It is useful to look at a trajectory of the changing attitudes of the ruling classes toward women's bodies and sexuality in order to understand the context from which these early feminist declarations arose.

Church and Governmental Controls over the Female Body in Puerto Rico from the Eighteenth to the Nineteenth Centuries

While the previous historical chapters of this study (Chapters 1 and 3) revealed that women's participation in the wars of independence marked a relatively clear transition from a period of agency to women's strictly and conservatively defined roles in the early republics, in Puerto Rico we cannot speak of such a clear-cut marker for transition. An examination of changes in certain social customs in the eighteenth and nineteenth centuries, however, renders visible an ever-growing awareness of and control over women's bodies over time.

In the eighteenth century the church pinpointed five areas of sexual behavior for correction among parishioners: promiscuity, incest, extramarital sex, prostitution, and abortion.[6] To correct these moral offenses, clergy supported limitations on social activities at which members of the opposite sex met. These limitations were likely leveled at people of the working classes, as elite and bourgeois women were more apt to have a select group of men from their social class from which to choose (or from which their parents chose) for marriage and were monitored and chaperoned very closely. There were likely many political reasons for limiting working-class extramarital relationships in addition to the religious motivation of minimizing so-called sins of the flesh. Controlling female reproductive bodies in late colonial Spanish America was a tool the ruling classes used to attempt to prevent miscegenation, to maintain wealth within racial groups and social classes, and to ensure a "healthy" population of virile citizens with a father/husband as the undisputed head of the family. During this period, women were the focus of limitations on sexual behavior because they were held responsible for permitting or prohibiting men from seducing and impregnating them (Barceló Miller 1987, 70).

The concern over what the church saw as immorally overt sexuality was reflected in its critiques of women's clothing. Ribes Tovar has found that in the eighteenth century, Puerto Rican *criollas* dressed in lighter attire than did European women because of the hot, humid climate. Women's dresses in Puerto Rico exhibited lower necklines and less voluminous and shorter skirts than those of European women. This lighter apparel caused San Juan's bishop in 1712 to accuse *criollas* of dressing provocatively to "induce lustfulness in men" (Ribes Tovar 1972, 65). This critique highlights the belief that women's bodies were the site of control over promiscuity. The physical and visual restraint of female bodies through clothing became one way the church attempted to stifle sexual activity occurring outside of the church- and state-sanctioned bond of marriage.

---

6. In 1526 Spain authorized, and the Catholic Church approved, the first house of prostitution in America (Flores Ramos 1998, 84). This is an early example of the way that the church condemned prostitution as an immoral activity, while at the same time it had a hand in controlling it (and perpetuating it) rather than fighting solely for its abolition.

Apparently the church's admonishments against low necklines yielded some success, because in the nineteenth century women's attire became more conservative. French influence brought "high-necked dresses, buttoned down the front, with pleats at the bust and lace collar and cuffs," better suited to a European climate than to the tropics (Ribes Tovar 1972, 99). In addition to this ample costume, women wore black shawls when going out in public (99). Hegemonic social policy succeeded in repressing the sexuality that apparently flowed too easily through Puerto Rican women's lighter garments.

The moral reforms that religious officials prescribed to control and limit the amorous meetings of young people were broad. They enacted restrictions for society as a whole, as well as particular limitations for women. In an obsessive effort to minimize contact between young unmarried people, the church disallowed festivals and other activities. For example, in 1729 a church mandate prohibited religious celebrations held at night in honor of the saints where young men and women could meet and enact "great offenses against God" (Pizarro cited in Barceló Miller 1987, 68; my translation). In 1760 *fandangos* (dances where young people socialized) were eliminated because they turned into a night of "profane diversions," and in 1787 the custom of singing the rosary was forbidden for the same reason (Barceló Miller 1987, 69–70). Religious officials hoped that by controlling social customs and public spaces they could also control the private sexual lives of its parishioners. The idea of controlling private aspects of citizens' lives overflowed into other areas.

The first cries for independence in the early nineteenth century and the subsequent successful battles waged by the Venezuelan independence leader Simón Bolívar and his followers led to stricter Spanish social and military control of the territories that were still governed by the Crown. Heightened control included limiting circumstances that could lead to social unrest and violence.

Like women's dress and social gatherings, dance took on a more conservative tone in the first decades of the nineteenth century. Back in the eighteenth century, *criollos* had transformed conservative traditional Spanish dances to fit the "Antillean environment": "the body was used to interpret intimate fantasies which expressed profound inner impulses" (Ribes Tovar 1972, 73). That is, dances became more sensual and closer to embodying sexual urges. By 1832, however, the sensual aspect of dance was curtailed. The dance of preference at the time was the Sevillian-style *contradanza*, whose final step was deemed too provocative: "[after changing partners] the original couple briefly reunited in a symbolical amorous embrace" (98). This last step "resulted in too many duels" and was thus eliminated (98). Although it is not clear from the historian's account who made the proclamation banning the dance, the important point is that the act reflects a conservative tendency in Puerto Rico, similar to those in the United States and Europe, aimed at repressing overt shows of sexuality in the national dances. Dances of the lower classes and those associated most with Afro–Puerto Ricans (such as the *danza*), however, remained erotic and were taboo for members of the so-called respectable classes.[7]

Cultural conservatism increased in Puerto Rican society as the century wore on, partially in conjunction with the intensification of Spanish efforts to squelch pro-independence activities. Although the aim was to limit opportunities for violence and prevent insurgencies, some of the Spanish decrees directly enforced the subordination of women by men through the physical control of their bodies. For example, General de la Torre, the highest government official on the island, prohibited prostitution in 1824 (although this decree was not strictly enforced until the 1890s [Flores Ramos 1998, 84]). Brothels had been legal in San Juan since the sixteenth century to "protect the honesty of married women in the city" and "to keep order among the settlers by avoiding confrontations that may have occurred in cases of kidnapping, rape, and infidelity" (84). By 1824, however, the need to moralize and control the population necessitated limiting opportunities for vice. Prostitution continued (sheltering or reforming prostitutes was not the objective), but with a closer monitoring of where women could go to sell their services, which prostitutes could stay on the street, and which had to be taken out of circulation. For years the adult male population on the island had outnumbered that of marriageable women. De la Torre's decree was accompanied by others like it. This excerpt paints a picture of the social and moral cleansing the government undertook to prevent insurrection and promote a moral and obedient society:

> In 1824, with the closing of the houses of prostitution and a wave of arrests of vagabonds and criminal elements, the artisans who frequented the gambling houses were fined, and games, with the exception of chess, checkers, backgammon and *chaquete,* were

---

7. For more on the elite's relationship to dances of the lower classes, see Suárez Findlay 1999, 56–57.

> banned even in private houses, which served as an excuse for police raids on meeting places. And other restrictions were imposed upon the population as fears of political revolt increased. Any person found on the street after 10 P.M. was fined, and all places of public entertainment were forced to close at that hour. It was forbidden to entertain house guests in private homes and penalties were imposed upon those who hid runaway slaves, minors or married women who left their legal owners, parents or husbands to live by themselves. (Ribes Tovar 1972, 108)

This excerpt demonstrates the invasion of public policy into the private spaces of citizens in efforts to limit opportunities for insurrection and impose a moral standard that was arbitrarily decided by local officials.[8] It is particularly noteworthy that the law reinforces the notion of a strong male head of the family; a father who let his wife or children wander from his home could be subject to fines. This excerpt also lumps women together with slaves and children, indicating that they were the "property" that the man of the house was responsible for controlling.[9]

In the mid-nineteenth century, church officials were especially concerned about the increase in premarital cohabitation, which, for the lower classes, mostly composed of black and mixed-race Puerto Ricans, was easier than finding time and money to marry.[10] Suárez Findlay claims that concubinage and serial long-term monogamy without marriage were so deeply

---

8. Ironically, starting in 1837 with the Spanish captain-general Angel Acosta, Spanish governors in Puerto Rico *encouraged* gambling and base entertainment to keep its inhabitants' minds off of insurrection and even built many gambling houses in San Juan for this purpose (Golding 1973, 82).

9. Similarly, the scholar of Latin American history and gender Florencia Mallon, in an article on Peru's transition to capitalism, has found that sexuality, along with control of women's property and labor, were ways that men asserted dominance in the public sphere in Peru in the era from 1830 to 1900: "Men . . . controlled women's sexuality both by defining what was 'proper' behavior and by making marriage decisions" (1987, 386). The case studies she lists include that of a man who would not allow his daughter to marry the father of her illegitimate children, as he was from a higher social class and was sure to disgrace her by parading around with other women publicly after their marriage (386). This is an interesting example because it shows that the father could control the sexuality of the women in his family—even if it meant an arbitrary disregard for traditional norms of keeping children within wedlock.

10. Despite church officials' efforts to moralize sexual behavior in the eighteenth and the first half of the nineteenth centuries, people of the working classes did not change their sexual mores. Barceló Miller cites the development of the single-crop plantation economy as an impediment to the church's edicts; the decline in quality of life and the rigorous planting schedule of slaves and workers prevented them from participating in religious rituals and from formalizing unions through marriage (1987, 74–77).

embedded in the culture of the lower classes that these incentives could not change people's behaviors. Nonetheless, the church sought to gain control over the moral formation of its congregation by reinforcing the importance of marriage and its vehicle was educating women to value holy matrimony. Marriage fees were also removed, to make the institution more accessible to the lower classes, whose lack of concern for formalizing sexual relationships alarmed social policy makers. Ironically, it would not be until the United States introduced divorce after the invasion that marriage would become more desirable to the population at large (Suárez Findlay 1999, 113–16). It was not financial incentive that would encourage couples to formalize their unions, but rather the legal possibility of dissolving the marriage if the partners were unhappy. One can speculate that women in particular might have viewed marriage as a more viable option once they had the possibility to legally separate from an abusive or indigent husband.

Church documents from this era show a two-pronged approach to women's role in this morally chaotic state of affairs: they both condemned women as immoral temptresses and proposed that their female parishioners subscribe to the cult of the Virgin Mary as a shining example to direct them away from evil impulses. The historian of women and gender in Puerto Rico María Barceló Miller uses a phrase to talk about this propagandistic shift in the characterization of women: "De la polilla a la virtud" (1987, 78) (From moth to virtue). The metaphor of woman as a moth—a pernicious insect that devours and ruins fine fabric (innocent men)—is taken from an 1864 ecclesiastic proclamation.[11] Arlene Díaz, historian of women's culture in Venezuela, finds a similar message in church documents after the wars of independence in Gran Colombia: "Not unlike the colonial ecclesiastic discourse on lust and chastity, nineteenth-century religious publications dwelt on the consequences of women's devilish behavior. . . . In sum, women were the . . . 'home of lust and administrator of the demons'; their [sexual] powers could make men lose their domination in society" (Pino Iturrieta 1993 cited in Díaz 2007, 33).[12] The message that women's sexuality was dangerous was found not only in church documents; Díaz notes that the liberator of the Americas himself, Simón Bolívar, often referred in his speeches

---

11. The analogy is from an 1864 ecclesiastic edict, "La polilla procede de los vestidos y de la mujer la iniquidad del hombre" (Fray José M. Fernández quoted in Barceló Miller 1987, 79) [Moths come from dresses and from woman comes the iniquity of man].

12. Díaz (2007) quotes the Venezuelan historian Elías Pino Iturrieta in the latter's book on women in Venezuelan history, *Ventaneras y castas, diabolicas y honestas* (Iturrieta 1993, 16–17).

to "the dangerous seductive powers of women" and that national rhetoric posited the passion that women could ignite as a force that "could corrupt both men and civilization" (33).

To counteract the socially damaging powers of women's sexuality, an organized and official cult of the Virgin Mary emerged in the mid 1800s. Barceló Miller has found that the Catholic Church vigorously projected the moral ideal of Mary as a corrective model against flirtatiousness and promiscuity. Two major institutions were founded to propagate the cult, the Primera Conferencia del Inmaculado Corazón de María (First Conference of the Immaculate Heart of Mary) in 1859 and the Congregación de las Hijas de María (Congregation of the Daughters of Mary) in 1870 (Barceló Miller 1987, 80–81). In 1861 religious retreats with a focus on Mary were organized for women from the capital (80). This impossibly self-sacrificing ideal, this heavenly version of the Angel of the House who gave birth through immaculate conception, set the standard for female asexuality and gained momentum throughout the nineteenth century.

Women's emulation of the Virgin Mary entailed, according to church documents of the era, the responsibilities of serving as a paradigm of religious devotion (to "save" society), encouraging love for and obedience to father or husband, and performing the role of faithful and docile servant within the family. In return for these services, women, instead of being scorned by the church and patriarchy (as the devouring moth), would receive "protection" and remain sheltered (Barceló Miller 1987, 78–83). Protection had a double meaning: material comforts that men could provide as well as the oppression that came from living in a patriarchal system while receiving some of its conditional benefits.

Another factor that affected political decision makers' manipulation of female roles in the nineteenth century was the decline in the economy and standard of living. This created a need for women of the lower classes to enter the workforce as housekeepers, seamstresses, and day workers (*jornaleras*). From 1871 to 1880 the number of women who were housewives decreased from 5,520 to 3,844 (a reduction of 1,676) while the number of women in the workforce increased from 299 to 2,184 (Barceló Miller 1987, 85). The church largely ignored this change in women's roles and continued to uphold Mary as the ideal model for all women. It is likely that women felt conflicted toward the intensification of moral standards set for them, with the promise of patriarchal "protection," when they were out in the workforce earning a living and working long hours for low wages rather than saying the rosary and attending mass. This clash between symbolic propaganda and real life was one of the circumstances that likely led women to begin or continue a process of questioning their circumstances. In particular, Capetillo was aware of and wrote about the hypocrisy of the ruling class toward women and the lower classes in her 1911 essay *Mi opinión sobre las libertades, derechos y deberes de la mujer* (My Opinion on the Liberties, Rights, and Responsibilities of Woman).

Woman Becomes Her Body: The Essentializing Nature of Medical Discourse, Social "Whitening," and the "Protection" of Women During Modernization

Both liberal and conservative social policies of the nineteenth century in Latin America focused on the female reproductive body as a symbolic and literal space where future generations of citizens could be molded to fit ruling class ideals of "whiteness" and morality, as the Caribbean historian of gender and sexuality Eileen Suárez Findlay, the scholar of eugenics in Latin America Nancy Leys Stepan, Trigo, and others have noted. This trend intensified notably from the 1880s through the early 1900s. While conservative politics often used the aforementioned religious discourses as its vehicle for moralizing women, liberals used Positivist and medical discourse to voice and justify policies that encouraged the erasure of feminine desire in the name of republican motherhood (as we have seen in the cases of Mexico and Peru). At the same time, women's sexualized bodies were a central focus of medical theories that heavily influenced marriage laws, education, and other social policies into the twentieth century with the politicization of eugenics.[13]

In nineteenth-century Latin America, as in Europe, the principal areas of university studies for men of the privileged classes were law and medicine, which meant significant overlap among professions in the ruling class. Doctors held weight in the political arena on questions of public health and morality.[14] Writers and politicians were sometimes trained as doctors or had influential friends or advisors who were trained in the medical profession (Stepan 1991, 40–42). Positivism (a philosophical approach to society and

---

13. See Stepan 1991.
14. Several examples are Zeno Gandía, a medical doctor who held several political posts and was a pro-independence advocate, and Drs. José Celso Barbosa and José E. Saldaña, who served on a committee addressing the prohibition of prostitution in the late 1890s (Flores Ramos 1998, 87).

government that focused on science and progress) and eugenics are two examples of how medicine drove social and political thought and practice. These policies sexually oppressed men (in particular, Afro–Puerto Rican men in regard to white women) and women of the lower classes and, to a lesser extent, women of the bourgeoisie in an effort to "whiten," moralize, cure (to use Trigo's term), and generally control the population. As Stepan put it, in Latin America around the 1870s "science became a rallying cry for the modern, secular elite" (41). Science was, to a large degree, perceived as a panacea for Spanish American social ills.

Social policies focused on women's sexuality logically manifested themselves in marriage laws. In 1805 "persons of recognized nobility" were permitted to marry people of "Negroid castes" (quoted in Ribes Tovar 1972, 96). This legislation was economically favorable to Afro–Puerto Rican women, because usually the person of higher social rank was a *criollo* man who married a woman of mixed or African origin; women of European descent were traditionally less likely to marry Afro-Cuban men.[15] The impetus for this law was likely twofold: to whiten the offspring of Afro–Puerto Rican women by allowing the latter to marry white men, and to legitimize cohabitation that carried on regardless of whether it was officially condoned.

While these social and political actions seem to have been aimed at protecting women by providing them with physical security in institutions and economic security through marriage to "whiter" partners, they also focus on women almost exclusively as reproductive bodies, rather than citizens with civil liberties. Few or no laws were upheld to protect Afro–Puerto Rican women from abuse by their white husbands, for example. The liberal policies the intellectual elite enacted carried as a subtext a strong desire to bring women's sexuality within bounds, whether by marriage or through segregated spaces within institutions. So, social policies of the times had a double result: greater opportunity for women's security (if we loosely define

---

15. Benigno Sánchez-Eppler (1994) analyzes policies of social whitening, or *blanqueamiento*, in nineteenth-century Cuba that encouraged women of all races to find the whitest partner possible for reproduction, leading to the social "castration" of black men, to use Sánchez-Eppler's term. It can be assumed that a similar process was under way in Puerto Rico, a country similar to Cuba in its interracial population being produced from the slave trade. Another legislative act aimed at favoring marriage in lieu of premarital cohabitation of interracial couples was the 1881 abolition of a law that forced people of different racial backgrounds to obtain special permission to marry (Ribes Tovar 1972, 96). Its elimination did away with additional fees and delays that prevented couples from legitimizing their unions.

security as the insurance of a bond of marriage with a domestic partner), accompanied by social codes of seclusion aimed at limiting women's social agency and private lives.[16] It is this social desire to contain the female body without considering women's well-being and happiness that Roqué's novel highlights and criticizes.

Early manifestations of medical theories in politics, which included social whitening, are explored by writers of the turn-of-the-century Spanish-speaking Caribbean. Social policies discouraged *mulata* and white women of the lower classes from having children with darker-skinned men, as the scholar of Caribbean and sexuality studies Benigno Sánchez-Eppler has shown in historical documents and in his reading of the well-known Cuban novel by Cirilo Villaverde *Cecilia Valdés* (1882), while marriage of light-skinned *mulata* women with *criollo* men was encouraged to whiten the population and create "legitimate" families.[17] Zeno Gandía's *La charca* offers a medicalized and essentializing perspective of the lack of control over the reproductive cycle of the *jíbara* (female Puerto Rican agricultural worker) and subsequent production of poorly cared for and illegitimate children. As Trigo puts it in his analysis of the Colombian Jorge Isaacs's widely read novel *María* (1867), "The sexual organs of women's bodies are not simply *an* aspect of the political crisis each author seeks to describe, but its determining aspect" (1995, 49). The public project of controlling women's sexuality was seen as one way of creating a healthy, virile nation vis-à-vis Spain and, later, the United States.

One of the ways that a medically derived social outlook manifested itself was in a marked increase in institutions throughout Spanish America intended to confine individuals who "contaminated" a population with sexual deviance, vagrancy, or mental illness.[18] Along with creating institutions to

---

16. Félix V. Matos Rodríguez (1999) views the creation of institutions for women workers in the second half of the nineteenth century as a way to perpetuate exploitative urban domestic labor after abolition.

17. For a detailed discussion of miscegenation in connection with racial and class issues in nineteenth-century Cuba, see Martínez-Alier 1989.

18. Foucault's (1988) *Madness and Civilization* is a book-length scholarly study that offers reflections on representations of madness in historical documents and fiction. Among the many functions and faces of madness, Foucault traces the institutionalization of madness as a scapegoat to replace leprosy in the mid-sixteenth century. Institutionalizing the insane served to marginalize them and thus protect the mentally healthy from alleged contamination. See also *The Birth of the Penitentiary in Latin America* (Salvatore and Aguirre 1996). For an analysis of the medical profession's exploitation of power to marginalize hegemonically undesirable segments of society in Argentina, see Salessi 1995. For a history of modern psychiatry's abuse and oppression of women, see Chesler 1997.

contain threatening subjects, authorities arbitrarily expanded their definition of crime to castigate women who had not in fact committed a crime, but who were suspected of engaging in sexual activity outside a committed relationship. Findlay's research shows that in Ponce authorities pursued a crackdown on any perceived "immoral" transgression by working-class women by labeling them prostitutes and persecuting them under the law: "By 1896 working women accused of nonmonogamy or unruly behavior were immediately labeled prostitutes and as a result suffered public harassment, fines, and imprisonment" (1997, 471). Similarly, as Trigo has shown, medical discourse on real and invented social diseases was inspired by intellectuals' fear of the Afro–Puerto Rican body and the lack of control over women's reproductive bodies. In turn, the social policies that the elite adopted to control these perceived ailments played upon the fears of the population at large, by discursively connecting social diseases with imagery of vampires and Medusas (Trigo 1995, 6, 69–89). Most of the institutionalized forms of social control were directed at the Afro–Puerto Rican population and lower classes for alleged criminal or deviant behavior and prostitution. Bourgeois and elite women faced harsh consequences for asserting their sexual desires or engaging in any behavior that questioned their decency, especially if their sexual agency took the form of adultery.

There are several types of institutional administrative action in the nineteenth century that indicate a greater concern for the control and confinement of reproductive female bodies. These were the segregation of women from men in state institutions that housed various types of social misfits (orphans, delinquents, people with mental illness), and legislative efforts made to facilitate marriage and limit concubinage. While sexual segregation in institutions benefited women because it greatly reduced the threat of rape, the driving factor was to monitor the movement and location of female bodies in society to impede the reproduction of morally weak, degenerate, and nonwhite Puerto Ricans. In the mid-1800s public health and service institutions began to segregate facilities by gender. One hospital specifically for women, called the Hospitalillo de la Concepción (Little Hospital of the Conception), had existed since 1615 and in 1823 was made co-ed municipal property (Ribes Tovar 1972, 95). In 1838 the hospital's administration segregated male and female prisoners. In 1872 the residents of the Asilo de Beneficencia (Asylum of Beneficence, an orphanage, institution for people with mental illness, reform home for prostitutes and criminals, and old-age home) were categorized and divided by sex and condition (Ribes Tovar 1972, 96). Prior to this, inhabitants of both sexes shared latrines in the *asilo*.

These changes were the result of medical theories of hereditary disease and miscegenation that drove social change.

Separating patients was not always enough to maintain hygienic categories; some medical institutions themselves had to be distanced from one another, literally and symbolically, to preserve the purity of the one from contamination by the other, as in the case of two women's hospitals in San Juan. The Hospital Especial de Mujeres (Women's Special Hospital) was established in 1895 to treat prostitutes for venereal disease and other conditions (Flores Ramos 1998, 87–89). As gender and sexuality scholars Donna Guy, Beatriz Calvo Peña, and others have found, stricter policies to regulate prostitution were common throughout Latin America near the end of the century and Puerto Rico underwent this process as well. In 1893 Spanish authorities approved a document of prostitution hygiene rules, which not only dictated sanitary conditions and disease control measures, but also controlled the location of prostitutes' bodies, as certain areas of the city were off limits to them in an effort to preserve these areas from the corrupting presence of the sinful women.[19] However, physical distancing of prostitutes was not enough. Irrational ruling-class fear of the corrupting presence of ambulatory female sexuality and its accompanying diseases, known under the name of "prostitute," is apparent in the dispute that arose in naming the Women's Special Hospital. Dr. Lugo Viñas, the director of the Women's and Children's Hospital, protested the similarity of the name of the prostitutes' hospital, where "women suffering from particular ailments would be assisted and cured," while his institution was established for the "assistance and cure of honest women in need of aid . . . and for the class of women who were able to afford the expenses of being treated at his hospital, for the cure of their ailments" (Archivo General de Puerto Rico, Fondos Municipales, Serie de San Juan quoted in Flores Ramos 1998, 89). In this dispute we see a sharp distinction between the class of honest and "decent" ill women and the grouping of those who were "indecent" and ill. What is interesting is that Lugo Viñas's fear (and the fear of the class whose interests he represents) is of the *symbolic* closeness of the two in the name, rather than any type of objective medical danger or contamination by physical contact (Dr. Lugo Viñas does not complain of the proximity of the Women's Special

---

19. Although the effort to regulate prostitution began under Spanish authority, Protestant influence under U.S. rule increased campaigns against both prostitution and drinking alcohol (just as temperance was sweeping through regions of the United States, so efforts were made to enforce the practice on the inhabitants of Puerto Rico [Flores Ramos 1998, 88]).

Hospital). Just as the police authority in Ponce arbitrarily defined prostitution to punish noncriminal yet transgressive behavior displayed by its women, Lugo Viñas is an example of a man of medicine in power reaching beyond the boundaries of empirical science to control the abstract elements of society to an ideological end: the symbolic distancing of overt, unclean female sexuality from a "protected" space inhabited by honorable women. As Flores Ramos points out, the doctor cannot even bring himself to use the word *prostitute* in his official letter (89), endeavoring to maintain a safe symbolic distance from it.

Although the examples above focus on the marginalization of women who belonged to lower social classes, they show us that discourses regarding women were obsessively focused on the reproductive body, and this outlook was projected onto women of the ruling classes as well. This essentializing view of woman as womb is clear in the enclosure policies for "decent" bourgeois women across Latin America, enforced to protect their virginity, and it is evidenced by the emphasis on teaching them proper hygiene and infant care rather than providing them with an education on par with that of the men of their social class.[20]

Traditional Women's Education, Bourgeois Women's Sexuality, and Early Feminists

A brief discussion of women's education is relevant to the following chapter in that Roqué taught school and actively proposed broader curricula for women to better match the academic formation of the men of their class. I will trace some history of women's education in Puerto Rico to show how, in response to liberalism, "Puerto Rican bourgeois feminists began to articulate their own moral vision of egalitarian elite marriages . . . and the white, wealthy women's right to intellectual and sexual fulfillment" (Suárez Findlay 1999, 15).[21]

As we have seen in the cases of Mexico, Peru, and elsewhere in Latin America, women's education was used in the nineteenth century as a nation-building tool for the new republics. Puerto Rico was under Spanish rule until

---

20. For a discussion of policies of enclosure for women, see Chapter 1 of this study.

21. As the tone of Suárez Findlay's (1999) quote indicates, early bourgeois feminists did not enfranchise their mixed-race sisters into these objectives. Instead, bourgeois and elite women helped lower-class women through charity and beneficent institutions, but it is not likely that they did it in an attempt to grant them equal rights and privileges.

1898 and that of the United States thereafter, so education did not have the same impetus as in independent nations. Discourses and educational policies implementing ideals for women of domestic household economy and motherhood were prevalent in efforts to push the island toward modernization and to mitigate social ills such as infant mortality and promiscuity: "Puerto Rican women of whatever class, it seemed, were [accused of being] unfit mothers, a major cornerstone of Puerto Rico's weakness" (Suárez Findlay 1999, 59). While in other Latin American countries the emphasis was on perfecting women to be mothers of future citizens of an independent nation, in Puerto Rico the Catholic, royalist, liberal, and Positivist discourses had an accusatory slant that focused on the sexually open female body.[22] Political treatises of the times aimed to better bourgeois women's preparation in domestic skills, religion, hygiene, and basic literacy as a way to protect their honor and push them toward rearing a community of intelligent and virile young men (future leaders and professionals) and obedient, prudent young women (future mothers).[23] A young woman's proper behavior and clean reputation were grave matters, as Spain's legal definition of virginity referred

22. The Catholic discourses that focus on women's dangerous seductiveness outlined in this chapter find their parallel, expressed in more objective terms, in writings such as Zeno Gandía's (1887) medical studies on Puerto Rican women and infant hygiene. Zeno Gandía's essentializing view of women conflates woman with their biological functions. This view is clear in his 1887 prize-winning study *Higiene de la infancia* (Hygiene During Infancy), in which he depicts the female body as a source of disease as well as nourishment.

23. For an overview of women's education in Puerto Rico from its origins to the 1980s, see Rivera (1987). For a thorough history of education for both sexes, see Osuna 1949. What follows is a brief summary of women's education on the island from the late eighteenth through the nineteenth century.

A mandate from Spain in 1783 called for the establishment of thirty-two schools for girls (Rivera 1987, 121). The results of this ruling were not seen until 1799, when four educational facilities for females were established in San Juan. The curricula of these first schools did not mandate reading and writing; they included catechism, needlework, and manners, while reading was only offered upon request (121). Rivera finds in Osuna's records that not only were women instructors paid a lower salary than male instructors, but five years later, in 1804, they had still not been remunerated (Osuna 1949, 19, cited in Rivera 1987, 121). Women's formation was limited to domestic and moral instruction.

In the early nineteenth century, liberal ideas entered Puerto Rico with the successes of the independence movement in South America, which resulted in increased importance being placed on public education for both sexes (Ribes Tovar 1972, 93). In 1820, a woman of modest means named Celestina Cordero y Molina founded a school for girls that included elementary reading and writing as well as Christian doctrine, sacred history, and domestic arts (Ribes Tovar 1972, 92). Great emphasis was placed on manners and decorum; girls were taught to respect their elders and be still in public. It is not so surprising that this narrow scope of subject matter was taught in the first girls' schools; this follows the evolutionary pattern of women's education seen in Peru and Mexico. What is remarkable about this school is that Cordero y Molina needed the approval of so many religious and political officials to teach such a traditional curriculum; approval had to be granted from the

to not only the intact hymen, but also the public recognition of her purity: "the *doncellez* [virginity] to which the law refers is that consisting of the state of respectability and the concept of such enjoyed by any young girl while she has not been dishonored in the eyes of society by an act that injures her respectability and constitutes an offence against customs and public morals" (Archivo Nacional de Cuba, Misc. Legal 2314/M quoted in Martínez-Alier 1989, 179–80). While for white Puerto Rican peasant women this meant a moral sexual education to "protect" them from mixing with men of African descent, for bourgeois women it meant jealously guarding their reputations, curbing their flirtatious and frivolous nature, and being transformed into diligent and prudent matrons of their homes.

---

bishop, the governor, the high police chief, and the deputies! (Ribes Tovar 1972, 92). This indicates an intensely conservative attitude toward even the most traditional and sanctioned teachings for women. In 1821 an educational facility for female citizens was founded by Vicenta Erickson (Ribes Tovar 1972, 93). Ribes Tovar claims that "[the] government of that period looked with disfavor on public education, since it counted upon ignorance as a protection for national integrity" (93). It was not until 1849 that the girls' school of the Hermanas del Oratorio de San Felipe (Sisters of the Oratory of Saint Phillip) opened (93).

According to a census from 1860, 40 percent of public schools and 36 percent of private schools were for girls, while 39 percent of all teachers were women (Rivera 1987, 121). By 1864, in San Juan there were eight public schools for girls and one private one, compared with twenty-four schools for boys (94). The teachers were primarily *mestiza* (of mixed Spanish and Indian descent) and Afro–Puerto Rican. Ribes Tovar adds that the teaching staff was "usually composed of one lady of good family," which can be assumed to mean *criolla*—of pure Spanish origin (94). In 1878, however, the number of girls' schools dropped to eight for a population of twenty-five thousand citizens (94).

Between 1865 and 1880 the Spanish government began to see education as a means of crushing separatist sentiments (Osuna 1949 cited in Rivera 1987, 122). It seems that influencing education was an ideological battle between the conservative royalists and liberal intellectuals. In 1874 the Spanish governor José Laureano Sanz fired all island-born teachers from the public school system and replaced them with instructors from Spain. An 1880 Spanish decree on education limited public education for girls of the *nivel superior* (highest level of education) to classes such as design, drawing, sewing, and domestic arts (Rivera 1987, 124). Spanish decision makers were even less interested in developing women's intellectual growth than were liberal intellectuals, who were driven by the ideal of republican motherhood.

Five schools of importance opened for girls between 1880 and 1886: Sagrado Corazón de Jesús (Sacred Heart of Jesus, 1880); Instituto de Segunda Enseñanza (Institute of Secondary Learning, 1883); and the Sociedad Protectora de la Inteligencia (Protectorate Society of Intelligence, 1886); the last being an organization that awarded scholarships to students to continue their studies in Spain (Ribes Tovar 1972, 94–95). These were all schools that shared the curricula of Catholic schools in other Latin American countries and shared the ideal that excluded advanced studies in all areas, and especially the sciences. Records show that during this time nuns also gave free instruction to a small number of female children from poor families (94). Women's overall participation in the education of their sex, however, was limited and underpaid. A survey from 1880 shows that women educators in girls' schools received, on average, only 67 percent of male educators' salaries in schools for boys (Rivera 1987, 124). This differential persisted in the surveys of following years.

Like marriage laws, the colonial interest in women's education was to aid in the process of whitening the culture. The ruling class believed that women's education was necessary to "purify the island's unhealthy heterogeneity and move beyond the economic and political stagnation in which they believed Puerto Rico was trapped" (Suárez Findlay 1999, 53). As Suárez Findlay has noted, and as was true in other Latin American societies, it was not just the color of a Puerto Rican's skin that determined that person's social standing or whiteness, but also his or her lifestyle and level of education. For instance, a white woman who allowed herself to be courted by a man of mixed race could have been considered less white, regardless of her family's social standing and the lightness of her skin. Educating women of all classes (with curricula guided by social status) would promote respectability (associated with socially desirable European qualities) and reduce adultery by men because they would esteem their wives more as partners.[24] The hope of liberals was that well-educated mothers "would then raise the de-Africanized, disciplined laborers, on the one hand, and assertive, virile white citizens, on the other, who were necessary to form a newly prosperous Puerto Rico" (59). This process of whitening through the rearing of so-called civilized, industrious citizens and the association of these ideals with white bodies of European immigrants was widespread in Latin America, where immigration laws provided incentives to these foreigners.

As Suárez Findlay notes, the "'dangers' [of women's sexual transgression] threatened many components of elite identity: familial honor; the alleged link between class privilege, racial purity, and female sexual control; and male claims to exclusive ownership of women's sexuality and sentiments" (1999, 62). She also points out that the characterization of woman as educated members of the elite class grew from the men of the ruling class's visions of what the "proper," "healthy" bourgeois Puerto Rican family should look like, *not* women's own ideas of self-fulfillment (62). Independently educated women of the bourgeoisie such as Roqué, however, contested these limiting goals of education, arguing that women needed intellectual stimulation for its own sake. Educating women thus yielded a result that male intellectuals had not anticipated, as Lola Rodríguez de Tió pointed out in 1875: "Women's education could be an obstacle to the ill-conceived ends of frivolous men, because a lettered woman will not always

---

24. The liberal elite perceived women of principally African heritage, however, to be too dominated by sensuality to reap the benefits of education (albeit the degree of perceived Africanness could vary depending on a woman's social status and lifestyle).

have the flexibility that the male ego requires" (cited in Suárez Findlay 1999, 63). Early feminists were aware, then, that efforts to educate them were not intended to encourage them to speak their minds and enter a process of subjectification through actualizing their desired selves, if these self-forged identities contradicted male-authored notions of their social roles.

Feminism in late nineteenth-century Puerto Rico grew out of this conflict between the liberal elite's political goals and bourgeois women's personal goals for self-realization. In the face of a strong push for conservative curricula for girls that focused on domestic and religious instruction, a handful of men and women were actively pursuing a broader range of courses for women as well as more facilities and instructors to reach a greater number of students. According to the Puerto Rican historian Yamila Azize Vargas, early feminist ideas came to Puerto Rico through male intellectuals such as Eugenio María de Hostos, Salvador Brau, Alejandro Tapia y Rivera, and Manuel Fernández Juncos.[25] Although they did not support the social equality of women, these men envisioned education as a means of bettering women's social condition and denounced their poor working conditions in the early 1900s (Azize Vargas 1987b, 19). Tapia also directed a journal for women, *La Azucena* (The White Lily), and defended women's rights. Azize Vargas recognizes Roqué, along with Rodríguez de Tió, as the first women to defend women's rights to better education and more participation in extradomestic spheres (19).[26] Rodríguez de Tió and Roqué both wrote about and supported the expansion of education for women, suffrage, and feminism. In 1872 in Santiago, Chile, Hostos made a declaration against the inferior position of women in which he used

---

25. These men are well-known figures in Puerto Rican letters. Eugenio María de Hostos (1839–1903) was an educator, novelist, literary critic, and thinker with a broad humanist background in sociology and philosophy whose thought influenced related fields, such as political science and economics. He was also an activist for the abolition of slavery and for Puerto Rican and Cuban independence from Spain. Salvador Brau (1842–1912) was a poet, novelist, essayist, playwright, journalist, and historian who also wrote about public education for peasant women. Alejandro Tapia y Rivera (1826–82) contributed to Puerto Rican letters an extensive opus of poetry, prose, and drama; he is among the most important figures in Puerto Rican literature. Manuel Fernández Juncos (1846–1928) was born in Spain and moved to Puerto Rico when he was twelve years old. He was a poet, writer, and journalist who founded several important liberal periodicals on politics and the arts. He was active in education reform and in politics as part of the Partido Autonomista, a liberal party in Puerto Rico that attempted to work with liberal Spanish politicians, but later abandoned his political career over a fallout with the party, focusing instead on education reform.

26. Young ladies of the wealthy class were not left completely uneducated, even before the era of education reform. They were taught catechism and some literacy and social skills and were expected to cultivate some special talent, such as painting, playing the piano, or embroidery.

scientific language to condemn women's traditional domestic and religious education (Ribes Tovar 1972, 113). He condemned society's pressure on women to be attractive (and little else) because it rendered them frivolous. Hostos denounced the government's neglect of women's education and its focus on them as reproductive bodies: "Woman has been reduced to the level of a two-legged mammal which procreates its kind, which feeds its biped offspring from its breasts, which sacrifices to the life of the species its own individual existence" (quoted in Ribes Tovar 1972, 113).[27] Hostos's words appear to be in dialogue with the objectifying discourses that focus more on women's wombs than on their status as whole individuals with intellectual, psychological, and emotional facets to their being. Since social degeneration was associated with the uncivilized, unevolved, or animalistic vocabulary with which Hostos imbues his speech, the word choice plays on a deep fear of the ruling class. The implication is that women pass these characteristics on to their children, thus breeding a degenerate and weak citizenry.

At the end of the century, bourgeois women in Puerto Rico took a relatively more active part in educating women from the lower classes by creating organizations to fund girls' educations. The 1886 pamphlet *Reglamento de la Asociación de Damas para la Instrucción de la Mujer* (Regulations of the Association of Ladies for the Instruction of Woman [1886]) contains government-approved rules for the Proyecto de Reglamento (Project of Regulation), which was carried out by the Women's Association for Women's Education.[28] The organization was under the patronage of the condesa de Verdú. It was a privately funded body, and the pamphlet seems to have served as a charter, with articles stating the goals, governing posts, sources of funding, and other rules for the association's actualization of funding and encouraging women's education.

The Women's Association's impetus for supporting education was the "notable desarrollo que va ganando en Europa y América la educación e instrucción de la mujer" (notable development that women's education is gaining in Europe and America). So one impetus for change, from the elite ladies' perspective, was to keep Puerto Rico up to date with cultural

---

27. Another man who rallied for the education of women and did so in terms of the importance of educating female citizens in order to achieve progress for the new nations was Tapia y Rivera (see Ribes Tovar 1972, 113).

28. This was an organization officially recognized in 1885 by the government and the Teachers' Association (Asociación de Maestros).

norms in Europe and North America. The association also recognized the responsibility of the "las más elevadas clases" (the most elevated classes) to take care of the education of "hijas de familia pobre o medianamente acomodadas que tengan vocación para la enseñanza" (5) [daughters of poor or lower middle-class families who have a vocation for teaching]. The tone in these statements is noteworthy because it is not one of solidarity with women of the working classes, but rather one of paternal (or maternal) protection, not unlike the discourse of the male liberal elite. While women of the upper classes recognized a responsibility to educate those of the lower classes, fear of racial and class conflict and differences prevented any real enfranchisement of lower-class women into bourgeois women's early feminist imaginings.

The Asociación de Damas did, nonetheless, promote job skills and literacy for women who may have otherwise remained ignorant. The goal of the organization was to finance the education of women who wanted to be teachers and administrators, and a future goal was to finance the education of women in commerce, telegraph operation, typography, bookbinding, obstetrics, and other areas (6).[29] The common ideology between upper-class women and the male intellectuals who were their relatives and acquaintances is apparent in the Asociación de Damas' interest in promoting medical advances advocated by the ruling class. For example, the charter states that individuals could earn the title of protector if they actively participated in efforts to vaccinate the population and promote proper hygiene.[30]

Roqué, who was carefully educated by her learned grandmother from a young age, was a feminist pedagogue who had the confidence to strive beyond male-dictated norms of education. She founded several girls' schools and spent her life educating young women of the island. Breaking out of the standard curricula of her day, she stressed the necessity that girls study the

---

29. Article 7 of the charter states that the funding will come from members' dues, "subvenciones" from the town hall and provincial government and other associations, personal or business donations, inheritances, proceeds from theater performances, conferences, sales ("bazar"), scholastic expositions, and interest accumulated on the funds from local branches (Reglamento 1886, 8). In addition to these sources of funding, article 10 sets down the different classes of members (*fundadores, natos, de mérito, protectores,* and so on), whose contributions include land, financing a young woman's education, lending one's professional services to the organization, writing essays propounding the merits of women's education or offering an award for such an essay, donating books, and donating items to sell in the bazaar, among others.

30. This is taken from the charter in article 10, number 4 (for the title of protector), item 7: "Las que procuren con todo celo y eficacia la propagación del virus vacuno y el cumplimiento de las disposiciones sobre la higiene" (*Reglamento* 1886, 12).

natural sciences, and she herself was a student of Positivism. Roqué used this philosophy, which had been exploited by men to essentialize women, to empower them instead, as we see in this quote from her 1888 textbook *Elementos de la geografía universal* (Elements of Universal Geography): "[Civilized are those] . . . who make progress in science, the arts, and all the fields of human knowledge; civilized peoples respect women, the law, and religion, rewarding talent, effort, service, and merit" (Roqué quoted and translated in García Padilla 1999, 50). In her study on Roqué as educator, the scholar of education María del Carmen García Padilla notes that Roqué "shared with Positivism the view that the systematic study of the natural sciences provides an objective approach to the order of the world and contributes to the adequate development of human rational capacities" (51). Unlike Comte, however, Roqué applied this view to women; in addition to opening girls' schools and spearheading suffrage, she also founded several important early feminist women's journals and vocational programs for women. Like Cabello and Pardo Bazán, Roqué embraced Positivism without abandoning her Catholic faith (García Padilla 1999, 51)—and, also similar to these women writers, it was in her best interest to do so, as women intellectuals who strayed too far from the norms of femininity were often scorned and shut out by their male peers, which diminished their power to enact positive change.

The U.S. presence after 1898 had a significant impact on education in Puerto Rico. Education was made universal, free, and available to children in rural areas, whereas prior to this time schools had been concentrated in the cities. It seems that Puerto Ricans had control over many of the decisions that were made in curricula and planning, as seven of the nine members of the Junta de Educación were Puerto Rican (Rivera 1987, 126); however, the process of Americanization, as it was called, was imposed upon Puerto Ricans. Roqué embraced U.S. intervention on the island at first, but later grew disillusioned as she discovered that the occupation and the advancements in technology and education brought with them a strong agenda of acculturation of Puerto Ricans to U.S. customs, including the use of English in the classroom (García Padilla 1999, 54). During the first decades of the twentieth century, with the expansion of the service sector and the need for more educated workers, women gained greater access to higher education. Until her death in 1933, Roqué remained "the most ardent feminist, the firmest defender of the rights of women, eroded by laws and societies created by men that have fallen prey to inhuman selfishness" (Roqué 1917 quoted and translated in García Padilla 1999, 56).

Conclusions

Under both Spanish and U.S. domination, ruling-class Puerto Ricans thought that by solving the population's numerous social "illnesses," that is, racial heterogeneity, promiscuity, alcoholism, and other undesirable traits that were considered hereditary, they could begin to eliminate these problems in future generations. In an attempt to stamp out such negatives, they focused on controlling women's bodies and sexuality because of their belief in the hereditary nature of degeneracy and delinquency, on the one hand, and industry and morality, on the other. Women could thus be socially conditioned and educated to choose lighter-skinned partners and ingrain hygienic morals in their children. Liberal and conservative politicians as well as the Catholic Church attempted to deny, stifle, or channel women's sexuality through marriage laws, education, recreation, and dress codes.

Medical discourse played a central role in the ability of the ruling class to enact social policies that limited women's and men's civil liberties. Medical language describing disease and heredity lent official-sounding justification and it inspired fear of the unhygienic consequences of ignoring its imperatives. These consequences could be revolts from a growing population of oppressed Afro–Puerto Ricans (the fear still lingered from the bloody Haitian revolt of 1791), a population unprepared for the independence it hoped to gain one day, or a nation of "too dark" illegitimate children whose mothers did not bestow upon them a hegemonic system of values. In all these policies of social regulation, the essentialized reproductive female body was the locus of control.

6

SEXUAL AGENCY IN ANA ROQUÉ'S *LUZ Y SOMBRA*: A SUBVERSION OF THE ESSENTIALIZED WOMAN

La sociedad siempre tiene un anatema para el que delinque, y sobre todo para la mujer, *a la que no se le permite ni un mal pensamiento;* y es porque las ciencias que de la moral tratan no son aún las mejor estudiadas.

Las fuerzas físicas de la Naturaleza producen innumerables estragos; el rayo mata, el huracán arrasa . . . *Pues también en nuestra naturaleza existen fuerzas instintivas muy poderosas, que son los principales móviles de nuestras acciones,* por lo que ya son objeto de estudio para los hombres pensadores.

[Society always has an anathema for those who are delinquent, and above all for women, *of whom nary an evil thought is permitted;* this is because sciences concerned with morality are still not adequately studied.

The physical forces of Nature produce immeasurable damage; lightning kills, hurricanes demolish . . . *Then very powerful instinctual forces exist in human nature as well; they are the prime motors of our actions,* and for this reason they are the object of study for thinkers.]

—Ana Roqué, *Luz y sombra*

THE PUERTO RICAN NOVELIST AND women's rights activist Ana Roqué fought for a change in the national standard for women that would include education, a variety of career options, the vote, and (through her fictional representations of women in the 1903 novel *Luz y sombra*) acceptance of female sexual desire.[1] Her conceptualizations of Puerto Rican female identity contradicted the angelic standard for women by attempting to grant them agency and greater opportunities to develop as individuals. Her fiction also condemned the abuse

---

1. In the preceding epigraph, the emphasis is mine. Ana Cristina Roqué Géigel de Duprey was born on April 18, 1853, in Aguadilla, Puerto Rico, and died October 3, 1933. When her mother died several years after her birth, she was educated and raised by her paternal grandmother, a teacher by profession who inspired the child's quest for knowledge in diverse areas of study. Roqué was self-educated and founded a private school in her home at the age of thirteen after mentoring with instructors. In 1885, at the age of thirty-two, she attended the Civil Institute for Secondary Education in San Juan. She married Luis Duprey when she was nineteen, and they had five children, three of whom survived to adulthood. Although the couple did not remain together physically (her husband lived with several different women during their marriage), they never divorced (Paravisini-Gebert 1994, 154). Later she founded the Colegio Mayagüezano (School of Mayagüez), the Liceo Ponceño

and exploitation of women. Roqué's 1895 short novel *Sara la obrera* is a tragic story of an unmarried *mulata* seamstress, Sara, whose best friend helps her own husband rape and drug the seamstress out of fear of the husband's abusiveness should she resist him. Roqué's short 1919 novel, *Un ruso en Puerto Rico,* also levels a critique of the sexual and economic domination of white men over Puerto Rican women and men of African and racially mixed heritage.[2]

Roqué was able to write about sexual transgression because of her social credibility and because she limited this topic to her fiction, which was carefully crafted within traditional discourses of womanhood, to soften the subversive material. Women activists who lobbied more directly for women's sexual freedom, such as Roqué's contemporary Luisa Capetillo, who openly supported women's right to leave their husbands and form new unions as they pleased, suffered harsh critique.[3] For example, in Capetillo's 1911 essay, *Mi opinión,* in the section called "On Honesty," she cites a Dr. Drysdall's view that women's sexuality is not animalistic or dangerous, but rather normal and healthy: "In women, as in men, the vigor of sexual appetites is a great virtue; it is the sign of a robust constitution, with healthy organs and a naturally-developed sexual disposition" (Drysdall quoted in Capetillo 2004, 50).

(Ponce Secondary School) in 1902, the organizations Liga Femenina Puertorriqueña (Puerto Rican Feminine League) in 1917, and the Puerto Rican Women's Suffrage Association in 1924. Roqué opposed the U.S. policy of teaching basic courses in English in public schools. She published articles in educational journals voicing her disagreement with this policy (Rivera 1987, 129). According to Delgado Votaw, Roqué estimated that she "granted degrees to 110 teachers, and educated 5,200 children in 23 years of public teaching, and 300 more in 10 years of private teaching" (1995, 76).

Delgado Votaw's short biography shows that Roqué published *Explicaciones de gramática castellana* (Explanations of Castilian Grammar [1889]). She also edited and founded the periodicals *La Mujer* (Woman [1893]), *La Evolución* (Evolution [1902]), *La Mujer del Siglo XX* (The Woman of the Twentieth Century [1917]), *Album Puertorriqueño* (Puerto Rican Album [1918]), and *El Heraldo de la Mujer* (The Woman's Herald [1918]). Her books *Geografía universal* (Universal Geography [1894]) and *La botánica en las indias occidentales* (Botany of the West Indies [for which I could not locate a date]) and the essay "Estudio sobre la flora puertorriqueña" (Study on Puerto Rican Flora [1908]) are some examples of her work in the natural sciences. Further evidence of her interest in the sciences is her study of meteorology and her membership in the Astronomy Society of Paris; she was even known to hold stargazing seminars in her home.

2. The summaries in this section are paraphrased from my forthcoming article "Ana Roqué de Duprey." Roqué published several other collections of fiction: *Pasatiempos* (Pastimes [1894]) and *Novelas y cuentos* (Novels and Short Stories [1895]).

3. Capetillo, a humbly born activist for workers and women's rights, was ostracized by feminists of the bourgeoisie, including Roqué, for her position on free love and women's right to dissolve an unhappy marriage and form a new union (Matos Rodríguez 2004, xix). It is likely that the suffragists viewed Capetillo as a danger to the reputation of their cause because of her radical views. Capetillo's views on free love were also attacked by the editor of the periodical *Brisas del Caribe* in 1917 (Matos Rodríguez 2004, xxiv–xxv).

Knowing the Positivist context of their era, it is not surprising that both women buttress their defense of female desire with the medical opinion of a doctor, one real and the other fictional. Roqué was far more subtle than Capetillo in her campaign for women's sexuality in that she safely hid behind the mask of fiction and was careful to denounce adultery at the same time that she asserted women's need for sexual fulfillment. The fact that Roqué was a civic leader also facilitated her intellectual peers' acceptance of her; she was extremely active in women's advocacy and was responsible for setting up many scholarship funds and programs for women's education and professional development.

In 1894 Roqué started a magazine about women titled *La Mujer* (Woman), which was the only periodical of its kind owned and edited by a woman (Suárez Findlay 1999, 65).[4] This was an important step toward forming solidarity among women of her class and providing a place for them to publish and exchange ideas. Later in her life Roqué founded the women's rights organizations Liga Femínea (League of Women, 1917) and the Asociación Puertorriqueña de Mujeres Sufragistas (Puerto Rican Association of Women Suffragists, 1924). She fought for suffrage throughout her life and lived to see the battle won. Roqué received for her numerous accomplishments an honorary doctorate in literature from the University of Puerto Rico.

Roqué's passionate study of the sciences partly explains her use of medical discourse in *Luz y sombra*.[5] As the first female member of the Ateneo Puertorriqueño, Roqué likely knew the work of the novelist, poet, historian, and independence activist Salvador Brau and she was a friend of Zeno Gandía's (two men of science who were also authors and politicians). Roqué's scientific and literary orientations are evidenced by her published studies in the natural sciences, as well as her creative writing and editing of five newspapers over the course of her lifetime (Delgado Votaw 1995, 76). A well-informed intellectual such as Roqué was surely aware of the male elite's employment of medical discourse to denounce miscegenation and unwed unions. Such discourse sough to control and objectify female bodies.[6] For instance, the medical doctor, novelist, and social policy reformer

---

4. Ribes Tovar (1972, 103) sets the date for *La mujer* at 1897.
5. For a discussion of Roqué's Positivism, see Chapter 5 of this study.
6. With the abolition of slavery in Puerto Rico in 1873, miscegenation was a particular threat to the "white" peasant population because of racial mingling with freed slaves, primarily in rural areas (Trigo 2000, 6). The medical doctor Francisco del Valle Atiles is one Puerto Rican thinker who expressed the fear of contamination of the white race by Afro-Cubans (whom he believed to be immune to anemia) in *The Puerto Rican Peasant,* published in 1887 (Trigo 2000, 81). For further information on essentialized conceptualizations of women by defining them in terms of

Zeno Gandía's perspective toward women focused largely on their maternal role. He was concerned with female promiscuity, population control, and sanitary conditions for child rearing; that is, his focus was women's biology and behavior as it affected society.[7]

Roqué's work, then, appears to be in dialogue with the Catholic Church's and liberal intellectuals' essentialized representations of female sexuality, as we saw them in the previous chapter. While Puerto Rican men of science made advances in overcoming disease and poor sanitation in a colony neglected by Spain and economically dominated by a small number of families, their treatises and fiction also had the negative effect of presenting an objectified subculture of femininity. It is not fortuitous, then, that Roqué's novel innovatively rearranges and reinterprets traditional gender traits within the female protagonist and dares the transgressive act of presenting the fulfillment of female sexual desire as a biological need in a female character who is a psychological and emotional subject, as well as a physical one.

Reclaiming the Self: *Luz y sombra*

Roqué navigated the waters of power, legitimacy, and subversion carefully by creating an outward fictional shell that appeared to uphold the status quo ("unfaithful women are punished") while reconstructing the essentialized images of women. She did this by manipulating literary commonplaces already familiar to the reader, such as the reason/emotion dichotomy and

---

reproduction (motherhood), see Chapter 5 of this study (the section "Church and Governmental Controls over the Female Body in Puerto Rico from the Eighteenth to the Nineteenth Centuries"), Barceló Miller 1987 and Suárez Findlay 1999.

7. Looking at a chronology of Zeno Gandía's life, one notes a consistent overlap between literature, medicine, social consciousness, and politics that included focused attention on the role of the female body in national health concerns. The son of Spanish royalist sugar plantation owners, Zeno Gandía was born 1855 in Arecibo. He began writing early, even while attending medical school in Madrid from 1870 to 1875. After graduating and traveling through Europe, he worked as a medical doctor in Ponce. From this point, around 1900, Zeno Gandía dedicated most of his time to politics and writing (Laguerre 1978, xviii). He became the president of the Education Committee in the Cámara de Delegados (House of Delegates), was appointed sanitation inspector in Ponce, and later worked in journalism. As I mention in Chapter 5, Zeno Gandía's formation as a doctor and his concern for infant health in Puerto Rico led his interest to women's roles in population control, health, and sanitation. A product of his times, he held an essentialistic view of women that equates women with their biological functions. In 1887 he published the prize-winning study *Higiene de la infancia* (Hygiene During Infancy) in which he depicts the female body as a source of disease as well as nourishment, as previously mentioned.

medical discourse. The advent of the Naturalist novel, which took up such unsavory characters as the prostitute, the opium addict, and the alcoholic, laid the foundation for Roqué to be able to talk about female sexuality in a positive way because Naturalism already opened the topic, albeit with a negative emphasis on sexual impulses and deviance (prostitution, promiscuity, and so on).[8] The erotic nature of the prose of some *modernista* writers, such as Julián del Casal (Cuba, 1863–1893), Darío, and Silva also aided in opening the door to writing about female sexuality in the literary circles of Latin America.

Roqué defends female sexual desire as a normal part of a healthy existence. She converts the dangerously contaminating abject female body into the "clean" or "hygienic" whole identity of the feminine self, thereby reversing the horror of the feminine abject in the Naturalist novel by normalizing, rather than marginalizing, women's sexuality.[9] *Normalizing* is a loaded term when applied to the feminine because, in the contexts of the novels in the study at hand, it acquires the meaning of "valorizing the feminine traits as its parallel masculine trait," but *normalizing* also means "equating with the masculine," where *normal* equals *male*. That is, women authors' views of equality often follow a masculine standard rather than creating alternative standards. In this sense, early feminists are not yet developing a sense of different but equal; nonetheless, they are clearly placing gender inequality in the center of intellectual ambiances and offering explanations and solutions to remedy the gross imbalance. Roqué's act of pointing out and rewriting gender inequality vis-à-vis sexuality was an important step for future generations of feminists.

The story of *Luz y sombra* sets up a false dichotomy between two friends: Julia is rational, worldly, Positivist, and materialist, while her friend and confidante is sentimental, maternal, self-abnegating, and domestic. While

---

8. In Puerto Rico, the primary example of the Naturalist novel is Zeno Gandía's *La charca*. Zeno Gandía's concern with the health, nutrition, and hygiene of infants and the mother's (often poorly executed) role manifests itself in the descriptions of the filthy conditions in which children are raised in *La charca*. While male laborers in the novel are also to blame for moral decline (several male characters are alcoholics and engage in the physical abuse of women), it is the impotent yet seductive female body that is most consistently under Zeno Gandía's Naturalist gaze. Other Naturalist writers, such as the Argentine Eugenio Cambaceres and the Mexican Federico Gamboa, also focus on the promiscuous and sexualized female body as a cite of barbarism and social decay.

9. I am using Kristeva's region of the cultural unconscious that comes about when such images are repressed. For Kristeva's definitions of the term *abject*, see *Powers of Horror* (1982) (as impure organic matter [1–2]; as an individual's memories [6]; as expressed in that which is considered socially taboo and in writing [16–18]).

Julia is tempted to the brink of adultery—presumably representing the *sombra* of the title—Matilde is the ideal of the spiritual and moral Angel of the House and, one assumes, represents *luz*. The dichotomy is carried into each woman's choices of residence and spouse. Julia is an elite urbanite and Matilde lives on a small farm in the countryside. (Here Roqué seems to convey that rural settings are more spiritually beneficial than the corruption of the city.) Julia marries Sevastel, an older yet handsome and distinguished military general, as a way to acquire a large fortune and social status. Matilde falls in love with and marries her cousin Paco, a man of modest means.

The main plot revolves around Julia's unsatisfying marriage and subsequent near-adultery. Not only is Sevastel significantly older than his wife, but he is also drained of spirit and vigor from carousing in his youth. He is therefore not able to satisfy Julia's need for physical love and passion. This lack in Julia's life sets the stage for her attraction to Sevastel's young, handsome friend Rafael. Despite temptation and a growing sexual awakening, Julia is determined to maintain her honor and resist Rafael's advances. She takes a trip to Spain with her husband, hoping the distance from Rafael will cool her feelings.

The second part of the novel resumes after Julia's stay in Spain, which did not mitigate her desire for Rafael as she had hoped. She finally agrees to meet him for an amorous encounter in his country home. She hesitates to go through with the meeting, but succumbs to Rafael's pleas. Once at Rafael's bachelor residence, Julia decides not to proceed with the affair. Before she can leave, the couple is surprised by Sevastel and two other soldiers. Although the soldiers do not recognize Julia, Sevastel does. He tries to kill her but the other men intervene. Sevastel and Rafael agree to duel over the anonymous "mistress" the following day. The dishonored husband administers a fatal wound to his opponent, who, before dying, assures Sevastel that he never consummated his relationship with Julia.

Julia becomes seriously ill upon hearing of Rafael's death. Sevastel calls on a young, handsome Guatemalan medical specialist to help his wife regain her health. Dr. Bernard (apparently a reference to the real-life French scientist and influence on Zola's Naturalism, Claude Bernard) prescribes a bizarre treatment to cure her. He reasons that, as the patient is dying from lack of love and passion, the only cure is seduction. Because her husband is not able to administer the prescription (implying, as the reader has suspected, that he is impotent), the doctor claims that the only way to cure Julia is for he himself, the doctor, to do the job. Bernard assures an uneasy Sevastel that he is a happily married man and has no impure intentions with Julia. The pseudoseduction/medical treatment is successful; Julia regains her strength, reconciles with Sevastel, and later gives birth to a daughter. (Although the doctor's seduction is supposed to be based on a performance of courtship, there is substantial suspicion in the mind of the reader about the identity of the baby's father.) Sevastel later dies of a "strange disease," a "general weakening that slowly turned him into a cadaver." Julia then dies of tuberculosis and finally her daughter dies of an unspecified illness (138). I will get back to Dr. Bernard's dubious medical treatments in a moment.

Matilde's is a secondary narrative that supports Julia's plot line; her words mainly express concern for Julia's well-being and voice the joys of simple living in a marriage filled with love and honest work. Matilde's one tragedy is the death of her infant son, Paquín, from diphtheria.

The epistolary structure of the novel is of utmost importance in the process of subjectivity. The exchange of letters lends itself to a reevaluation of feminine identity because of its intimate tone and the metafictional effect that reading the correspondence between the two women creates. The exchange of missives is mainly between Julia and Matilde, although some letters circulate among the women and their spouses as well. (For example, Sevastel corresponds with Matilde about Julia's health.) In a collection of studies that considers the question of feminine style and themes in the epistolary form in eighteenth- and nineteenth-century France, Christine Planté finds that letters were an appropriate space for individuals to disregard conventional gender norms; for example, women wrote about politics or men wrote on sentimental themes (1998, 17). This is true in Roqué's novel, as Julia transgresses gender norms by talking openly about her desire for Rafael (permissible for men but taboo for women) and by describing her rational nature in terms considered masculine at the time.

In Roqué's novel the epistle creates an intimate, private ambiance that makes the reader feel as if he or she were spying into private lives of strangers. (I will discuss this voyeuristic effect in more detail later in my analysis.) As the letters progress, the reader becomes familiar with the characters in this personal mode and he or she is drawn more deeply into the plot; we are witness to their innermost desires and conflicts *as the female characters tell them*—not as they are related by the masculine perspective of a third-person narrator. Psychologically, the blurring between fiction and reality that one experiences upon reading a novel composed of letters aids the rewriting of the female identity.[10] That is, the characters/authors of the letters seem to become the reader's acquaintances as the story progresses. The epistolary

---

10. Vivienne Mylne has noted the epistolary novel's ability to grant verisimilitude to fiction to assuage eighteenth-century France's distrust of the untruth of fiction (cited in Gurkin Altman 1982, 6).

form is a vehicle for convincing the reader that transgressive women like Julia exist in one's society, while it also draws him or her in as a witness or accomplice to this transgression, thus implicating the reader in the feminist rewriting at hand.

In an epistolary novel, then, readers experience the text more interactively than when they read fiction with a central narrator's voice because of the illusion that one is discovering private documents and also because of the added verisimilitude. Setting up the reader's psychological investment in the story is an effective authorial strategy for presenting subversive symbolic material. The theoretical work of Leon Festinger and James Carlsmith, well-known psychologists who investigate cognitive dissonance, aids in understanding the literary strategy of the epistolary style in *Luz y sombra*. The theory of cognitive dissonance aims to explain how the human brain adopts certain ideals in order to maintain consistency between an individual's behavior and his or her belief system, thus eliminating dissonance between the belief and the action; it explores the question "What happens to a person's private opinion if [one] is forced to do or say something contrary to that opinion?" (Festinger and Carlsmith 1959, 1). For our exploration of literary strategy, the question could be, What happens when a reader with patriarchal views on gender willingly "spies" on letters in epistolary fiction that defend transgressive behavior for women? According to the theory of cognitive dissonance, "the private opinion changes so as to bring it into closer correspondence with the overt behavior the person was forced to perform" (Festinger and Carlsmith 1959, 1). So, one may argue that a reader who becomes a party to fictional transgression, as is the case in the epistolary novel, begins to sympathize with the feminist sentiments contained in the letters.

As I have mentioned, an important function of the epistolary structure of *Luz y sombra* lies in most of the textual voice coming from the female characters Julia and Matilde. In Roqué's novel, *women are the subjects of their own narratives*; they present and analyze their own problems and one another's dilemmas, provide comfort to one another, and criticize oppressive aspects of their society. In Roqué's novel women author their own lives and create their own symbolic selves. They are authors of their own identities. By using their agency to fulfill their desires (albeit accompanied by negative consequences, in the case of Julia), they are engaging in their own subjectification.

Although *Luz y sombra* includes an omniscient narrator in the second part of the novel, Roqué's narrator often speaks in the first person plural to continue the intimate textual voice from the letters. The narrator's use of *we* continues the invitation from the first part into the private sphere of the two female characters and is an extension of the familiar tone of the epistolary structure. The narrative voice is an important addition to the letters, because it serves as a sympathetic voice of authority that judges and emphasizes what the various characters in the novel have to say.

Roqué's disassembly of gender stereotypes is channeled through two literary mechanisms: a redistribution of male and female characteristics and defense of women's sexual desire and sexual agency. The mixing of masculine and feminine characteristics mainly concerns male objective logic versus female romantic sentiment and masculine sexual love as opposed to feminine emotional love. Comparable to a typical educated male's outlook (the example of *La charca*'s grounded, somewhat jaded Juan del Salto comes to mind), Julia faces life with a clear, rational, analytical outlook. She says of herself, "Creo soy yo la que estoy en el terreno firme de la vida; pues con mis diecisiete años precoces, me inclino siempre a lo práctico, a lo que me reporte utilidades positivas; y dejo o ahogo los sueños vagos" (31) [I believe I am the one on life's firm ground; at the precocious age of sixteen, I am always inclined toward that which is practical, those things that bring me positive gains, and I abandon or smother vague dreams]. Julia determines, in her rational and dispassionate way, to follow society's example and marry the wealthiest and most prestigious suitor.[11] Roqué's use of language that rings of Positivism and progress is not fortuitous; her own great interest in Positivism, outlined in Chapter 5, links her sympathetically to the character of Julia, despite the latter's shortcomings. Julia's goal is to lead a comfortable and luxurious life and hold a high position in society; she is not concerned with what she considers ephemeral and sentimental love. She disdains the "feminine" language that Matilde uses in her letters; in response to her friend's flowery proclamation of love for her cousin Paco, she writes: "¡Oh, qué idilio, amiga Matilde, es tu carta de ayer! ¡Cuánto me he reído al pensar de que manera tan tonta te has enamorado de . . . el amor!" (39)

---

11. Although Julia is somewhat similar to Cabello's character Balanca Sol in her rational way of following society's example in regard to marriage, there are some significant differences. Julia is not interested in social climbing; she is already a member of society's elite. Also, Julia marries an elegant man and harbors hope for a romantic awakening toward her husband, while Blanca Sol's husband is a buffoon. Julia admires Sevastel but feels frustrated by his cool attitude toward her, whereas Blanca Sol is more malicious toward her clumsy bourgeois mate, her malice being the fault of the superficial society that misguided her. Julia is dispassionate about the prospect of love; Blanca Sol disregarded a love she had in favor of social climbing, which leads her to resent Serafín and Lima society in general.

[Oh! How idyllic, Matilde, my friend, is your letter from yesterday! How I have laughed upon thinking in what a silly way you have fallen in love . . . with love!]. Another time she gruffly taunts Matilde for "hacer el oso" (62) [engaging in traditional courtship] with her fiancé.

This objective, logical outlook and derisive stance toward the weak, emotional response is not unlike the response of conservative literary critics of the era to the so-called effeminate *modernista* poetry of del Casal or Darío, calling their writing *preciocista* and criticizing them for being overly focused on aesthetics, rather than attending to practical nationalist themes. While it is not my goal here to develop such a comparison, I use this example to show that Julia describes herself and interacts with Matilde in terms that were considered virile for the times, as opposed to the artful and artificial prose of the *modernistas* or the sentimental style of Romanticism.[12] Thus Roqué's creation of Julia's rational, Positivist character was likely an attempt to enfranchise women into the ruling class's ideal of masculine power.

Renouncing Angelic Self-Abnegation: Roqué's Claim on Female Sexual Desire

In addition to logical intellect and disdain for the sentimental, sexual desire is another typically male-dominated sphere that Julia boldly enters. Choosing women's sexuality for her critical redefinition of gender norms put Roqué in dialogue with a significant issue of her time; as I discussed in the previous chapter, heavy emphasis was placed on chastity for women as Angels of the House, to the point of restricting women's social movement and limiting women to modest styles of clothing.

Roqué uses her descriptions of nature to buttress social messages in the novel. In *Luz y sombra* nature reflects Julia's awakened sexual desire. The chapter preceding Julia's rendezvous with Rafael closes with references to Julia's sexual frustration. It describes her desperation, rapidly circulating blood, and fiercely beating heart that "wastes her organism" (110).[13] At the

---

12. For example, the pages of José Enrique Rodó's 1900 book-length essay *Ariel* (1968) are filled with references to the importance of rational judgment and virility for the future of a strong Latin America. The Mexican Positivist Barreda's (1991) essay on women in the early twentieth century (addressed in Chapter 1 of this study), in turn, seriously questions women's capacity for intellectual (masculine) thought.

13. The following segment opens with a description of the dark night, with resplendent stars gleaming behind black clouds that would not yield drops of rain. This imagery reminds the reader

same time, a storm is brewing and threatens to erupt but maintains itself on the threshold of fruition:

> Ese cariz tempestuoso es muy común en nuestros veranos. Mas la tempestad suele resolverse en relámpagos sin ruido, a las que acompaña un calor asfixiante que hace decir a los más: "¡Oh y qué cargada está la atmósfera!" cuando lo que pasa es que está demasiado enrarecida a causa de la absorción del vapor de agua por las nubes, y la respiración se hace difícil, sintiéndose una anhelosa sensación de angustia. (111)
>
> [This tempestuous atmosphere is very common in our summers. Moreover the storm tends to dissolve in silent lightening, which is accompanied by an asphyxiating heat that makes everyone exclaim "How stuffy it is!" when what is actually happening is that the air has expanded owing to the clouds' absorption of the water vapor, and this makes one experience difficulty breathing and a breathless sensation of anguish.]

While this passage reflects Roqué's great interest in the natural sciences, it is not difficult to read the metaphor beneath the thin veneer of *costumbrismo* writing (a form of writing in the nineteenth century in Latin America that described local customs or ambiances). The analogy is between the natural phenomenon of the suffocating summer heat, produced by a brewing storm whose energy is held prisoner within the clouds, and Julia's physical decline and anguish produced from her brewing passion.

There are many passages in which Julia's need for sexual fulfillment is expressed in a direct manner. While after 1900 some Latin American male writers acknowledged female sexual desire in their fiction (although they rarely used a bourgeois housewife to exemplify this), women writers avoided the topic to save their reputations and good standing in the literary

---

of the soiled-dress metaphor that marked the deconstruction of the light/shade dichotomy; the dress was white with a dark spot, but here the black cloud is sprinkled with white stars. The mixing of black and white is repeated to emphasize the mix of virtue and vice within everyone. A reading of the deconstruction of the dichotomy between black and white obviously lends itself to a racial reading of the symbolism as well. This would be particularly relevant given Roqué's fight for humane treatment of the slaves on her husband's plantation in 1872 and her support and celebration of their emancipation in 1873 (Paravisini-Gebert 1994, 154).

community.[14] In one often-quoted passage of *Luz y sombra,* nonetheless, the narrator plainly states Julia's right to physical satisfaction within her marriage:

> Dios y el mundo le habían concedido un esposo para que satisficiera los sueños de su mente, las aspiraciones de su alma, y los impulsos de su ardiente temperamento. Tenía, pues, derecho al amor, teníalo a los goces legítimos de su estado, y de casi todo eso estaba privada por una burla sangrienta del destino. . . . La esposa se abrasaba de pasión mientras el marido dormía como un bendito. (76–77)
>
> [God and the world had granted her a husband to satisfy her mind's dreams, her soul's aspirations, and her burning temperament's impulses. She had, then, the right to love, she had the right to the legitimate enjoyment of her married status, and she was deprived of almost all of this because of a cruel hoax of destiny. . . . The wife burned with passion while the husband slept the sleep of the just at her side.]

The narrator blames Sevastel for denying his wife her "right to love," which, to add legitimacy to the narrator's words, is sanctioned by God. The word choice ("right") lends a legal tone to a woman's privilege to sexual satisfaction within marriage, which minimizes Julia's responsibility in her stumble with Rafael in the moral economy of the novel.

---

14. Several novels by male writers in the late nineteenth and early twentieth centuries explore female sexuality directly. Federico Gamboa published the novel of the prostitute *Santa* (Mexico, 1901), while Silva's *De sobremesa* (written 1895–96, published 1925) presents a disdainful view of female promiscuity in the lovers of the decadent protagonist Fernández. The Guatemalan *modernista* writer Enrique Gómez Carrillo is one of few authors who unambiguously present proper bourgeois women as agents of sexual desire (although with some degree of sensationalism, in decadent style) in his collections of short fictions *Almas y cerebros* (1898) and *Del amor, del dolor y del vicio* (1898; revised edition 1901), to offer two examples. His wife, the Peruvian writer Zoila Aurora Cáceres, in 1914 explores an affair of a proper bourgeois woman in her novel *La rosa muerta*. Roqué, then, was an early female advocate of a woman's right to sexual fulfillment within marriage. Rather than present this desire as a decadent urge (Gómez Carrillo) or as a symptom of a marginalized character (such as a prostitute or a female stage performer), Roqué writes this desire into a female character who is otherwise recognizable and not terribly unusual in the eyes of her reader. As I discuss in Chapter 5, her defense of female sexuality is partially in line with her contemporary and fellow Puerto Rican Luisa Capetillo (although Roqué disagreed with Capetillo's advocacy of free love for women outside marriage).

In another scene, Julia is the subject of this legitimating narrative. She intimates to Matilde the frustration she experiences in Sevastel's bed:

> Las caricias frías y convencionales de mi esposo me exasperaban, me enardecían: me abrasaba, una desesperación sin nombre se apoderaba de mí, y después de dar vueltas en mi lecho solitario, y de despedazar a mordiscos los encajes de mis almohadas, o de mi pañuelo, . . . por fin el sueño, sobreponiéndose sobre mi naturaleza exuberante de juventud, rendía mi materia. (65)

> [My husband's cold and conventional caresses exasperated me, they enflamed me; I was burning up, an unknown desperation took hold of me, and after tossing and turning in my solitary bed and biting the lace on my pillowcase or handkerchief to shreds, . . . finally sleep, overcoming my exuberant and young nature, subdued my flesh.]

In this scene Roqué overtly represents a young woman of the dominant social class as the subject of sexual desire. In this way, the narrative reverses the suppression of extramarital, or even extrareproductive, sexual behavior advocated by the Catholic Church.[15] Roqué embraces female sexual pleasure that social policy has suppressed, prefiguring by more than a half century this discursive gesture in Cixous ("Laugh of the Medusa"), Irigaray, and Kristeva. Like later thinkers, Roqué employs sexual awakening as an integral part of the character's development of the self.[16]

The narrative strategy in the passage above is noteworthy. Roqué leads the reader three levels deep into the text. The first level is the narrator's

---

15. For more information on the governmental and clerical suppression of the female body, see Chapter 5 of this study.

16. For Kristeva the concept of *jouissance* is part of the subject's becoming: "The overt expression of jouissance, a pleasure emerging outside the structures of the social order, is . . . a sign of woman gaining her own identity and entering the sphere of the subject as opposed to that of the passive object" (Kristeva 1974a, 138–52). Similarly, for Irigaray the female libido is "one symptom of something outside that threatened the signs, the sense, the syntax, the systems of representation of meaning and a praxis designed to the precise specifications of the (masculine) 'subject'" (1985, 43). The "story" to which Irigaray refers here is Freud's Oedipal myth to describe the process of adult heterosexuality. One of the many aspects of the Oedipal model that Irigaray critiques is the absence of focus and explanation of the female libido: "Woman would thus find no possible way to represent or tell *the story of the economy of her libido*" (43). For Irigaray, Freud's idea of the libido may be neuter or masculine, but never female (43).

observing from outside, the second is the first-person stories of the letters, and the third is Julia's narration of a scene within the epistle. The reader is a voyeur to this scene not only because he or she is allowed to "spy" on Julia's letter, but also because the reader gains entry into the intimate area of her bedchamber. Rather than reading a scientificesque narrator's account of aphasic women who are continually victimized and sexually violated, as in *La charca,* the reader is the witness to a woman's expressing her need for passion. Roland Barthes, who likens the reader to a "spectator in a nightclub," recognizes as an authorial strategy the act of rendering the reader voyeur: "The text is a fetish object, *and this fetish desires me.* The text chooses me, by a whole disposition of invisible screens . . . : vocabulary, references, . . . etc. and, lost in the midst of the text . . . there is always the . . . author" (1975, 11, 27). As participatory witnesses to this desire, the reader, to quell the cognitive dissonance between accepted social norms (women are self-abnegating and men are desirous), may begin to sympathize subconsciously with the subversive message and begin to believe, in fact, that women are as desirous as men. He or she is lured into the spectacle of the text and is thus psychologically invested in its content.

Julia gives voice to her physiological sexual lack, which is causing her health to deteriorate visibly: friends and acquaintances comment upon her sickly appearance (65–66). Her apparent symptoms of frustration are dark circles under her eyes, pallor, and weight loss. While a strong sex drive in a woman is portrayed as aberrant in male-authored texts of the period, lack of sexual fulfillment is unhealthy here. By assigning visually detectable evidence to Julia's problem, Roqué is "rendering the invisible visible," to use Fernando Feliú's phrase; the protagonist's problem takes on greater importance when it seems to fall under a label created by and maintained by medical doctors (2002, 154). The terms "enardecer" (enflame) and "abrasar" (burn) clearly suggest the physical nature of her dissatisfaction with Sevastel, and if that is not clear enough she states that sleep finally conquers her "materia" (matter), the physical source of her suffering. The chaste Angel of the House Matilde, rather than dismissing Julia's problem, is devastated to hear of such suffering, when she herself experiences all the pleasures and comforts of love with Paco (69). The epistolary style implicates the reader in this exchange as a third-party confidante to these problems; he or she gravitates to sympathize with Matilde's compassionate position toward Julia, since she, after all, is the shining example of virtue.

A Woman Writes the Doctor: Medical Justifications for Female Sexual Desire

To make her case to the bourgeois readership of Puerto Rican society, Roqué has various unlikely characters in the novel rally for the legitimacy of Julia's physical desire. Rafael, the doctor, Matilde, the narrator, and even Sevastel all recognize in some way that Julia's unreleased passion is unhealthy and morally debilitating. Rafael is the least convincing of the group to defend Julia's sexuality, because he has selfish motives for his argument (he would be the fortunate recipient of Julia's passion). However, the dialogue between the two as he is trying to convince her to submit seems to serve as a general message to the reader. This is suggested through an interesting use of italics in the dialogue between Julia and Rafael:

> [Julia, hablando de Sevastel] No puedo amarle a él, pero tampoco *debo* amar a otro.
> —¿Y por qué? ¿No sabe Ud., señora, que la naturaleza tiene sus leyes, y que *nadie* puede contravenirlas sin que le traicione su propio corazón? (101–2)

> [(Julia, about Sevastel) "I cannot love him, but neither *should* I love another."
> "And why not? Do you not know, Madame, that nature has its laws and that *nobody* can contravene them without cheating one's own heart?"]

The italics on *nadie* draw the reader's attention to it for a closer analysis of the statement. *Nobody* is a relevant choice for emphasis because it is genderless, implicating both men and women. When Rafael says that *nobody* can go against nature's laws, he is equalizing women and men. While we cannot assume that Roqué was condoning adultery, for either men or women, in the context of the novel the reader gets a clear message that when women are tempted by adultery, it may be because they are not sexually fulfilled in their marriage, rather than because they are deviant or malicious. As I mentioned earlier, women were punished for sexual transgression; local law called for prison terms of up to six years for elite women who were convicted of adultery, but this was not the case for men (Suárez Findlay 1999, 27).

Thus Roqué's message could be read as a way of bringing this injustice to the attention of her readers.

While the idea of sexual equality is implicit above, the narrator is daring in her explicit communication of this view. The narrator's use of the word *angel* below is ideologically loaded; it is a deliberate attempt to wipe away the artificially pure and perfect façade of the Angel of the House, acknowledging that this model is the basis for gross inequality between the sexes:

> Hay que convencerse de que *la mujer no es un ángel; es un ser lleno de pasiones lo mismo que el hombre;* y no basta a veces la buena educación moral que en teoría se les da, para preservarlas del desvarío que le imponen sus propias pasiones. . . . Y no atendiendo a estas leyes poderosas que dominan nuestro organismo . . . se las expone a todos los peligros de la imprevisión, a luchar como heroínas, *y pocas llegan a la cúspide sin mancharse en el camino, aunque sea con una leve sombra, su blanca vestidura.* (103; my emphasis)

> [One must convince oneself that *women are not an angels; they are beings filled with passions just like men* and at times the proper moral education that, in theory, we give them is not enough to save them from the whims their own passions impose upon on them. . . . And ignoring these powerful laws that dominate their organisms . . . they are exposed to all the dangers caused by this lack of foresight, abandoned to struggle like heroines, *and few arrive at the cusp without soiling their white dresses on the way, even if it is with a trivial spot.*]

The metaphorical soiled white dress that nearly every woman must wear is a deconstruction of the dichotomy of the virginal white of a wedding gown and the marring spot of the moral slip, light and shade, or female virtue versus deviance. The emphasis is on the inhuman standard inherent in the Angel of the House. Here the dichotomy is deconstructed; light and shadow are inextricably mixed within women, as in men. The narrator stresses the moral equality of men and women and that it is just as difficult—and unrealistic—for women to maintain impeccable moral conduct as it is for men.

This is a groundbreaking statement for early feminism for two reasons. First, it takes away the ideological crutch of female moral superiority—a claim that many educated women used or implied in order to lobby for power and rights in the 1800s across Europe as well as in the Hispanic world (Groneman 1995, 226). Second, it is performing reversals of masculine discourse, while giving place and prominence to female sexuality, much as French poststructural feminist critics perform in the 1970s.[17] As Paravisini-Gebert (1994) points out, Roqué is innovative in Spanish American early feminist fiction in that she recognizes that writing female sexuality as a healthy component of human existence forcefully undermines patriarchal control, by removing women from the Virgin Mary pedestal and placing them on equal moral footing with men.

To buttress this stance, the angelic Matilde, who is idealized as a perfect nurturing wife, mother, and friend, reiterates it. When Julia becomes ill after Rafael's death, Sevastel is shocked to learn of her passionate nature, thinking that her "proper upbringing" would have dampened her desires. To this the Angel of the House, Matilde, replies:

> Eso sucederá, le repliqué yo, si la mujer fuera un ser distinto de los demás seres, y la educación pudiera sustraerla a las leyes propias de nuestra naturaleza imperfecta. *Pero desgraciadamente estamos formadas de la misma sangre y con los mismos vicios de organización que ustedes.* No somos seres distintos de los demás, y por lo general se nos exige que seamos como las conveniencias sociales nos quisieran, *y no como Dios o la naturaleza nos han formado.* (122; my emphasis)

> [That would happen, I replied to him, if Woman were a different being from the rest of the beings, and education could separate her from the very laws of our imperfect natures. *But unfortunately we are formed from the same blood and with the same physical organization as you.* We are not beings different from the rest, and in general we are required to be the way social conventions want us to be, *and not the way God or nature have formed us.*]

---

17. For example, in her 1974 *Speculum of the Other Woman* Irigaray (1985) reclaims female sexuality by deconstructing Freud's theory that all sexuality is masculine. However, it is important to note that, unlike the poststructural feminist Irigaray (and Hélène Cixous [1981] in "Laugh of the Medusa"), Roqué does *not* celebrate what masculine discourse sublimates as the abject. That is, while these twentieth-century feminists celebrate women's reproductive bodies as a way of reclaiming them from the marginalized spaces into which masculine discourse projects them, Roqué's novel provides a new discourse of women's sexuality for her time, that *omits,* as a political gesture, the essentialized representations of masculine notions of female reproduction.

Although the words are subversive because they equate the sexual physical needs of the sexes, they are tempered because they are spoken by a character who upholds all the most highly valued patriarchal qualities of female citizenship and motherhood. Matilde is self-abnegating, adores her family, and works diligently on her small farm—but she also happens to believe that women have the same temptations and urges as men. For Roqué's character and the narrator, God and nature are the authors of this equal desire; the reader may thus infer that the ruling class (social conventions) is *unnatural, unhealthy, and ungodly* to deny this truth.

Taking an elite discourse used to legitimatize the words of characters in Naturalist writing, Dr. Bernard (the doctor Sevastel calls upon to cure his wife) justifies Julia's suffering from a medical standpoint.[18] As we saw in Chapter 5 of this study, the figure of the medical doctor and medical discourse held a privileged place in a Puerto Rico poised for Positivist-style modernization. Therefore it is not fortuitous that Roqué chooses Dr. Bernard as the mouthpiece for her early feminist messages. Although the appearance of Bernard and his unusual treatment may seem an "artificio . . . que le quita fuerza y verosimilitud del relato" (Saldivia Berglund 2000, 201) [an artificial plot element . . . that detracts from the strength and believability of the story], it has clear basis in Roqué's historical context. While medical discourse in both medical and nonmedical settings was used at the turn of the century to uphold patriarchal ideology, here Roqué employs it in the service of her subversive character: "Bien dice el sabio doctor: 'Había mucho fuego en los ojos de Julia, y no había rendido aún tributo a las leyes naturales, gozando de la vida del amor con la fuerza de sus veinte años, para que estuviera ya hastiado de todo'" (122) [So says the wise doctor: "A fire burned in Julia's eyes and, not having yet rendered tribute to natural laws by enjoying life's love with the force of a twenty-year-old, she was now completely weakened"]. The doctor repeats this diagnosis, emphasizing the biological reasoning behind Julia's behavior: "Esta joven no ha tenido expansiones en la edad en que la naturaleza impone como ley ineludible los dulces goces del amor" (131) [This young woman has not had experiences at the age when nature imposes the sweet pleasures of love as an ineluctable law]. Despite its Romantic tone, the message is expressed in medical but also

---

18. A popularized form of medical discourse started to appear at the end of the nineteenth century and was used to diagnose the illness of the marginalized classes and contained as part of its subtext a transfer of contemporary bourgeois values (Trigo 1995, 134). As I discussed in the preceding chapter, female chastity was one of these values.

legal terms ("law"), likely to speak to the two areas of expertise of the ruling class: law and medicine.

Given, then, the numerous voices sympathetic to Julia's plight and the messages, both embedded and explicit, regarding women's human and imperfect character (which is even tolerated by God), she is not as guilty as she may appear on a superficial reading of the novel. Sevastel, however, does not escape as unscathed. He is arguably a better candidate to represent *sombra,* or punishable vice, than is Julia. It is because of his promiscuous past that he is unable to satisfy his wife:

> Si Sevastel hubiera sido un hombre apasionado, que hubiese podido apagar la sed de goces de aquella naturaleza sensual, al menos, dominada la materia, sólo el espíritu divagaría falto también de satisfacciones. (76)

> [If Sevastel had been a passionate man who had been able to quench that sensual nature's thirst for pleasure, at least, with the body sated, only the spirit would wander lacking satisfaction.]

This quotation is emphasized by the image of Sevastel's saintly (*bendito*) *sleep,* while his wife "burned with passion" by his side—with an ironic usage of biblical moral imagery, here used to represent a former carouser (77). His punishment is emasculation: Sevastel is sexually impotent, at least to the extent of not carrying out his husbandly duties of attending to Julia's desire. He is also emasculated by Rafael's conquest of his wife (although he does clean this stain on his honor with Rafael's blood) and by Dr. Bernard, who literally must publicly court his wife back to life, as Sevastel is incapable. This scene, perhaps the most perplexing of the novel, is worth a closer look:

> [Dr. Bernard a Sevastel]:—Para despertar esa alma dormida, aletargada, es necesario hacerla sentir, y yo voy a intentar la prueba.
> —¡¡Ud.!! Dijo aún más admirado Sevastel. ¿Se va Ud. de enamorar de mi mujer?
> —Enamorarme, no. Voy a curarla. . . . voy a hacer el amor a Julia . . . a fin de conmover las fibras más sensibles de su alma enferma.
> . . . Sevastel bajó la cabeza hondamente preocupado. (132)

[(Dr. Bernard to Sevastel): "In order to awaken that sleeping, benumbed soul it is necessary to make it feel, and I am going to carry out the experiment."

"You!!" said Sevastel, even more bewildered. "You are going to fall in love with my wife?"

"No, not fall in love with her; I am going to cure her. . . . I am going to make love to Julia . . . in order to stir her infirm soul's most sensitive fibers."

. . . Sevastel bowed his head, deeply concerned.]

This must have struck a very sensitive chord with contemporary readers; to have a medical doctor, a pillar of society, engaging in one of the most condemnable acts among gentlemen—dishonoring an elite officer by seducing his wife—and justifying it medically! In the novel the doctor and Sevastel must devise a plan to fool society so that the husband is not publicly humiliated; however, the reader has already witnessed Sevastel's double dishonor. Here Roqué reverses the usual role of doctors and science in literature, as the scientist and literary critic Laura Otis has recognized them. Otis identifies a scientific fear of the penetrability or corruptibility of cells (which she terms "feminization")—and a literary fear of corruption of ideologies. Female sexuality plays an important role in maintaining national purity: "The sexual paranoia inherent in the membrane model . . . has its basis in two interrelated cultural prejudices: (1) depreciation and misreading of female sexuality as passive penetrability, and (2) exaggerated esteem for the intact hymen, whose rupture initiates one into the realm of the passive, the penetrated, and the impure" (Otis 1999, 7). This doctor-of-love tangent in *Luz y sombra* is a daring tactic that positions the doctor as the advocate for lovemaking, toying with the reader's expectations of morality of the elite and rewriting a more realistic notion of sexuality and womanhood.

Conclusions

The ending of *Luz y sombra* may seem anticlimactic for contemporary feminists because Julia, her baby, and Sevastel all die, while the traditional female prototype Matilde is exalted. However, the early feminist messages lie in the treatment of Julia's character and others' positions in relation to her. This circuitous manner of questioning ruling-class ideals was one way in which criticism was executed in Roqué's time.[19] Although Matilde is the ideal domestic Angel of the House, she changes and molds national discourse about women from within this superficial shell of the "perfect" hardworking, modest, self-sacrificing woman by defending female sexual desire, rather than condemning Julia. The wayward protagonist is forgiven by her husband, who blames himself for her moral slip. In light of these major rewritings of hegemonic identity politics on women's sexuality, Roqué's novel challenges the power structure by encouraging women to attend to their happiness rather than maintaining wealth through marital ties.

Another question to consider is that, if the death of Julia's child is meant as a punishment (Chen Sham 1999, 174–75; Saldivia Berglund 2000), then why does Matilde's child also die, seeing that she is blameless of any transgression? One explanation for the deaths of Julia and her family could be that Roqué was borrowing a standard plot of Naturalism, which incorporated death (often vividly and medically depicted) as one more part of life, just like birth, eating, working, and loving. A Naturalist depiction of death generally differs from a Romantic demise in that the latter typically appeals to emotions, is sanitized, is described with spiritual language, and is much further removed from the way fatal illnesses or accidents look in the real world, whereas death in Naturalism is studied as the result of hereditary illness, accidents caused by poor working conditions, or socially derived disease. Death is a very common physiological (rather than spiritual, or moral) phenomenon in the works of Zola, Zeno Gandía, Brau, the Spaniard Emilia Pardo Bazán, and many other Naturalist writers of the era, in which characters' deaths are common. It does not necessarily indicate that a character is being punished, but rather that he or she is the victim of a violent society,

---

19. Zavala recognizes the act of building upon accepted literary norms to voice opposition to traditional ideology as a common strategy of nineteenth- and early twentieth-century authors: "It is important to identify the oppositions used to organize the . . . discursive field, the politics behind a style of writing . . . *the reverse discourse, the polymorphous exploits of tropes to exercise critical power.* . . . *The already spoken and already written triggers the imaginary to re-write the same narrative, with different images, portraits, expressions, idiolects*" (1992, 179). Zavala identifies how authors write against an existing power structure by taking literary commonplaces from it and using them in an altered form to make a statement, to "ring changes" (179). Molloy has recognized that women authors engage in critique by appropriating male language and using it to lend authority to their discourse: "More than excluding women, that [phallocentric] language assigns women to a subordinate place, and, from that position of authority, deauthorizes woman's word. That is, it includes that word but in a position of weakness. . . . What women can do and, in fact, have done is establish a new praxis, subverting the authoritarian language that puts them 'in their place' dislocating it in different ways depending on the time period" (1991, 143; my emphasis). In Roqué's novel using a medical-doctor character and medical discourse to voice her social critique is a sort of pirating of male discourse for a feminist cause.

hereditary illness, environmentally caused accidents, or poverty. Another explanation could be the many deaths in Roqué's immediate family (which was common for the times): her mother died when she was a child, and two of her own children died at a young age.

If the language, characters, and structure of the novel are studied in the context of contemporary texts and how women were written into fiction, and if we consider Roqué's intent and constant advocacy of women's rights throughout her life, we cannot read Julia's death as a poetic punishment. Based on the text, in which Julia's error is blamed on social norms and Sevastel's frigidity by three different legitimizing voices (the omniscient narrator, the virtuous Matilde, and Dr. Bernard), we can hardly conclude that Julia dies because she "soils and distorts the sacrosanct institution of marriage" or that the ending "figures perfectly into a patriarchal logic: the defense of matrimony and the condemnation of adultery" (Chen Sham 1999, 175–76) or that "este castigo tiene un fin claramente moralizador porque se apega a los valores morales y religiosos sin cuestionar sus bases" (Saldivia Berglund 2000, 202) [this punishment has a clearly moralizing end because it clings to moral and religious values without questioning their bases]. On the contrary, the reader sympathizes with Julia and understands her actions as the consequences of patriarchal social rules that limited women's options for financial support and their ability to find a true and equal love. As I have mentioned, the character who represents *sombra* is most likely Sevastel.

In *Luz y sombra* Roqué presents a logical, intelligent female character who is both sexually desirous and justified in her sexuality by several supporting characters and the narrator. In so doing, she is rearranging in a new way the traditional scripts of scientific discourse that presented women as passive objects requiring society's protection. The narrative strategy, similar to the comparative literary critic Katie Arens's reading of Cixous's strategy in "The Laugh of the Medusa," engages in critically "violating 'customary' assumptions of her culture rather than exploring two 'natural' categories [male and female]" (1998b, 238–39). Thus Roqué's Julia "renders herself visible; she is no longer engaged in the mimicry of disguise," but is poised to make her own mark in the symbolic (244). Casting female sexuality as a necessary part of an intelligent and vocal woman's mental and physical health was an answer to literary texts such as *La charca* that were densely packed with dangerous and oppressive stereotypes. This was a step in the right direction to gain ground for the social change, to attempt to redefine gender boundaries, and in so doing, equalize women's right to social freedoms and agency with those of men.

CONCLUSIONS

THIS JOURNEY HAS LED US through the times and minds of Refugio Barragán, Mercedes Cabello de Carbonera, and Ana Roqué. We have rediscovered their texts; traveled into the past to recognize the symbolic social value of their fiction; and analyzed their revolutionary rewritings of womanhood, produced at a time when women who dared to desire higher learning, recalling the biblical Eve plucking the fruit from the tree of knowledge, were ridiculed, deemed masculine, and persecuted. My goal has been to show the cultural, social, and historical value of these women writers (and others like them), as their efforts to redefine the Angel of the House held a wide audience and an important place in the symbolic economy of their times. While the preceding studies of each individual novel and writer illuminate the specificities of the project within the country of origin, a comparative overview yields insight about common approaches to early feminist production.

Women writers of the 1880s and early 1900s witnessed the disruptions of power that arose from the processes of modernization. The rhetoric of equality and education that accompanied ideals of democracy planted the seeds in the minds of women across the region to question the bases of their social and legal inequality. While masculinist discourse relied upon essentializing views of women in Positivist writings to define the limits of women's capacity to learn, writers such as Cabello and Roqué, along with their contemporaries Matto, Capetillo, and others, were drawn to the scientific logic of Positivism for its rhetoric of progress and perfectibility and used scientific-sounding language in their essays and fiction to lobby for the advancement of their sex. Unlike the majority of women in Spanish America of their time, the women discussed in this study were well read and continued to learn and think critically beyond formal instruction. Barragán and Roqué were advocates and reformers of girls' education, while Cabello's essays and fiction emphasized the educated woman's role in civilizing the nation. This shared value points to the essential role of education in expanding young women's horizons—not only so women would better the nation as homemakers (as ruling-class intellectuals hoped), but also to give them the confidence to critique authority and move beyond their prescribed roles. Education sparked the desire for further exploration, and the Angel of the House's emphasis on abnegation and blind obedience came into stark conflict with the inquiring minds of women. The dynamic fictional female characters who engage in intelligent dialogue and pursue their desires as a means of actualizing themselves as individuals embody the frustration of their authors and their efforts to change the status quo. These lasting fictional models opened doors in the minds of generations of women readers and created examples for future generations of defiant women writers.

Life often resembles literature and this appears true for the writers of this study and others. Cabello, Barragán, and Matto were widowed at a young age, while Roqué and Gorriti were estranged from their husbands. It is probable that the absence of a male head of household allowed these women the privacy to write, free from critical eyes watching over them. The lacuna of male authority in their own lives lent itself to imagining female characters who defy the subservient position of Angel of the House. Indeed, the three women protagonists we have examined break free from the influence of their male Others in their alternative imagined worlds.

Barragán, Roqué, and Cabello draw on similar techniques, using language and imagery to undermine the power of the Angel of the House as a primary social signifier. While patriarchal social forces were behind the dreaming of the angelic domestic ideal, desire for self-realization, fulfillment, and independence fueled this early feminist fiction. Common desires for change pick a common target, and so we have similar literary strategies in play to vie for symbolic power.

All the writers here include and confront the Angel of the House ideal. They present—and glorify—a woman who, at least superficially, resembles an Angel of the House. Although the tenets of virtuous womanhood are contradicted in the narrative or in the actions that the character performs (Barragán's María), or the Angel of the House is put to the task of defending the transgressive character (Cabello's Josefina and Roqué's Matilde), the angelic woman must be included in the narrative as a decoy for fending off negative reactions to the novel. The Angel of the House was unavoidable because she was so intimately linked to these writers' desires, as an obstacle to liberation or because of the frustration she inspired as an unattainable ideal. In any case, because of the reactionary climate for women's social positions in the 1880s–early 1990s, the circumstances were only suitable for presenting subversive messages couched in a discourse recognizable to the ruling elite and to the typical bourgeois reader. Including the angelic housewife or daughter provided this familiarity and safeguard.

All three writers stripped the Angel of the House of her authority by deconstructing the artificiality of the model or by showing what life would be like outside the model. By handicapping the father figure, Barragán's protagonist engages in a level of agency about which readers could only dream. In the fictions of Cabello and Roqué, each chooses to set up false dichotomies through character development (Blanca/Josefina in Cabello and Julia/Matilde in Roqué) to then show how each model sets an unrealistic standard that their characters cannot achieve as real, mortal humans. The moral downward spiral that the "bad" characters suffer, then, is read as a humanizing representation of women who suffer because of the artificial demands society makes of them. Cabello's focus is on deconstructing the dichotomy of virtue and vice (namely, virgin/whore, Mary/Eve) and critiquing women's education, while Roqué, bolstered by a longer tradition of early feminism by 1903, tackles the onerous task of defending women's sexuality as a natural part of her formation as a subject.

The appeal of the novel to a wide readership was essential to the early feminist project, so creating interest through plot features was necessary in all cases. For Barragán we may point to *costumbrismo* (which inspired local pride and nationalism) and sheer action-packed entertainment—replete with murders, robberies, intrigue, love, and overall drama—that earned her success. Cabello was thought to have drawn on a local personality as the model for her story; thus her novel had gossip appeal to 1880s *limeños*. In addition, she was thought to be one of the first novelists of Peru, drew vaguely on the model of Flaubert's well-known romantic novel *Madame Bovary,* and also included plot fixtures of the time-honored fairy tale of Cinderella (which she reworked into an early feminist version of the tale). The Peruvian's novel was widely read because of her talent for drawing on popular models and giving them a subversive twist. Roqué may have been the most well connected of our writers; she was the first woman ever to be invited into the Ateneo, Puerto Rico's prestigious intellectual organization, and was granted an honorary doctorate from the University of Puerto Rico at the end of her life. Her reputation likely lent name recognition to her work among her peers. Undeniably, the theme of adultery (or, in this case, the verge of adultery), sparked readers' interest, just as readers of Nathaniel Hawthorne's *The Scarlet Letter* (1850) still enjoy today the piquant draw of sexual transgression. The Positivist, medical theme of "curing" female sexual desire, the epistolary style, and the positive example of female bonding between the two close friends formed a unique and provocative combination that humanized the wayward Julia to readers. Our authors considered their art as well as their social goals when it came to their subversive projects. A large readership meant power over the imaginations of many.

Barragán, Cabello, and Roqué were of a generation of women writers of the last decades of the nineteenth century who, bolstered by the zeitgeist of the era, the rhetoric of progress, and increasing (albeit spotty) governmental attention to the education of women, formed literary groups, began protofeminist periodicals, and published their woman-centered writing. Almost all of the women novelists of this era focused on female characters and their plights, and did so in a variety of styles and genres. Several women successfully cultivated the extremely popular travel narrative (both real-life and fictional versions). Flora Tristán, Juana Manuela Gorriti, Eduarda Mansilla, the condesa de Merlín, Barragán, and Zoila Aurora Cáceres all experienced (or imagined) and wrote about the thrill of travel in a period when women's place was in the home. Finding or imagining oneself in a new culture forces a self-reflection and redefinition through new eyes that is only possible in deep cultural interaction with the Other, giving way to processes of imagination of oneself as a subject. Women's precarious place in modernization sparked the content of the novels of writers such as Emma de la Barra, Carmela Eulate Sanjurjo, Cabello, and Roqué, whose protagonists struggle with the superficial demands upon them along with the pressures of conforming to the Angel of the House model. While many women writers exposed and mourned women's emotional and physical suffering through their writing (Roqué, María Néstora Téllez Rendón, Laura Méndez de Cuenca, Matto, Gorriti, and others), some women chose to imagine dynamic women whose agency results in positive life outcomes for them (Barragán, Soledad Acosta de Samper). Gertrudis Gómez de Avellaneda took up many of these themes and approaches in her novels and plays, so many of which champion the intelligence and passion of women (not unlike herself). Still another way that women writers sought to challenge the status of their sex was by publishing histories of famous European, Asian, and Latin American women; this was true in the case of Zoila Aurora Cáceres, Gertrudis Gómez de Avellaneda (in her periodical), Soledad Acosta de Samper, and others. In all these cases one element is constant: they gave voice and agency to fictional women or the "I" of the author, and they as writers presented an example of intelligent, ambitious women whose thoughts and imaginations could not be silenced by an imposed domestic life.

In *Rewriting Womanhood* we have begun to establish what drove women at the turn of the nineteenth century to risk ridicule and alienation by publishing alternative models for female identity. Barragán, Cabello, Roqué, and their contemporaries are on a continuum that can be traced back to the 1500s, in the writing of the Spaniard Santa Teresa de Avila (Spain, 1515–1582), and the 1600s, in the work of María de Zayas y Sotomayor (Spain, 1590–1661) and Sor Juana (colonial Mexico, 1651?–1695), among others, and whose work would set a literary base for later subversive women poets and novelists such as Delmira Agustini (Uruguay, 1886–1914), Teresa de la Parra (Venezuela, 1889–1936), María Luisa Bombal (Argentina, 1910–1980), Alfonsina Storni (Argentina, 1892–1938), Gabriela Mistral (Chile, 1889–1957), Rosario Castellanos (Mexico, 1925–1974), and Rosario Ferré (Puerto Rico, 1938–). While all these women wrote their desires and subverted patriarchal law, each one did so in a way that responded to her social, geographical, and historical context, as we have seen in the case of women writers at the turn of the nineteenth century in the specific examples of this study.

The emergence of a nascent, yet patently formalized, Latin American brand of feminism is discernable in the narratives of Barragán, Cabello, and Roqué. New, empowered visions of female identity present modern images of women in the novels we have examined. Our authors' goals were to redefine womanhood to create an individual as an imagined subject within a symbolic social formation—to write the consciousness of a fictional individual who could work herself into the social scripts of the symbolic order. Their efforts to rewrite womanhood later dovetailed with the endeavors of pioneers of suffrage, editors of feminist periodicals, and educational and legal reformists to pave the road for bourgeois women to advance into the twentieth century equipped with the symbolic tools to achieve greater civic and legal rights.

WORKS CITED

Abreu Gómez, Ermilo. 1938. "La crítica." In *Semblanza de Sor Juana*, 9–17. Mexico City: Ediciones Letras de México.

Acosta de Samper, Soledad. 1895. *La mujer en la sociedad moderna*. Paris: Garnier Hermanos. Also available at http://books.google.com.

———. 2006. *Novelas y cuadros de la vida sur-americana*. 1869. Edited by Flor María Rodríguez-Arenas. Buenos Aires: Stockcero.

Adams, Clementina. 1999. "Rescatando la obra de Virginia Elena Ortea: Una voz combativa en pro de la mujer fin-de-siglo." In *La voz de la mujer en la literatura hispanoamericana fin-de-siglo* [Woman's Voice in Turn-of-the-Century Hispanic Literature], edited by Luis Jiménez, 115–26. San José: Editorial de la Universidad de Costa Rica.

Agosín, Marjorie. 1999. Introduction to *Magical Sites: Women Travelers in Nineteenth-Century Latin America*, edited by Marjorie Agosín and Julie H. Levison, 9–22. Buffalo, N.Y.: White Pine Press.

Aldaraca, Bridget. 1982. "*El Ángel del Hogar*: The Cult of Domesticity in Nineteenth-Century Spain." In *Theory and Practice of Feminist Literary Criticism*, edited by Gabriela Mora and Karen S. Van Hooft, 62–87. Ypsilanti, Mich.: Bilingual Press.

———. 1991. *El Ángel del Hogar: Galdós and the Ideology of Domesticity in Spain*. Chapel Hill: University of North Carolina Press.

Almeida, Marcelina. 1998. *Por una fortuna una cruz*. 1860. With "Los orígenes del feminismo en Uruguay" by Virginia Cánova. Göteborg, Sweden: Chalmers University of Technology.

Alvarado, Lourdes. 1991. Introduction to *El siglo XX ante el feminismo: Una interpretación positivista*, by Horacio Barreda, 7–30. 1909. Edited by Lourdes Alvarado. Mexico City: Universidad Autónoma de México.

Alvarez, Ernesto. 1987. *Manuel Zeno Gandía: Estética y sociedad*. Santo Domingo, Dominican Republic: Corripio.

Alzate, Carolina, ed. 2005. *Soledad Acosta de Samper: Escritura, género y nación en el siglo XIX*. Madrid: Iberoamericana.

Álzaga, Florinda. 1997. *La Avellaneda: Intensidad y vanguardia*. Miami: Ediciones Universal.

Arambel-Guiñazú, María Cristina. 2004. Introduction to *Blanca Sol: Novela social*, 1–24. 1888. Madrid: Iberoamericana.

Arana Soto, S. 1969. *Los desafíos y los médicos puertorriqueños y otros artículos afines*. Barcelona: Tipografía Miguza.

Arango-Ramos, Fanny. 1994. "Mercedes Cabello de Carbonera: Historia de una verdadera conspiración cultural." *Revista Hispánica Moderna* 47:306–23.
Araujo, Nora. 1993. "Raza y género en *Sab*." *Casa de las Americas* 190:42–49.
Archivo General de Puerto Rico, Fondos Municipales, Serie de San Juan. 1905. "Registro de Carta de del Dr. Lugo Viñas, solicitando un cambio de nombre para el Hospital Especial de Mujeres, 19 de junio de 1905."
Arens, Katherine. 1998a. "Discourse Analysis as Critical Historiography: A Sémanalyse of Mystic Speech." *Rethinking History* 2, no. 1:23–50.
———. 1998b. "From Callois to 'The Laugh of the Medusa': Vectors of a Diagonal Science." *Textual Practice* 12, no. 2:225–50.
———. 1998c. "The Linguistics of French Feminism: *Sémanalyse* as Critical Discourse Analysis." *Intertexts* 2, no. 2:171–84.
Arrom, Silvia Marina. 1985. *The Women of Mexico City, 1790–1857*. Stanford: Stanford University Press.
Azize Vargas, Yamila, ed. 1987a. *La mujer en Puerto Rico: Ensayos de investigación*. Río Piedras, Puerto Rico: Ediciones Huracán.
———. 1987b. "Mujeres en lucha: Orígenes y evolución del movimiento feminista." In *La mujer en Puerto Rico: Ensayos de investigación*, edited by Yamila Azize Vargas, 11–25. Río Piedras, Puerto Rico: Ediciones Huracán.
Azua, Néstor Tomás. 1988. *Periodismo y feminismo en la Argentina: 1830–1930*. Buenos Aires: Amecé Editores.
Barceló Miller, María F. de. 1987. "De la polilla a la virtud: Visión sobre la mujer de la iglesia jerárquica de Puerto Rico." In *La mujer en Puerto Rico: Ensayos de investigación*, edited by Yamila Azize Vargas, 50–88. Río Piedras, Puerto Rico: Ediciones Huracán.
Barragán de Toscano, Refugio. 1934. *La hija del bandido o los subterráneos del Nevado*. 1887. Mexico City: Editorial México.
———. 2007. *La hija del bandido*. 1887. Edited by María Zalduondo. Buenos Aires: Stockcero.
Barreda, Horacio. 1991. *El siglo XIX ante el feminismo: Una interpretación positivista*. 1909. Edited by Lourdes Alvarado. Mexico City: Universidad Autónoma de México.
Barrera, Trinidad. 1996. "La fantasia de Juana Manuela Gorriti." *Hispamérica: Revista de Literatura* 25, no. 74:103–11.
Barrios de Chungara, Domitila, and Moema Viezzer. 1978. *"Si me permiten hablar": Testimonio de Domitila, una mujer de las minas de Bolivia*. Mexico City: Siglo XXI.
Barthes, Roland. 1975. *The Pleasure of the Text*. Translated by Richard Miller. New York: Hill and Wang.
Batticuore, Graciela. 1999. *El taller de la escritora: Veladas literarias de Juana Manuela Gorriti, Lima–Buenos Aires (1876/7–1892)* [The Writer's Workshop: The Literary Soirées of Juana Manuela Gorriti]. Rosario, Argentina: Beatriz Viterbo.
Baum, Rob. 2000. "After the Ball Is Over: Bringing *Cinderella* Home." *Cultural Analysis* 1:69–83.
Bennett, Barbara. 2002. "Thelma and Louise in Wonderland: Feminist Revisions of Fairytales in McCorkle's 'Sleeping Beauty, Revised.'" *Pembroke Magazine* 34:7–12.
Berg, Mary. 1990. "Clorinda Matto de Turner (1852–1909)." In *Spanish American Women Writers: A Bio-Bibliographical Source Book*, edited by Diane E. Marting, 303–15. New York: Greenwood Press.

———. 1995. "Writing for Her Life: The Essays of Clorinda Matto de Turner." In *Reinterpreting the Spanish American Essay: Women Writers of the Nineteenth and Twentieth Centuries,* edited by Doris Meyer, 80–89. Austin: University of Texas Press.

———. 2003. "César Duayen and Early Twentieth-Century Argentina." *Studies in Honor of Enrique Anderson Imbert,* edited by Nancy Abraham Hall and Lanin A. Gyurko, 305–15. Newark, Del.: Cuesta.

———. 2004. "La mujer moderna en las novelas de César Duáyen [sic]." *Revista Iberoamericana* 70, no. 206:197–209.

Bergmann, Emilie, Janet Greenberg, Gwen Kirkpatrick, Francine Masiello, Francesca Miller, Marta Morello-Frosch, Kathleen Newman, and Mary Louise Pratt. 1990. "Toward a History of Women's Periodicals in Latin America: Introduction." In *Women, Culture, and Politics in Latin America: Seminar on Feminism and Culture in Latin America,* 173–81. Berkeley and Los Angeles: University of California Press.

Bettelheim, Bruno. 1976. *The Uses of Enchantment: The Meaning and Importance of Fairytales.* New York: Vintage.

Boggs, Ralph S. 1929. "Seven Folktales from Porto Rico." *Journal of American Folklore* 42:157–66.

Bonfiglio, Giovanni. 1994. *Los italianos en la sociedad peruana: Una visión histórica.* Lima: Asociación de Italianos del Perú.

Brushwood, John. 1981. *Genteel Barbarism.* Lincoln: University of Nebraska Press.

Butler, Judith. 1999. *Gender Trouble: Feminism and the Subversion of Identity.* Rev. ed. New York: Routledge.

Cabello de Carbonera, Mercedes. 1889a. *Blanca Sol: Novela social.* Lima: Universo.

———. 1889b. *Las consecuencias.* Lima: Imprenta de Torres Aguirre.

———. 1948. *La novela moderna: Estudio filosófico.* 1892. Lima: Ediciones Hora del Hombre.

———. 2001. *El conspirador: Autobiografía de un hombre público.* 1892. Prologue by Oswaldo Voysest. Lima: Kavia Cobaya.

———. 2004. *Blanca Sol: Novela social.* 1889. Edited and with an introduction by María Cristina Arambel Guiñazú. Madrid: Iberoamericana.

———. 2005. *Sacrificio y recompensa.* 1886. Buenos Aires: Stockcero.

———. 2007. *Blanca Sol: Novela social.* 1889. Edited and with an introduction by Oswaldo Voysest. Buenos Aires: Stockcero.

Cáceres, Zoila Aurora. 2007. *La rosa muerta.* 1914. Edited and with an introduction by Thomas Ward. Buenos Aires: Stockcero.

Caillet-Bois, Julio, ed. 1958. *Antología de la poesía hispanoamericana.* Madrid: Aguilar.

Calvo Peña, Beatriz. 2005. "Prensa, política y prostitución en La Habana finisecular: El caso de La Cebolla y la 'polémica de las meretrices.'" *Cuban Studies* 36:23–49.

Campuzano, Luisa, ed. 1997. *Mujeres latinoamericanas: Historia y cultura siglos XVI al XIX* [Latin American Women: History and Culture from the Sixteenth to the Nineteenth Centuries]. 2 vols. Havana: Casa de las Américas.

———. 2004. *Las muchachas de la Habana no tienen temor de Dios . . . : Escritoras cubanas (siglo XVIII al XXI).* Havana: Ediciones Unión.

Cánova, Virginia. 1998. "Los orígenes del feminismo en Uruguay." In *Por una fortuna una cruz* [1860, by Marcelina Almeida]/*Los orígenes del feminismo en Uruguay,* 1–265. Göteborg, Sweden: Chalmers University of Technology.

Cantú, Norma Elia. 2000. *La Quinceañera: Towards an Ethnographic Analysis of a Life-Cycle Ritual*. San Antonio, Tex.: Guadalupe Cultural Arts Center.

Capetillo, Luisa. 2004. *A Nation of Women: An Early Feminist Speaks Out; Mi opinión sobre las libertades, derechos y deberes de la mujer*. Edited and with an introduction by Félix V. Matos Rodríguez. Translated by Alan West-Durán. Houston: Arte Público Press.

Carner, Françoise. 1987. "Estereotipos femeninos en el siglo XIX." In *Presencia y transparencia: La mujer en la historia de México*, edited by Carmen Ramos Escandón, 95–110. Mexico City: Colegio de México.

Carrilla, Emilio. *El romanticismo en la América hispánica*. Madrid: Gredos.

Cepeda, Alejandro Felix R. P. 1909. Introduction to *La mujer*, by Antonio de P. Moreno and Domingo Elizalde, v–viii. Mexico City: José Ignacio Durán.

Cervantes Saavedra, Miguel de. 1985. "El licenciado vidriera." 1613. In *Novelas Ejemplares II*, edited by Harry Sieber, 41–74. Madrid: Cátedra.

Chambers Gooch, Fanny. 1998. "Keeping House in Northern Mexico" [in *Face to Face with the Mexicans* (1887)]. In *Women Through Women's Eyes: Latin American Women in Nineteenth-Century Travel Accounts*, edited by June E. Hahner, 131–55. Wilmington, Del.: Scholarly Resources.

Charnon-Deutsch, Lou. 1994. *Narratives of Desire: Nineteenth-Century Spanish Fiction by Women*. University Park: Pennsylvania State University Press.

Chen Sham, Jorge. 1999. "Sanción moral y castigo: Contradicciones ideológicas en la narrativa de Ana Roqué." In *La voz de la mujer en la literatura hispanoamericana fin de siglo* [Woman's Voice in Turn-of-the-Century Hispanic Literature], edited by Luis Jiménez, 167–80. San José: University of Costa Rica Press.

Cherpak, Evelyn. 1978. "The Participation of Women in the Independence Movement in Gran Colombia, 1780–1830." In *Latin American Women: Historical Perspectives*, edited by Asunción Lavrin, 219–34. Westport, Conn.: Greenwood Press.

Chesler, Phyllis. 1997. *Women and Madness*. New York: Four Walls Eight Windows.

Cixous, Hélène. 1981. "The Laugh of the Medusa." 1975. Translated by Keith Cohen and Paula Cohen. In *New French Feminisms: An Anthology*, edited and with introductions by Elaine Marks and Isabelle de Courtivron, 245–64. New York: Schocken.

Cixous, Hélène, and Catherine Clément. 1986. *The Newly Born Woman*. 1973. Translated by Betsy Wing. Minneapolis: University of Minnesota Press.

Colomar, Orencia. 1974. *Fisiognomía*. Barcelona: Plaza and Janes.

Copjec, Joan. 1994. *Read My Desire: Lacan Against the Historicists*. MIT Press.

Cornejo Polar, Antonio. 2005. *Literatura y sociedad en el Perú: La novela indigenista/Clorinda Matto de Turner, novelista: Estudios sobre* Aves sin nido, Indole *y* Herencia. Lima: Latinoamericana Editores.

Cristal. 1985. Screenplay by Delia Fiallo. Directed by Daniel Farías, Arturo Páez, and Tito Rojas. Television program. Radio Caracas Televisión, Caracas.

Cruz, Anne J. 2005. "La sororidad de Sor Juana: Espiritualidad y tratamiento de la sexualidad femeninas [femenina] en España y el Nuevo Mundo." In *Literatura y femenismo en España (s. XV–XXI)*, edited and with an introduction by Lisa Vollendorf, 95–106. Barcelona: Icaria.

Cruz, Sor Juana Inés de la. 1985. "Arguye de inconsecuentes el gusto y la censura de los hombres que en las mujeres acusan lo que causan." 1689. In *Obras completas*, 109. Mexico City: Porrúa.

Cuesta Jiménez, Valentín. 1943. "Sangre en los Labios: Contribución al estudio de la vida de Gertrudis Gómez de Avellaneda." Pamphlet. Güines, Cuba: Tosco.
da Cunha, Gloria. 2006. *Pensadoras de la nación* [Women Thinkers of the Nation]. Madrid: Iberoamericana.
Darío, Ruben. 1994. *Azul. . . .* 1888. Mexico: Espasa-Calpe.
de la Barra, Emma (pseudo. César Duayén). 2005. *Stella: Una novela de costumbres argentinas.* Introduction by Mary Berg. Buenos Aires: Stockcero.
de Leon, Luis. 1872. *La perfecta casada.* 1583. Prologue by Miguel Ginesta. Madrid: Imprenta de Miguel Ginesta.
Delgado Votaw, Carmen. 1995. *Puerto Rican Women/Mujeres puertorriqueñas.* Washington, D.C.: Lisboa.
Denegri, Francesca. 1996. *El abanico y la cigarrera: La primera generación de mujeres ilustradas en el Perú* [The Fan and the Cigarette Seller: The First Generation of Learned Women in Peru]. Lima: Flora Tristán Centro de la Mujer Peruana.
Díaz, Arlene J. 2007. "Vicenta Ochoa, Dead Many Times: Gender, Politics, and a Death Sentence in Early Republican Caracas, Venezuela." In *Gender, Sexuality, and Power in Latin America Since Independence,* edited by William E. French and Katherine Elaine Bliss, 31–51. Lanham, Md.: Rowman and Littlefield.
Dill, Hans-Otto. 2001. "El primer Yo latinoamericano es femenino: A los 350 años del nacimiento de Sor Juana Inés de la Cruz." *Taller de Letras* 29:101–13.
Domenella, Ana Rosa, Luzelena Gutiérrez de Velasco, and Nora Pasternac. 1991. "Laura Méndez de Cuenca: Espíritu positivista y sensibilidad romántica." In *Las voces olvidadas: Antología crítica de narradoras mexicanas nacidas en el siglo XIX,* edited by Ana Rosa Domenella and Nora Pasternac, 117–38. Mexico City: Colegio de México.
Domenella, Ana Rosa, and Nora Pasternac, eds. 1991. *Las voces olvidadas: Antología crítica de narradoras mexicanas nacidas en el siglo XIX.* Mexico City: Colegio de México.
Dore, Elizabeth. 2000. "One Step Forward, Two Steps Back: Gender and the State in the Long Nineteenth Century." In *Hidden Histories of Gender and the State in Latin America,* edited by Elizabeth Dore and Maxine Molyneux, 3–32. Durham: Duke University Press.
Dore, Elizabeth, and Maxine Molyneux, eds. 2000. *Hidden Histories of Gender and the State in Latin America.* Durham: Duke University Press.
Dowling, Colette. 1981. *The Cinderella Complex: Women's Hidden Fear of Independence.* New York: Summit.
Dworkin, Andrea. 1974. *Woman Hating.* New York: Dutton.
Encinales de Sanjinés, Paulina. 1997. "La obra de Soledad Acosta de Samper: ¿Un proyecto cultural?" In *Mujeres latinoamericanas: Historia y cultura siglos XVI al XIX* [Latin American Women: History and Culture from the Sixteenth to the Nineteenth Centuries], edited by Luisa Campuzano, 2:227–32. Havana: Casa de las Américas.
Epple, Juan Armando. 1980. "El naturalismo en la novela latinoamericana." *Cuadernos Universitarios* 6:15–21.
———. 1987. "Mercedes Cabello de Carbonera y el problema de la 'novela moderna' en el Perú." In *Doctores y proscritos: La nueva generación de latinoamericanistas chilenos en U.S.A.,* edited by Javier Campos and Silverio Muñoz, 23–48. With an introduction by Jaime Concha. Minneapolis: Institute for the Study of Ideologies and Literature.

Erskine Inglis Calderón de la Barca, Frances. 1970. *Life in Mexico.* 1834. New York: Dutton.
Feliú, Fernando. 2002. "Rendering the Invisible Visible and the Visible Invisible: The Colonizing Function of Bailey K. Ashford's Antianemia Campaigns." Translated by María Elena Cepeda. In *Foucault and Latin America,* edited by Benigno Trigo, 153–68. New York: Routledge.
Fernández de Lizardi, José Joquín. 1942. *La educación de las mujeres o La Quijotita y su prima: Historia muy cierta con apariencias de novela.* 1818. Mexico City: Cámara Mexicana del Libro.
Festinger, Leon, and James M. Carlsmith. 1959. "Cognitive Consequences of Forced Compliance." *Journal of Abnormal and Social Psychology* 58:203–10. http://psychclassics.yorku.ca/Festinger/ (accessed June 15, 2003).
Findlay, Eileen J. 1997. "Decency and Democracy: The Politics of Prostitution in Ponce, Puerto Rico, 1890–1900." *Feminist Studies* 23, no. 3:471–99.
Fiscal, María Rosa. 1991. "Reencuentro con María Enriqueta." In *Las voces olvidadas: Antología crítica de narradoras mexicanas nacidas en el siglo XIX,* edited by Ana Rosa Domenella and Nora Pasternac, 181–99. Mexico City: Colegio de México.
Fletcher, Lea, ed. 1993. *El ajuar de la patria: Ensayos críticos sobre Juana Manuela Gorriti.* Buenos Aires: Feminaria.
———. 1994. *Mujeres y cultura en la Argentina del siglo XIX.* Buenos Aires: Feminaria.
Flores, Angel, and Kate Flores, eds. 1986. *The Defiant Muse: Hispanic Feminist Poems from the Middle Ages to the Present; A Bilingual Anthology.* New York: The Feminist Press at the City University of New York.
Flores Ramos, José. 1998. "Virgins, Whores, and Martyrs: Prostitution in the Colony, 1898–1919." In *Puerto Rican Women's History: New Perspectives,* edited by Félix V. Matos Rodríguez and Linda C. Delgado, 83–104. London: M. E. Sharpe.
Fort, Amelia, ed. 1993. *Mujeres peruanas: La mitad de la población del Perú a comienzos de los noventa.* Lima: Centro Instituto de Estudios Socioeconómicos y Fomento del Desarrollo.
Foster, David William, and Daniel Altamiranda, eds. 1997. *From Romanticism to Modernism in Latin America.* New York: Garland.
Foucault, Michel. 1988. *Madness and Civilization: A History of Insanity in the Age of Reason.* Translated by Richard Howard. New York: Random House.
Fox-Lockert, Lucía. 1979. "Mercedes Cabello de Carbonera." *Women Novelists in Spain and Spanish America,* 147–55. Metuchen, N.J.: Scarecrow Press.
Franco, Jean. 1989. *Plotting Women: Gender and Representation in Mexico.* New York: Columbia University Press.
Frederick, Bonnie. 1991. "In Their Own Voice: The Women Writers of the Generación del '80 in Argentina." *Hispania* 74, no. 2:282–89.
———. 1998. *Wily Modesty: Argentine Women Writers, 1860–1910.* Tempe, Ariz.: Center for Latin American Studies.
French, William E., and Katherine Elaine Bliss, eds. 2007. *Gender, Sexuality, and Power in Latin America Since Independence.* Lanham, Md.: Rowman and Littlefield.
Freud, Sigmund. 1995. *The Basic Writings of Sigmund Freud.* 1904–14. Translated and edited by Abraham Arden Brill. New York: Modern Library.
Friedan, Betty. 1983. *The Feminine Mystique.* 1963. New York: Norton.

García Calderón, Ventura. 1910. *Del romanticismo al modernismo.* Paris: Sociedad de Ediciones Literarias y Artísticas.

García Padilla, María del C. 1999. "Ana Roqué de Duprey: Let Us, Sisters, *Make* Another Life." In *Women's Philosophies of Education: Thinking Through Our Mothers,* edited by Connie Titone and Karen E. Maloney, 43–64. Upper Saddle River, N.J.: Prentice Hall.

García y García, Elvira. 1924. *La mujer peruana a través de los siglos: Serie historiada de estudios y observaciones.* Vol. 1. Lima: Impresora Americana.

Gardner, Fletcher, and W. W. Newell. 1906. "Filipino (Tagalog) Versions of Cinderella." *The Journal of American Folklore* 19:268–80.

Gaussin, Jean. 1973. *Conocer a los demás por el rostro.* Paris: Centre d'Étude et de Promotion de la Lecture.

Ghose, Indira. 1998. *Women Travellers in Colonial India: The Power of the Female Gaze.* Calcutta: Oxford University Press.

Gilbert, Sandra M., and Susan Gubar. 1979. *The Madwoman in the Attic: The Woman Writer and the Nineteenth-Century Literary Imagination.* New Haven: Yale University Press.

Ginesta, Miguel. 1872. "Prólogo." In *La perfecta casada,* by Luis de León. 1583. Madrid: Imprenta de Miguel Ginesta.

Glave, Luis Miguel. 1999. "Diez años de soledad: Vida y muerte de Mercedes Cabello de Carbonera." In *Juanamanuela, mucho papel: Algunas lecturas críticas de textos de Juana Manuela Gorriti,* edited by Amelia Royo, 91–109. Salta, Argentina: Ediciones del Robledal.

Golding, Morton J. 1973. *A Short History of Puerto Rico.* New York: New American Library.

Gómez de Avellaneda, Gertrudis. 2000. *Dos mujeres.* 1843. Introduction by Antón Arrufat. La Habana: Letras Cubanas.

Gonzáles Ascorra, Martha Irene. 1997. *La evolución de la conciencia femenina a través de las novelas de Gertrudis Gomez de Avellaneda, Soledad Acosta de Samper y Mercedes Cabello de Carbonera* [The Evolution of Feminine Consciousness Through the Novels of Gertrudis Gómez de Avellaneda, Soledad Acosta de Samper, and Mercedes Cabello de Carbonera]. New York: Peter Lang.

González Boixo, José Carlos. 1995. "La poesía de la 'inteligencia' en la poesía de Sor Juana: Su proyección desde el ideario feminista." *Colonial Latin American Review* 4, no. 2:125–38.

González-Quevedo, Lydia Margarita. 1996. "A Postcolonial Approach to a Colonial Literature? The Case of Puerto Rico." Ph.D. diss., University of Texas at Austin.

Gorriti, Juana Manuela. 1865. *Sueños y realidades.* Edited by Vicente G. Quesada. Introduction by José María Torres Caicedo. 2 vols. Buenos Aries: Casavalle.

———. 1876. *Panoramas de la vida: Colección de novelas, fantasias, leyendas y descripciones americanas.* 2 vols. Prol. Mariano Pelliza. Buenos Aires: Casavalle.

———. 1991. "Lo íntimo." In *La mujer salteña en las letras: Juana Manuela Gorriti y Lo íntimo,* edited by Alicia Martorell. Salta, Argentina: Fundación del Banco del Noreste.

———. 2003. *Dreams and Realities: Selected Fiction of Juana Manuela Gorriti.* Edited by Francine Masiello. Translated by Sergio Waisman. New York: Oxford University Press.

———. 2006. *Peregrinaciones de una [sic] alma triste.* Edited by Mary Berg. Buenos Aires: Stockcero.

Gourman, Jack. 1996. *Gourman Report.* 7th ed. Los Angeles: National Education Standards.
Gran enciclopedia aragonesa. 2007. "Sinués y Navarro, María del Pilar." http://www.enciclopedia-aragonesa.com/voz.asp?voz_id=11811 (accessed July 17, 2007).
Greenberg, Janet. 1990. "Toward a History of Women's Periodicals in Latin America: A Working Bibliography." In *Women, Culture, and Politics in Latin America: Seminar on Feminism and Culture in Latin America,* 182–231. Berkeley and Los Angeles: University of California Press.
Groneman, Carol. 1995. "Nymphomania: The Historical Construction of Female Sexuality." In *Deviant Bodies: Critical Perspectives on Difference in Science and Popular Culture,* edited by Jennifer Terry and Jacqueline Urla, 219–50. Bloomington: University of Indiana Press. http://emedia.netlibrary.com (accessed June 12, 2003).
Grosz, Elizabeth. 1989. *Sexual Subversions: Three French Feminists.* St. Leonards, Australia: Allen and Unwin.
———. 1990. *Jacques Lacan: A Feminist Introduction.* New York: Routledge.
Guardia, Sara Beatriz. 1985. *Mujeres peruanas: El otro lado de la historia.* Lima: Editora Humboldt.
Guerra, Lucía. 1985. "Estrategias femeninas en la elaboración del sujeto romántico en la obra de Gertrudis Gómez de Avellaneda." *Revista Iberoamericana* 15, no. 132–33: 707–22.
———. 1987a. "Mercedes Cabello de Carbonera: Estética de la moral y los desvíos nodisyuntivos de la virtud." *Revista de Crítica Literaria Latinoamericana* 26:25–41.
———. 1987b. "Visión marginal de la historia en la narrativa de Juana Manuela Gorriti." *Ideologies and Literature* 2, no. 2:59–76.
Gurkin Altman, Janet. 1982. *Epistolarity: Approaches to a Form.* Columbus: Ohio State University Press.
Gutiérrez Nájera, Manuel. 1896. "Para un menú." 1888. *Obras de Manuel Gutiérrez Nájera: Poesía,* 274. Mexico City: Impresora del Timbre.
Guy, Donna J. 1990. *Sex and Danger in Buenos Aires: Prostitution, Family, and the Nation in Buenos Aires.* Lincoln: University of Nebraska Press.
———. 2000. *White Slavery and Mothers Alive and Dead: The Troubled Meeting of Sex, Gender, Public Health, and Progress in Latin America.* Lincoln: University of Nebraska Press.
Hahner, June E. 1998. Introduction to *Women Through Women's Eyes: Latin American Women in Nineteenth-Century Travel Accounts,* edited by June E. Hahner. Wilmington, Del.: Scholarly Resources.
Herrick, Jane. 1957. "Periodicals for Women in Mexico During the Nineteenth Century." *Americas* 14, no. 2:135–44.
Heyes, Cressida. 2002. "Identity Politics." In *The Stanford Encyclopedia of Philosophy.* Fall 2002 ed., edited by Edward N. Zalta. http:plato.stanford.edu/archives/fall2002/entries/identity-politics/ (accessed August 14, 2003).
Huidobro Azua, Esther. 1904. [Unnamed article.] *La Mujer Mexicana.* February 1, 1.
Hunefeldt, Christine. 2000. *Liberalism in the Bedroom: Quarreling Spouses in Nineteenth-Century Lima.* University Park: Pennsylvania State University Press.
Irigaray, Luce. 1985. *The Speculum of the Other Woman.* 1974. Translated by Gillian C. Gill. Ithaca: Cornell University Press.
Jagoe, Catherine. 1990. "María del Pilar Sinués de Marco (1835–1893)." In *Spanish Women Writers: A Bio-Bibliographical Source Book,* edited by Linda Gould Levine,

Ellen Engelson Marson, and Gloria Feiman Waldman, 473–83. Westport, Conn.: Greenwood Press.
Jaramillo Flores, Renán. 1977. *El otro rostro de América*. Madrid: Editora Nacional.
Jiménez, Luis. 1999a. "La estética del 'ave rara' en *La muñeca* de Carmela Eulate Sanjurjo." In *La voz de la mujer en la literatura hispanoamericana fin-de-siglo* [Woman's Voice in Turn-of-the-Century Hispanic Literature], edited by Luis Jiménez, 181–90. San José: Editorial de la Universidad de Costa Rica.
———, ed. 1999b. *La voz de la mujer en la literatura hispanoamericana fin-de-siglo* [Woman's Voice in Turn-of-the-Century Hispanic Literature]. San José: Editorial de la Universidad de Costa Rica.
Kentner, Janet R. 1975. "The Socio-political Role of Women in the Mexican Wars of Independence, 1810–1821." Ph.D. diss., Loyola University of Chicago.
Kirk, Pamela. 1998. *Sor Juana Inés de la Cruz: Religion, Art, and Feminism*. New York: Continuum.
Kirkpatrick, Gwen. 1995. "El feminismo en los tiempos del cólera." *Revista de Crítica Literaria Latinoamericana* 42:45–55.
Kirkpatrick, Susan. 1989. *Las Románticas: Women Writers and Subjectivity in Spain, 1835–1850*. Berkeley and Los Angeles: University of California Press.
———. 1990. "Gómez de Avellaneda's Sab: Gendering the Liberal Romantic Subject." In *In the Feminine Mode: Essays on Hispanic Women Writers*, edited by Noël Valis and Carol Maier, 115–30. Lewisburg: Bucknell University Press.
Kristeva, Julia. 1974a. "About Chinese Women." Translated by Anita Barrows. In *The Kristeva Reader*, edited by Toril Moi, 138–59. New York: Columbia University Press.
———. 1974b. "Revolution in Poetic Language." Translated by Margaret Waller. In *The Kristeva Reader*, edited by Toril Moi, 89–136. New York: Columbia University Press.
———. 1982. *Powers of Horror: An Essay on Abjection*. Translated by Leon S. Roudiez. New York: Columbia University Press.
———. 1984. *Revolution in Poetic Language*. Translated by Margaret Waller. Introduction by Leon S. Roudiez. New York: Columbia University Press.
———. 1986. *The Kristeva Reader*. Edited by Toril Moi. New York: Columbia University Press.
Lacan, Jacques. 1977. *Écrits: A Selection*. 1953–73. Translated by Alan Sheridan. New York: W. W. Norton.
———. 1982. *Feminine Sexuality*. 1966–75. Translated by Jacqueline Rose. Edited by Juliet Mitchell and Jacqueline Rose. New York: W. W. Norton.
LaGreca, Nancy. 2006a. "Feminist Literary Criticism of Latin American Women's Writing: Context, Approaches, and Analysis of the 1990s and Early 2000s." *Revista de Estudios Hispánicos* 40:379–403.
———. 2006b. "Literatura y conciencia: El suicidio femenino en el *Album cubano de lo bueno y lo bello* (1860) y *Dos mujeres* (1842) de Gertrudis Gómez de Avellaneda." *Revolución y Cultura* 3:12–16.
———. 2007. "Ana Roqué de Duprey." In *Latin American Writers: An Encyclopedia*, edited by María Claudia André and Eva Paulino Bueno. New York: Routledge.
Laguerre, Enrique. 1978. Introduction to *La charca*, by Manuel Zeno Gandía, ix–li. 1894. Caracas: Biblioteca Ayacucho.

Landes, Joan B. 1988. *Women and the Public Sphere in the Age of the French Revolution.* Ithaca: Cornell University Press.
Laqueur, Thomas. 1990. *Making Sex: Body and Gender from the Greeks to Freud.* Cambridge: Harvard University Press.
Lavrin, Asunción, ed. 1978. *Latin American Women: Historical Perspectives.* Westport, Conn.: Greenwood Press.
Leader, Darian, and Judy Groves. 1998. *Introducing Lacan.* New York: Totem.
Lichtblau, Myron. 1959. *The Argentine Novel in the Nineteenth Century.* New York: Hispanic Institute in the United States.
Lieberman, Marcia. 1987. "'Some Day My Prince Will Come': Female Acculturation Through the Fairy Tale." In *Don't Bet on the Prince: Contemporary Feminist Fairy Tales in North America and England,* edited by Jack Zipes. New York: Routledge.
Lindstrom, Naomi. 2007. "El convento y el jardín: La búsqueda de espacios alternativos en *Sab*." *Decimonónica* 4, no. 2:49–60.
Lorenz, Charlotte M. 1941. "Translated Plays in Madrid Theatres (1808–1818)." *Hispanic Review* 9, no. 3:376–82.
Macías, Anna. 1982. *Against All Odds: The Feminist Movement in Mexico to 1940.* Westport, Conn.: Greenwood Press.
Maguire, Gregory. 1995. *Wicked: The Life and Times of the Wicked Witch of the West.* New York: Regan Books.
Mallon, Florencia E. 1987. "Patriarchy in the Transition to Capitalism: Central Peru, 1830–1950." *Feminist Studies* 13, no. 2:379–407.
Mansilla de García, Eduarda. 2006. *Recuerdos de viaje.* 1882. Introduction by J. P. Spicer-Escalante. New York: Stockcero.
Martínez-Alier, Verena. 1989. *Marriage, Class, and Colour in Nineteenth-Century Cuba: A Study of Racial Attitudes and Sexual Values in a Slave Society.* Ann Arbor: University of Michigan Press.
Marting, Diane E., ed. 1990. *Spanish American Women Writers: A Bio-Bibliographical Source Book.* New York: Greenwood Press.
Masiello, Francine. 1992. *Between Civilization and Barbarism: Women, Nation, and Literary Culture in Modern Argentina.* Lincoln: University of Nebraska Press.
———. 1996. "Melodrama, Sex, and Nation in Latin America's *fin de siglo.*" *Modern Language Quarterly: A Journal of Literary History* 57, no. 2:269–78.
Mason, Alden J. and Aurelio M. Espinosa. 1925. "Porto Rican Folk-Lore: Folk-Tales; Cuentos de Encantamiento." *The Journal of American Folklore* 38:507–618.
Mathews, Cristina. 2005. "The Masquerade as Experiment: Gender and Representation in Mercedes Cabello de Carbonera's *El conspirador: Autobiografía de un hombre público.*" *Hispanic Review* 73, no. 4:467–89.
Matos Rodríguez, Félix V. 1999. *Women and Urban Change in San Juan, Puerto Rico, 1820–1868.* Gainesville: University Press of Florida.
———. 2004. Introduction to *A Nation of Women: An Early Feminist Speaks Out; Mi opinión sobre las libertades, derechos y deberes de la mujer,* by Luisa Capetillo, translated by Alan West-Durán, vii–li. Houston: Arte Público Press.
Matos Rodríguez, Félix V., and Linda C. Delgado, eds. 1998. *Puerto Rican Women's History: New Perspectives.* London: M. E. Sharpe.
Matto de Turner, Clorinda. 1884. "La industria nacional." 1882. In *Perú: Tradiciones cuzqueñas.* Arequipa, Peru: "La Bolsa."

———. 1996. *Birds Without a Nest*. Translated by J. G. Hudson. Emended by Naomi Lindstrom. Austin: University of Texas Press.
———. 2004. *Aves sin nido*. 1889. Buenos Aires: Stockcero.
———. 2006a. *Herencia*. 1895. Introduction by Mary Berg. Buenos Aires: Stockcero.
———. 2006b. *Indole*. 1891. Introduction by Mary Berg. Buenos Aires: Stockcero.
Mazquiarán de Rodríguez, Mercedes. 1990. "Mercedes Cabello de Carbonera (1845–1909)." In *Spanish American Women Writers: A Bio-Bibliographical Source Book*, edited by Diane E. Marting, 94–104. New York: Greenwood Press.
McCorkle, Jill. 1992. "Sleeping Beauty, Revised." In *Crash Diet: Stories*, 197–214. Chapel Hill, N.C.: Algonquin.
Méndez Rodenas, Adriana. 1998. *Gender and Nationalism in Colonial Cuba: The Travels of Santa Cruz y Montalvo, Condesa de Merlín*. Nashville: Vanderbilt.
Menon, Elizabeth K. 2006. "Les Filles d'Eve in Word and Image." In *Writing and Seeing: Essays on Word and Image*, edited and with an introduction by Rui Carvalho Homem, 157–73. Amsterdam: Rodopi.
Merrim, Stephanie. 1999. *Early Modern Women's Writing and Sor Juana Inés de la Cruz*. Nashville: Vanderbilt University Press.
Meyer, Doris, ed. 1995. *Reinterpreting the Spanish American Essay: Women Writers of the Nineteenth and Twentieth Centuries*. Austin: University of Texas Press.
Meyer, Michael C., and William L. Sherman. 1991. *The Course of Mexican History*. 4th ed. New York: Oxford University Press.
Miller, John C. 1977. "Clorinda Matto de Turner and Mercedes Cabello de Carbonera: Societal Criticism and Morality." In *Latin American Women Writers: Yesterday and Today*, 25–32. Pittsburgh: The Review.
Mitterand, Henri. 1986. *Zola et le naturalisme*. Paris: Presses Universitaires de France.
Moi, Toril. 1998. *Sexual/Textual Politics*. New York: Routledge.
Molloy, Sylvia. 1991. Interview. In *Women Writers of Latin America: Intimate Histories*, by Magdalena García Pinto, translated by Trudy Balch and Magdalena García Pinto, 125–44. Austin: University of Texas Press.
———. 1992. "Too Wilde for Comfort: Desire and Ideology in Fin-de-Siècle Spanish America." *Social Text* 10:187–201.
———. 1996. *Acto de presencia: La escritura autobiográfica en Hispanoamérica*. Mexico City: Fondo de Cultura Económica–Colegio de México.
Montero Sánchez, Susana. 1993. "Estrategia y propuesta de un periodismo marginal." In *Ensayo Letras Cubanas*. Havana: Letras Cubanas.
Moreno, Antonio de P., and Domingo Elizalde. 1909. *La mujer*. Introduction by R. P. Félix Alejandro Cepeda. Mexico City: José Ignacio Durán.
Munsch, Robert. 1980. *The Paper Bag Princess*. Toronto: Amick Press.
Mylne, Vivienne. 1965. *The Eighteenth-Century Novel: Techniques of Illusion*. Manchester: Manchester University Press.
Nagy-Zekmi, Sylvia. 1999. "Silencio y ambigüedad en *Blanca Sol* de Mercedes Cabello de Carbonera." In *La voz de la mujer en la literatura hispanoamericana fin-de-siglo* [Woman's Voice in Turn-of-the-Century Hispanic Literature], edited by Luis Jiménez, 49–59. San José: Editorial de la Universidad de Costa Rica.
Nombela, Julio. 1909. *Impresiones y recuerdos*. 4 vols. Madrid: Casa Editorial de "La Ultima Moda."

Ochoa, John. 2002. "Bordering on Madness: The *Licenciado vidriera*, Guillermo Gómez-Peña, and the Performance of Liminality." In *Foucault and Latin America*, edited by Benigno Trigo, 83–102. New York: Routledge.

Oliver, Kelly. 1993. *Reading Kristeva: Unravelling the Double-Bind*. Bloomington: Indiana University Press.

Ordóñez, Montserrat. 1997. "Soledad Acosta de Samper: ¿Un intento fallido de literatura nacional?" In *Mujeres latinoamericanas: Historia y cultura siglos XVI al XIX* [Latin American Women: History and Culture from the Sixteenth to the Nineteenth Centuries], edited by Luisa Campuzano, 2:233–41. Havana: Casa de las Américas.

Ordóñez, Montserrat, and Betty Osorio, eds. 1997. *Colombia en el contexto Latinoamericano* [Colombia in the Latin American Context]. Bogotá: Instituto Caro y Cuervo.

Orjuela, Héctor H., ed. 2000. *Las sacerdotistas: Antología de la poesía femenina de Colombia en el siglo XIX* [The Priestesses: Anthology of Colombian Women's Poetry of the Nineteenth Century]. Bogotá: Quebecor.

Osuna, Juan José. 1949. *A History of Education in Puerto Rico*. San Juan: Universidad de Puerto Rico.

Otis, Laura. 1999. *Membranes: Metaphors of Invasion in Nineteenth-Century Literature, Science, and Politics*. Baltimore: Johns Hopkins University Press.

Panttaja, Elisabeth. 1993. "The Poor Girl and the Bad Man: Fairytales of Feminine Power." *Kentucky Review* 12, no. 1–2:29–37.

Paravisini-Gebert, Lizabeth. 1994. "Introducción" and "Esquema biográfico." In *Luz y sombra*, by Ana Roqué, 1–16, 151–59. 1903. Río Piedras: University of Puerto Rico Press.

Parcero, María de la Luz. 1992. *Condiciones de la mujer en México durante el siglo XIX*. Mexico City: Instituto Nacional de Antropología e Historia.

Pastor, Brígida. 2003. *Fashioning Feminism in Cuba and Beyond: The Prose of Gertrudis Gómez de Avellaneda*. New York: Peter Lang.

Paz, Melchor de. 1796. *Crónica de la sublevación de Tupac Amaru*. Madrid.

Peluffo, Ana. 2002. "Las trampas del naturalismo en *Blanca Sol*: Prostitutes y costureras en el paisaje urbano de Mercedes Cabello de Carbonera." *Revista de Crítica Literaria Latinoamericana* 55:37–52.

———. 2004. "Bajo las alas del ángel de caridad: Indigenismo y beneficencia en el Perú republicano." *Revista Iberoamericana* 70, no. 206:103–15.

———. 2005. *Lágrimas andinas: Sentimentalismo, género y virtud republicana en Clorinda Matto de Turner*. Pittsburgh: Instituto Internacional de Literatura Iberoamericana.

Pérez Petit, Victor. 1943. *Las tres catedrales del naturalismo*. Montevideo, Uruguay: C. García.

Perry, Mary Elizabeth. 1995. "Crisis and Disorder in the World of María de Zayas y Sotomayor." In *María de Zayas: The Dynamics of Discourse*, edited by Amy R. Williamsen and Judith A. Whitenack, 23–39. Madison: Fairleigh Dickinson University Press.

Piccato, Pablo. 2007. "'Such a Strong Need': Sexuality and Violence in Belem Prison." In *Gender, Sexuality, and Power in Latin America Since Independence*, edited by William E. French and Katherine Elaine Bliss, 87–108. Lanham, Md.: Rowman and Littlefield.

Picón Garfield, Evelyn. 1992. "Periodical Literature for Women in Mid-Nineteenth Century Cuba: The Case of Gertrudis Gómez de Avellaneda's *Álbum cubano de lo bueno y lo bello*." *Studies in Latin American Popular Culture* 11:13–28.
Pino Iturrieta, Elías. 1993. *Ventaneras y castas, diabolicas y honestas*. Barcelona: Planeta.
Pinto Vargas, Ismael. 2003. *Sin perdón y sin olvido: Mercedes Cabello de Carbonera y su mundo*. Lima: Universidad de San Martín de Porres.
Planté, Christine, ed. 1998. *L'epistolaire, un genre féminin?* Paris: Honoré Champion.
Poot Herrera, Sara. 1991. "Dolores Bolio: Figura literaria de vuelta de siglo." In *Las voces olvidadas: Antología crítica de narradoras mexicanas nacidas en el siglo XIX*, edited by Ana Rosa Domenella and Nora Pasternac, 227–46. Mexico City: Colegio de México.
Portugal, Ana María. 1987. "Mercedes Cabello o el riesgo de ser mujer." In *La mujer en la historia*. Lima: Centro de Documentación de la Mujer.
Prado, Gloria María. 1991. "*Staurofila* de María Néstora Téllez Rendón." In *Las voces olvidadas: Antología crítica de narradoras mexicanas nacidas en el siglo XIX*, edited by Ana Rosa Domenella and Nora Pasternac, 33–58. Mexico City: Colegio de México.
Pratt, Mary Louise. 1992. *Imperial Eyes: Travel Writing and Transculturation*. London: Routledge.
El privilegio de amar. 1998. Original story by Delia Fiallo. Adapted by Liliana Abud. Directed by Miguel Córcega and Mónica Miguel. Television program. Televisa, Mexico.
Rama, Angel. 1984. *La ciudad letrada*. Hanover: Ediciones del Norte.
Ramos Escandón, Carmen, ed. 1987a. *Presencia y transparencia: La mujer en la historia de México*. Mexico City: Colegio de México.
———. 1987b. "Señoritas porfirianas: Mujer e ideología en el México progresista, 1880–1910." In *Presencia y transparencia: La mujer en la historia de México*, edited by Carmen Ramos Escandón, 143–62. Mexico City: Colegio de México.
Reglamento de la Asociación de Damas para la Instrucción de la Mujer. 1886. San Juan, Puerto Rico: Tipografía de González.
Rendall, Jane. 1984. *The Origins of Modern Feminism: Women in Britain, France, and the United States, 1780–1860*. New York: Schocken.
Ribes Tovar, Federico. 1972. *The Puerto Rican Woman: Her Life and Evolution Throughout History*. Translated by Anthony Rawlings. New York: Plus Ultra.
Riley, Denise. 1988. *"Am I That Name?" Feminism and the Category of "Women" in History*. Minneapolis: University of Minnesota Press.
Rivera, Marcia. 1987. "El proceso educativo en Puerto Rico y la reproducción de la subordinación femenina." In *La mujer en Puerto Rico: Ensayos de investigación*, edited by Yamila Azize Vargas, 113–38. Río Piedras, Puerto Rico: Ediciones Huracán.
Rivers, Christopher. 1994. *Face Value: Physiognomical Thought and the Legible Body in Marivaux, Lavater, Balzac, Gautier, and Zola*. Madison: University of Wisconsin Press.
Rodó, José Enrique. 1968. *Ariel, Liberalismo y Jacobinismo. Ensayos: Rubén Darío, Bolívar, Montalvo*. Mexico City: Porrúa.
———. 1993. *Ariel*. 1900. Translated by Margaret Sayers Peden. Austin: University of Texas Press.
Romero Aceves, Ricardo. 1982. *La mujer en la historia de México*. Mexico City: Costa-Amic.

Roqué, Ana. 1888. *Elementos de la geografía universal*. Humacao, Puerto Rico: Imprenta de Otero.
———. 1894. *Pasatiempos*. Humacao, Puerto Rico.
———. 1895a. *Novelas y cuentos*. Ponce, Puerto Rico.
———. 1895b. *Sara la obrera y otros cuentos*. Ponce, Puerto Rico: Imprenta Manuel López.
———. 1919. *Un ruso en Puerto Rico*. Ponce, Puerto Rico: Imprenta Manuel López.
———. 1941. "A mis compatriotas." 1917. *Revista de la Asociación de Mujeres Graduadas* 7, no. 1:19–20.
———. 1994. *Luz y sombra*. 1903. Río Piedras: University of Puerto Rico.
Rosas Lauro, Claudia. 1999. "Jaque a la Dama: La imagen de la mujer en la prensa limeña de fines del siglo XVIII." In *Mujeres y género en la historia del Perú*, edited by Margarita E. Zegarra, 143–71. Lima: Centro de Documentación Sobre la Mujer.
Rose, Jacqueline. 1982. "Introduction II." In *Feminine Sexuality*, by Jacques Lacan, 27–58. 1966–75. Translated by Jacqueline Rose, edited by Juliet Mitchell and Jacqueline Rose. New York: W. W. Norton.
Ruiz Cabañas, Samuel. 1934. Foreword to *La hija del bandido o los subterráneos del Nevado*, by Refugio Barragán de Toscano, i–ii. 1887. Mexico City: Editorial México.
Salas, Elizabeth. 1990. *Soldaderas in the Mexican Military: Myth and History*. Austin: University of Texas Press.
Saldivia Berglund, Marcela. 2000. "Género y representación: La presencia moral masculina y el discurso de la sexualidad femenina en la novela *Luz y sombra* de Ana Roqué (1853–1933)." *Revista Mexicana del Caribe* 10:180–210.
Salessi, Jorge. 1995. *Médicos maleantes y maricas: Higiene, criminología y homosexualidad en la construcción de la nación argentina; Buenos Aires, 1871–1914*. Rosario, Argentina: Beatriz Viterbo.
Salvatore, Ricardo D., and Carlos Aguirre, eds. 1996. *The Birth of the Penitentiary in Latin America: Essays on Criminology, Prison Reform, and Social Control, 1830–1940*. Austin: University of Texas Press, Institute of Latin American Studies.
Sanborn, Helen. 1884. "Character and Customs of the People." In *A Winter in Central America*, edited by Marjorie Agosín and Julie H. Levison, 207–15. Buffalo, N.Y.: White Pine Press.
Sánchez, Luis Alberto. 1951. *La literatura peruana: Derrotero para una historia espiritual del Perú*. Vol. 6. Paraguay: Editorial Guarania.
Sánchez-Eppler, Benigno. 1994. "'Por causa mecánica': The Coupling of Bodies and Machines and the Production and Reproduction of Whiteness in *Cecilia Valdés* and Nineteenth-Century Cuba." In *Thinking Bodies*, edited by Juliet Flower MacCannell and Laura Zakarin, 78–86. Stanford: Stanford University Press.
Sánchez-Llama, Iñigo. 1999. "Representaciones de la autoría intelectual femenina en las escritoras isabelinas del siglo XIX peninsular." *Hispania* 82, no. 4:750–60.
Scarano, Francisco A. 1993. *Puerto Rico: Cinco siglos de historia*. New York: McGraw-Hill.
Schade, George. 1989. "Eugenio Cambaceres." In *Latin American Writers*, 1:269–76. New York: Scribner.
Showalter, Elaine. 1990. *Sexual Anarchy*. New York: Viking.
Siess, Jürgen. 1998. "Effusion amoureuse et échange intellectuel: La pratique épistolaire de Julie de Lespinasse." In *L'epistolaire, un genre féminin?* edited by Christine Planté, 117–29. Paris: Honoré Champion.

Silva, José Asunción. 1992. "Crepúsculo." 1895. In *Obra completa: Edición crítica*, edited by Héctor H. Orjuela, 14–16. Mexico City: Archivos.
Silvestrini, Blanca, and María Dolores Luques Sánchez. 1991. *Historia de Puerto Rico: Una trayectoria de un pueblo*. San Juan, Puerto Rico: Ediciones Cultural Panamaericana.
Sinués de Marco, María del Pilar. 1859. *El ángel del hogar*. Madrid.
Solá, María M. 1987. "Angel, arpía, animal fiero y tierno: Mujer, sociedad y literatura en Puerto Rico." In *La mujer en Puerto Rico: Ensayos de investigación*, edited by Yamila Azize Vargas, 194–227. Río Piedras, Puerto Rico: Ediciones Huracán.
Sommer, Doris. 1991. *Foundational Fictions: The National Romances of Latin America*. Berkeley and Los Angeles: University of California Press.
Sprengnether, Madelon. 1989. "(M)other Eve: Some Revisions of the Fall in Fiction by Contemporary Women Writers." In *Feminism and Psychoanalysis*, 298–322. Ithaca: Cornell University Press.
Stepan, Nancy Leys. 1991. *"The Hour of Eugenics": Race, Gender, and Nation in Latin America*. Ithaca: Cornell University Press.
Stephens, John. 1999. "Constructions of Female Selves in Adolescent Fiction: Makeovers as Metonym." *Papers* 9, no. 1:5–13.
Suárez Findlay, Eileen J. 1999. *Imposing Decency: The Politics of Sexuality and Race in Puerto Rico, 1870–1920*. Durham: Duke University Press.
Tamayo Vargas, Augusto. 1940. *Perú en trance de novel: Ensayo crítico-biográfico sobre Mercedes Cabello de Carbonera*. Lima: Ediciones Baluarte.
Tatar, Maria. 1987. *The Hard Facts of the Grimms' Fairy Tales*. Princeton: Princeton University Press.
Tauzin Castellanos, Isabelle. 1988. "La educación femenina en el Perú del siglo XIX." In *Peruanistas contemporáneos: Temas, métodos, avances*, vol. 1, edited by Wilfredo Kapsoli, 97–109. Lima: Consejo Nacional de Ciencia y Tecnología.
Teixidor, Felipe. 1970. Introduction to *La vida en México durante una residencia de dos años en ese país*, by Frances Erskine Inglis Calderón de la Barca, vii–lxvii. 1834. Translated by Felipe Teixidor. Mexico City: Porrúa.
Tenorio-Trillo, Mauricio. 1996. *Mexico at the World's Fairs: Crafting a Modern Nation*. Berkeley and Los Angeles: University of California Press.
Torres-Pou, Joan. 1998. "Positivismo y feminismo en la producción narrativa de Mercedes Cabello de Carbonera." In *Estudios en honor de Janet Pérez: El sujeto femenino en escritoras hispánicas*, edited by Susana Cavallo, 245–53. Potomac: Scripta Humanistica.
Tosi, Laura. 2001. "Smart Princesses, Clever Choices: The Deconstruction of the Cinderella Paradigm and the Shaping of Female Cultural Identity in Adult and Children's Contemporary Rewritings of Fairy Tales." *Miscelánea: A Journal of English and American Studies* 24:93–106.
Trazegnies Granda, Fernando de. 1987. "Law and Modernization in Nineteenth-Century Peru." *Legal History Program Working Papers*, ser. 1, 1, no. 8:1–31. Madison, Wis.: Institute for Legal Studies.
Trigo, Benigno. 1995. "La función crítica del discurso alienista en *De sobremesa* de José Asunción Silva." *Hispanic Journal* 15:133–45.
———. 2000. *Subjects of Crisis: Race and Gender as Disease in Latin America*. Hanover: University Press of New England.

———, ed. 2002. *Foucault and Latin America*. New York: Routledge.
Tristán, Flora. 1983. *Les pérégrinations d'une paria. 1833–34*. Paris: La Découverte/Maspero.
———. 1998. "Travels Through Peru." 1833–34. Translated by Jean Hawkes. In *Women Through Women's Eyes*, edited by June E. Hahner, 21–42. Wilmington, Del.: Scholarly Resources.
Trottner, Josefina W. 1963. "Diálogo con los mexicanos: Visión histórica de Fanny Chambers Gooch." Diss., Universidad Autónoma de México.
Tuñón Pablos, Julia. 1999. *Women in Mexico: A Past Unveiled*. Translated by Alan Hynds. Austin: University of Texas Press.
Turner, Victor. 1969. *Ritual Process: Structure and Anti-Structure*. Chicago: Aldine.
———. 1977. "Variations on the Theme of Liminality." In *Secular Ritual*, edited by Sally Moore and Barbara G. Myerhoff, 36–52. Amsterdam: Van Gorcum.
Urraca, Beatriz. 1999. "Juana Manuela Gorriti and the Persistence of Memory." *Latin American Research Review* 34, no. 1:151–73.
Van Deusen, Nancy E. 1999. "Determinando los límites de la virtud: El discurso en torno al recogimiento entre las mujeres de Lima durante el siglo XVII." In *Mujeres y género en la historia del Perú*, edited by Margarita E. Zegarra, 39–58. Lima: Centro de Documentación Sobre la Mujer.
Vidal, Hernán, ed. 1989. *Cultural and Historical Grounding for Hispanic and Luso-Brazilian Feminist Literary Criticism*. Minneapolis: Institute for the Study of Ideologies and Literature.
Villavicencio, Maritza. 1992. *Del silencio a la palabra: Mujeres peruanas en los siglos XIX y XX*. Edited by Margarita Zegarra. Lima: Flora Tristán Centro de la Mujer Peruana.
Vitale, Luis. 1987. *La mitad invisible de la historia latinoamericana: El protagonismo social de la mujer*. Buenos Aires: Sudamericana/Planeta.
Voysest, Oswaldo. 1998. "Clorinda Matto and Mercedes Cabello: Reading Emile Zola's Naturalism in a Dissonant Voice." *Excavatio: Emile Zola and Naturalism* 11:195–201.
———. 2001. "Prólogo." In *El conspirador: Autobiografía de un hombre público*, by Mercedes Cabello de Carbonera, 5–9. Lima: Kavia Cobaya.
———. 2005. "Ejemplo de un naturalismo literario peruano heterodoxo: El caso de Mercedes Cabello de Carbonera." In *La ventana: Portal Informativo de la Casa de las Américas*. http://laventana.casa.cult.cu/modules.php?name=News&file=article&sid=2524 (accessed April 28, 2005).
Werlich, David P. 1978. *Peru: A Short History*. Carbondale: Southern Illinois University Press.
Woolf, Virginia. 1981. *A Room of One's Own*. 1929. Foreword by Mary Gordon. New York: Harcourt Brace.
Zalduondo, María. 2001. "Novel Women: Gender and Nation in Nineteenth-Century Novels by Two Spanish American Women Writers." Ph.D. diss., University of Texas at Austin.
———. 2007. "(Des)orden en el porfiriato: La construcción del bandido en dos novelas desconocidas del siglo XIX mexicano." *Decimonónica* 4, no. 2:77–94.
Zavala, Iris M. 1992. *Colonialism and Culture: Hispanic Modernisms and the Social Imaginary*. Bloomington: Indiana University Press.

Zayas y Sotomayor, María de. 1950. *Desengaños amorosos, parte segunda del sarao y entretenimiento honesto*. 1646. Edited and with a foreword by Agustín G. de Amezua y Mayo. Madrid: Aldus.

Zea, Leopoldo. 1949. *Dos etapas del pensamiento en Hispanoamérica: Del romanticismo al positivismo*. Mexico City: Colegio de México.

———. 1963. *The Latin-American Mind*. Translated by James H. Abbott and Lowell Dunham. Norman: University of Oklahoma Press.

Zegarra, Margarita E., ed. 1999. *Mujeres y género en la historia del Perú*. Lima: Centro de Documentación Sobre la Mujer.

Zeno Gandía, Manuel. 1978. *La charca*. 1894. Introduction by Enrique Laguerre. Caracas: Biblioteca Ayacucho.

Zipes, Jack. 1987. *Don't Bet on the Prince: Contemporary Feminist Fairy Tales in North America and England*. New York: Routledge.

Žižek Slavoj. 1992a. *Enjoy Your Symptom! Jacques Lacan in Hollywood and Out*. New York: Routledge.

———, ed. 1992b. *Everything You Always Wanted to Know About Lacan (But Were Afraid to Ask Hitchcock)*. London: Verso.

Zola, Émile. 1964. "The Experimental Novel." 1893. *The Experimental Novel and Other Essays*. Translated by Belle M. Sherman. New York: Haskell House.

———. 1998. *Nana*. 1880. Translated by Douglas Parmee. Oxford: Oxford University Press.

Zorilla, José. 1990. *Don Juan Tenorio*. 1844. Edited by Aniano Peña. Madrid: Cátedra.

INDEX

Acosta de Samper, Soledad, 17–18, 174
adultery, 163, 173
agency
   in *Blanca Sol*, 112–13, 122
   chora concept and, 12 n. 5
   in *La hija del bandido*, 53, 60, 68–75
   marginal spaces and, 60
   of women in Peru, 79–82
Agustini, Delmira, 175
Aldaraca, Bridget, 5, 6–7
Almeida, Marcelina, 4 n. 2
Álzaga, Florinda, 19
Amaru, Tupac, 78
American Realism, 96–97
Amézaga, Mariano, 91
Angel of the House
   in *Blanca Sol*, 108, 114–15, 122
   Catholic Church and, 41–44
   cult of Virgin Mary and, 134
   definition of, 3, 10
   as domestic ideal, 5–6
   female writers and, 12–13, 172–73
   in Hispanic literature, 6–11
   in *La hija del bandido*, 73–75
   in *Luz y sombra*, 162, 163
   in Mexico, 34–35
   national morality and, 11
   in Peru, 81–82, 83–88
   primary school teachers and, 39 n. 10
   Spain and, 88 n. 8
   thinking women and, 11–12
   trope of, 12, 25, 119 n. 19
Anthony, Susan B., 39
Arambel-Guiñazú, María Cristina, 22
Arens, Katie, 170
Argentina, writers from, 16–17, 23 n. 27
Arona, Juan de, 4 n. 2, 106 n. 7

Avila, Santa Teresa de, 75–76, 175
Azize Vargas, Yamila, 144

Barceló Miller, Rico María, 133–34, 162
Barragán de Toscano, Refugio. *See also La hija del bandido*
   birth and life of, 54–55
   critical attention toward, 21–22
   essay on, 20
   foreign travel and, 40
   marriage of, 55
   Mexican politics and, 54
   subject matter of, 2, 3
   success of, 53
   travel narratives of, 174
   as widow, 36, 55
Barreda, Horacio
   El siglo XX ante el feminismo, 1, 45–52, 158 n. 12
   Positivism and, 99
Barthes, Roland, 162
Bastidas, Micaela, 78
Batticuore, Graciela, 14
beaterios, 38, 83–84
Beauvoir, Simone de, 3
Bennett, Barbara, 121 n. 21
Berg, Mary, 17
Bernard, Claude, 94
Blanca Sol (Cabello de Carbonera)
   acquisition of power and, 112–13
   Cinderella fairy tale in, 103, 105, 108–10, 113, 114–16, 122
   critical attention to, 103–4 n. 2, 122
   education for women in, 110–19, 122–23
   experimental space in, 97
   female solidarity in, 120
   historical setting for, 90

Luz y sombra compared to, 157 n. 11
  narrator in, 116–17, 118–19
  Naturalism in, 112
  secondary plot of, 87
  stepmother figure in, 110–21
  stereotyping in, 116
  story of, 106–8, 121–22
Bolívar, Simón, 81, 83, 98 n. 13, 130, 133–34
Bombal, María Luisa, 175
bourgeois women, in Peru, 79–82, 103–4 n. 2
Bracetti, Mariana, 126, 127
Brau, Salvador, 144, 151, 169
Brushwood, John, 96 n. 12
Butler, Judith, 25

Cabello de Carbonera, Mercedes. *See also* *Blanca Sol*
  as advocate for women, 104
  American Realism and, 96–97
  biographies published on, 90 n. 10
  critical attention toward, 22
  cultural myths and, 104–5
  as declared insane, 101
  education of, 91–92
  El conspirador, 112
  "Influencia de la mujer en la civilización," 98, 104, 123 n. 23
  intellectual and literary strategies of, 100–101
  "La novela moderna," 110
  Las consecuencias, 96 n. 12
  modernization and, 174
  Naturalism and, 94, 95–96, 97
  negative criticism of, 101, 106 n. 7, 116–17 n. 17
  Positivism and, 89, 97, 98–99, 110
  pseudonym of, 93
  slander of, 4 n. 2
  subject matter of, 2, 3
  veladas and, 14
  as widow, 36, 92
  works of, 16 n. 14, 93
Cáceres, Zoila Aurora, 15 n. 10, 160 n. 14, 174
Calvo Peña, Beatriz, 139
Cambaceres, Eugenio, 94, 153 n. 8
Campuzano, Rosita, 79–80
Cánova, Virginia, 4 n. 2
Capetillo, Luisa, 128, 135, 150–51, 160 n. 14
Carlsmith, James, 156
Carner, Francoise, 31–32, 36, 37
Carrillo, Josefa, 80
Castellanos, Rosario, 3, 40, 72, 175

Catholic Church
  marriage and, 132–33
  prostitution and, 129 n. 6
  in Puerto Rico, 126, 129–30
  reactions against feminism by, 41–44
  Roqué and, 152
  Virgin Mary, cult of, 5 n. 3, 104–5, 133, 134
  women and, 84, 133–34
cave, as metaphor, 65–66, 68, 165 n. 17
Cepeda, Alejandro Felix R. P., 42
Chambers Gooch, Fanny, 40–41, 41 n. 13
characterization of women, in Puerto Rico, 133–34, 143
Charnon-Deutsch, Lou, 4–5
chastity, 6, 36, 141–42. *See also* virginity
Cherpak, Evelyn, 28 n. 1
Chocano, José Santos, 101
chora, concept of, 12 n. 5, 65
científicos in Mexico, 29, 33, 43, 47
Cinderella story
  in *Blanca Sol*, 103, 105, 108–10, 113, 114–16, 122
  Electra fantasies and, 120 n. 20
  versions of, 105
Cixous, Hélène, 72, 161, 165 n. 17, 170
clothing for women
  in Mexico, 36–37
  in Puerto Rico, 129–30
cognitive dissonance, 156, 162
Colón, Cristóbol, 57
Columbia, writers from, 17–18
comportment manual, 6–7
Comte, Auguste, 45, 97
convent life, 75–77
costumbrismo writing, 56, 159, 173
criollas/criollos, 57, 60, 80–81, 130
Cuba
  social whitening policies in, 136 n. 15
  writers from, 18–19
cultural myths, manipulation of, 104–5

dance, in Puerto Rico, 130–31
Darío, Ruben, 153, 158
death, in *Luz y sombra*, 169–70
de Erauso, Catalina, 76
de la Barra, Emma, 17, 174
de la Cruz, Sor Juana Inés, 75–76, 115 n. 15, 175
de la Parra, Teresa, 175
del Casal, Julián, 153, 158
de León, Luis, 6–7

de Lequanda, José Ignacio, 84
del Valle Atiles, Francisco, 151 n. 6
Denegri, Francesca, 5, 13–14, 99, 100
de Zarco, María Sandoval, 39
Díaz, Arlene, 133
Díaz, José de la Cruz Porfirio, 29, 30, 32–33, 35
Domenella, Ana Rosa, 20
Dore, Elizabeth, 2
Dowling, Collette, 121 n. 22
Duprey, Luis, 149 n. 1
Dworkin, Andrea, 120 n. 21, 121

ecclesiastic separation, 35, 85
education for women
   Blanca Sol and, 110–19, 122–23
   Catholic Church and, 43
   limitations on, 3
   in Mexico, 30–34
   in Peru, 88, 89–92
   in Puerto Rico, 140–44, 145–46
   role of, 171–72
   Tristán on, 87
Elizalde, Domingo, 40–44
enclosure. *See* seclusion of women
Epple, Juan Armando, 22, 95 n. 12
equality, Barreda definition of, 51
Erskine Inglis Calderón de la Barca, Fanny, 36, 40–41, 41 n. 13
Étienne, Charles-Guillaume, 105
eugenics, 136
Eulate Sanjurjo, Carmela, 19, 107 n. 8, 174
Eve, biblical story of, 105, 171

fairy tales, 103, 105 n. 5, 120–21. *See also* Cinderella story
Feliú, Fernando, 162
feminine ideal. *See* Angel of the House
feminism
   Barragán and, 72
   ecclesiastic reactions against, 41–44
   in *Luz y sombra*, 164–65
   in Mexico, 38–41
   Positivism and, 44–52
   in Puerto Rico, 144–45
feminist literary scholarship on Latin American writing, 22–23 n. 27
Fernández Juncos, Manuel, 144
Ferré, Rosario, 3
Ferreyros, Petronila, 80–81
Festinger, Leon, 156
financial ruin, commonplace of, 107 n. 8

Flaubert, Gustave, 107 n. 8, 173
Fletcher, Lea, 17, 23 n. 27
Flores Ramos, José, 140
foreign travel, in Mexico, 40–41
Foucault, Michel, 137 n. 18
Fox-Lockert, Lucía, 112
Franco, Jean, 22–23 n. 27
Frederick, Bonnie, 6, 16–17, 23 n. 27, 25
freedom
   Barreda definition of, 48–51
   in *La hija del bandido*, 64
   travel as metaphor for, 70–71
Freire de Jaimes, Carolina, 15
Freud, Sigmund, 23–24 n. 28, 57–58 n. 7, 161 n. 16
Freudian theory. *See* psychoanalytic theory
Friedan, Betty, 3

Gamboa, Federico, 153 n. 8, 160 n. 14
Gamboa, Ignacio, 52
García, Genaro, 35, 39 n. 10
García, Juana and Candelaria, 80
García Calderón, Ventura, 95 n. 12, 96 n. 12
García Padilla, María del Carmen, 147
García y García, Elvira
   biography by, 82
   Cabello and, 101
   women's history study by, 79, 80–81, 85, 92–93
gender, segregation by, 138–40
Ghose, Indira, 41
Gilbert, Sandra M., 25
Glave, Luis Miguel, 90 n. 10, 101
Gómez Carrillo, Enrique, 160 n. 14
Gómez de Avellaneda, Gertrudis
   characterization of, 4 n. 2
   in Hispanic literary canon, 18–19
   journal of, 10–11
   orphans in novels of, 59
   as poet, 3, 13 n. 6
   Sinués de Marco on, 8
   themes of, 174
González Ascorra, Martha Irene, 22
González de Fanning, Teresa, 15
González Prada, Manuel, 14, 95 n. 12, 98, 106 n. 7
Gorriti, Juana Manuela
   on Cabello, 96 n. 12
   critical works on, 23 n. 27
   as early feminist, 72
   novels of, 22
   Positivism and, 89, 97, 99–100

198 INDEX

Sueños y realidades, 100
travel narratives of, 174
veladas of, 13–15, 93
works of, 13
Gubar, Susan, 25
Guerra, Lucía, 22, 95 n. 12, 108, 113
Gutiérrez, Rita Cetina, 39
Guy, Donna, 139

Herrmann, Claudine, 72–73
Hostos, Eugenio María de, 144–45
Hunefeldt, Christine, 83, 84, 87

identity politics of women, 22–25
immobility of women
 in Mexico, 36–37
 in Peru, 83–84
independence period, in Peru, 78, 79–82
institutionalized social control, 137–40
intellectual deficiencies of women, assertions about, 1–2
Irigaray, Luce, 24 n. 28, 66, 72, 161, 165 n. 17
Isaacs, Jorge, 5 n. 3, 137
Isouard, Nicholas, 105

Jalisco, Mexico, 54
Jaramillo Flores, Renán, 78, 79
journals for women
 Angel of the House standard and, 11
 Gómez de Avellaneda and, 10–11
 Gorriti and, 15
 in Mexico, 39–40
 in Puerto Rico, 128
 Roqué and, 151
 Sinués de Marco and, 9
Juárez, Benito, 54 n. 3

Kristeva, Julia
 chora, 12 n. 5, 65
 feminine desire and, 24 n. 28
 region of cultural unconscious, 153 n. 9
 Roqué and, 161
 symbolic order and, 24 n. 29

Lacan, Jacques, 24 nn. 28, 29, 27, 57, 58 n. 7
La charca (Zeno Gandía), 125, 137, 162, 170
La hija del bandido (Barragán)
 angelic ideal in, 73–75
 description of, 53, 77
 female agency in, 53, 60, 68–75
 genre and, 56

 liminoid, and reconnection with mother in, 63–68
 name-of-the-father in, 57–60
 narrator of, 70–72
 perpetuation of liminality in, 75–77
 story of, 56–57
 strategic liminality in, 60–63
 travel in, 57, 68, 69–70, 73
liberty, Barreda definition of, 48–51
Lima, Peru, 70–81, 83, 117–18
liminality in *La hija del bandido*
 coming of age of heroine and, 60–61, 62–63
 perpetuation of, 75–77
 reconnection with mother and, 63–68
 Turner theory and, 61–62
literary salons (*veladas*), 13–15, 93
Lizardi, José Joaquín Fernández, 30–31
Luz y sombra (Roqué)
 Blanca Sol compared to, 157 n. 11
 doctor-of-love tangent in, 167–68
 ending of, 168–70
 epostolary structure of, 155–56
 female sexual desire in, 158–62
 gender stereotypes in, 157–58
 medical discourse in, 163–68
 narrator of, 156–57
 Naturalism in, 166–67
 Positivism in, 173–74
 story of, 153–55

Macías, Anna, 33
Maguire, Gregory, 121
Mansilla de García, Eduarda, 17, 23 n. 27, 174
Manso, Juana, 17, 23 n. 27
marriage
 in Mexico, 34–35
 in Peru, 84–85
 in Puerto Rico, 132–33, 136
 quinceañera and, 61
"masculine" characteristics ascribed to female novelists, 4–5, 116–17 n. 17
Masiello, Francine, 6, 17, 23 n. 27, 104 n. 2
Mathews, Cristina, 112
Matto de Turner, Clorinda
 Catholicism and, 95
 as early feminist, 72
 "La industria nacional," 99
 "La mujer y la ciencia," 99
 negative criticism of, 106 n. 7
 as newspaper editor, 15–16
 novels of, 22

Positivism and, 89, 97, 99
Sinués de Marco and, 11
veladas and, 14
Maximilian Joseph, Ferdinand, 54
McCorkle, Jill, 121
medical discourse
 in *Luz y sombra*, 163–68
 in politics, 137–40
 on public health and morality, 135–36
 Roqué and, 151–52
Méndez de Cuenca, Laura, 20–21, 174
Merino, Rosa, 80
Merlín, condessa de, 19 n. 22, 174
Mexican Revolution, 30
Mexico. *See also* Barragán de Toscano, Refugio
 Angel of the House ideology in, 34–35
 early feminism in, 38–41
 education for women in, 30–34
 French influence in, 29, 43–44
 Jalisco, 54
 marriage in, 34–35
 modernization in, 30
 power struggles in, 28–29
 status of women in, 34–38
 Wars of Independence, 28
 writers from, 20–21
Mill, John Stuart, 39
Miller, John, 104 n. 2
Mistral, Gabriela, 175
Mitterand, Henri, 96 n. 12
modernista movement, 15 n. 10, 56 n. 5, 103 n. 1
modernization, 30, 128, 171, 174
morality
 gender and, 74–75, 113
 as weapon, 87
Moreno, Antonio de P., 40–44
mother
 reconnection with, in *La hija del bandido*, 63–68
 stepmother figure in *Blanca Sol*, 110–21
Munsch, Robert, 121

Nájera, Manuel Gutiérrez, 31
narrator
 in *Blanca Sol*, 116–17, 118–19
 in *La hija del bandido*, 70–72
 in *Luz y sombra*, 156–57
nation building
 definition of gender and, 5–6
 education as tool for, 140–41
 lexicon of, 98–99

Naturalism
 in *Blanca Sol*, 112
 Cabello and, 94, 95–96, 97
 death and, 169
 in Latin America, 94–97
 in *Luz y sombra*, 166–67
 novels and, 153
 Zeno Gandía and, 94, 153 n.8
normalizing, definition of, 153
novelists, female. *See also specific novelists*
 from Argentina, 17, 23 n. 27
 challenges faced by, 3–4
 from Colombia, 17–18
 common approaches to feminist production, 171–75
 criticism within boundaries of domestic topics by, 12–13, 119 n. 19, 172–73
 from Cuba, 18–19
 experience of community for, 14
 "masculine" characteristics ascribed to, 4–5, 116–17 n. 17
 from Mexico, 20–21
 as negative example, 8
 from Peru, 13–15
 Positivism and, 171
 from Puerto Rico, 19–20
 rewards of, 2–3
 risks taken by, 2

Oedipal complex, 57–58 n. 7, 161 n. 16
orphans and orphan-bandits, in novels, 59–60
Otis, Laura, 168

Palma, Ricardo, 14, 101, 106 n. 7
Paravisini-Gebert, Lizabeth, 22, 165
Pardo Bazán, Emilia, 95, 169
Pasternac, Nora, 20
Pastor, Beatriz, 19
Patmore, Coventry, 6
patriarchal authority
 female writers and, 172
 in *La hija del bandido*, 67, 75–77
 in Mexico, 36
 in Puerto Rico, 132
 Sinués de Marco on, 8, 9
Paz, Melchor de, 78
Paz Soldán, Pedro, 106 n. 7. *See also* Arona, Juan de
Peluffo, Ana
 on *Blanca Sol*, 108
 on Cabello, 22, 96 n. 12, 104 n. 2, 106 n. 7
 critical work by, 23 n. 27

Pérez Galdós, Benito, 107 n. 8
Perrault, Charles, 105
Peru. *See also* Cabello de Carbonera, Mercedes
   Argentina and, 16
   education of women in, 88, 89–92
   French influence in, 100
   Naturalism in, 93–97
   in nineteenth century, 88–93
   political structure of, 112
   Positivism in, 89, 97–100
   postindependence period in, 83–88
   status of women in, 78–79, 87–88
   veladas in, 13–15
   war with Chile, 92–93
   writers from, 13–15
Peruvian Ladies' Society, 80
Piérola, Nicolás, 16
Pinto Vargas, Ismael, 105
Planté, Christine, 155
Plato, cave of, 65–66, 165 n. 17
poetry, 3
poets, female, 13 n. 6, 75–76
Positivism
   antifeminist rhetoric of, 44–52
   Catholic Church and, 42–43
   female writers and, 171
   Gorriti and, 89, 97, 99–100
   in *Luz y sombra*, 173–74
   Matto de Turner and, 89, 97, 99
   medical discourse and, 136
   in Peru, 89, 97–100
   Revista Positiva, 1, 45
   Roqué and, 147, 157
Prado, Gloria María, 20
Pratt, Mary Louise, 70
pre-liminal state, 63–64, 68
press, woman-centered, 15
progress
   Barreda definition of, 47–48
   for women, 2, 10, 30–38, 87–88
pro-independence activities, in Puerto Rico, 131–32
prostitution, 129 n. 6, 131, 135 n. 14, 139
psychoanalytic theory
   connection between unconscious and language, 23–24 n. 28
   identity formation, 53
   Oedipal complex, 57–58 n. 7, 161 n. 16
   rebellion against father for love of mother, 67
   subconscious and fairy tales, 103
public voice, women and, 4

Puerto Rico. *See also* Roqué Géigel de Duprey, Ana Cristina
   controls over female body in, 128–35
   early feminism in, 144–45
   economy of, 124–25, 134–35
   education of women in, 140–44, 145–46
   modernization in, 128
   political climate of, 125–27
   social regulation in, 148
   status of women in, 135–40
   U.S. intervention on, 147
   writers from, 19–20

quinceañera, 53, 60–61, 64

rabonas, 78–79, 92
Rama, Angel, 4
Ramón, Ignacio, 38–41
Ramos Escandón, Carmen, 37
recogimiento, 37, 68, 83–84
reproductive partners, choice of, 6, 129
Ribes Tovar, Federico, 126, 129
Ricuarte, Genoveva, 81
Riley, Denise, 25
Rivera, Columba, 39
Rodó, José Enrique, 98 n. 13, 158 n. 12
Rodríguez de Tió, Lola, 3, 13 n. 6, 126–27, 128, 143–44
Roqué Géigel de Duprey, Ana Cristina. *See also Luz y sombra*
   Catholic Church and, 152
   connections of, 173–74
   critical attention toward, 22
   education and career of, 146–47
   Elementos de la geografía universal, 147
   essentialized images of women and, 152–53
   fiction of, 149–50
   La Mujer magazine, 151
   life of, 140, 149–50 n. 1
   marriage of, 36
   modernization and, 174
   Positivism and, 147, 157
   Sara la obrera, 150
   sexual transgressions in works of, 150, 151, 153
   subject matter of, 2, 3
   suffrage and, 151
   works and interests of, 19–20, 150 n. 1
ruling class
   European culture and, 100
   fears of, 99, 122–23, 139, 144
   as literate public, 4

Sáenz, Manuela, 81
Salas, Elizabeth, 28
Sanborn, Helen, 40–41, 41 n. 13, 69
Sánchez-Eppler, Benigno, 136 n. 15, 137
San Martín, José de, 79, 80
Santa Cruz y Montalvo, María de las Mercedes, 19 n. 22
Sarmiento, Domingo Faustino, 6, 98 n. 13, 99 n. 14, 123 n. 23
Schade, George, 94
seclusion of women. *See also* immobility of women
　in *La hija del bandido*, 68
　in Mexico, 36–37
　national policies and, 6
　in Peru, 84
segregation by gender, 138–40
sexual activity of women
　Catholic Church and, 129–30
　claim for, in *Luz y sombra*, 158–62
　control over, 37–38, 137–40, 141–42
　as dangerous, 133–34
　medical justifications for, 163–68
　writings about, 150, 151, 153
Silva, 153, 160 n. 14
Silva, José Asunción, 102–3, 105
Silva de Ochoa, Brígida, 82
Sinués de Marco, María del Pilar, 7–11
social mobility, and angelic ideal, 87
social whitening, policies of, 136, 143
Sommer, Doris, 85
Spencer, Herbert, 98
Stanton, Elizabeth Cady, 39
Stepan, Nancy Leys, 135, 136
stereotyping
　in *Blanca Sol*, 116
　in *Luz y sombra*, 157–58
Storni, Alfonsina, 175
Suárez Findlay, Eileen, 132–33, 135, 138, 140, 143
subjectivity, female, 25, 27
suffrage, 151
symbolic order
　in *La hija del bandido*, 59
　Name-of-the-Father and, 57–58 n. 7
　Naturalism and, 97
　women's place in, 23–24

Tamayo Vargas, Augusto, 90 n. 10, 91, 93, 95 n. 12, 117 n. 17
Tapia y Rivera, Alejandro, 144, 145 n. 27

Tatar, Maria, 120 n. 20
Téllez Rendón, María Néstora, 20, 174
Tió y Segarra, Bonicio, 127 n. 5
Todd, Janet, 25
Torres-Pou, Joan, 96 n. 12, 101
Toscano, Salvador, 55
Toscano Arreola, Estéban, 55
travel by women
　control of, 37
　in *La hija del bandido*, 57, 68, 69–70, 73
　as metaphor for freedom, 70–71
travel narratives, 19 n. 22, 40–41, 86, 174
Trigo, Benigno, 126, 135, 138
Trinidad Enríquez, María, 91
Tristán, Flora, 86–87, 174
Tuñón Pablos, Julia, 46
Turner, Victor, 61–62, 63, 75

Ugarteche de Prado, Magdalena, 93
United States, and Puerto Rico, 147

Van Deusen, Nancy, 37–38
veladas (literary salons), 13–15, 93
Verdú, condesa de, 145
Villaverde, Cirilo, 137
Viñas, Lugo, 139
virginity, 37, 141–42. *See also* chastity
Virgin Mary
　cult of, 104–5, 133, 134
　as example of Angel of the House, 5 n. 3
virtue, of women
　debunking of, in *Blanca Sol*, 110–19
　in Mexico, 36
　unrealistic standards of, 87
voyeur, reader as, 162
Voysest, Oswaldo, 22, 89, 93–94, 96 n. 12, 97

War of the Pacific, 92–93
wartime, women in, 28, 78–79, 92–93
widows, in Mexico, 35–36
Women's Association for Women's Education, 145–46
Woolf, Virginia, 3, 72
workforce, women in
　masculinist rhetoric and, 52
　in Mexico, 31–32, 33, 34, 39 n. 10
　in Puerto Rico, 134–35
Wright de Kleinhans, Laureana, 20 n. 23, 39, 72
writing, and feminine space, 72–73

Zalduondo, María, 31
Zapata, Dolores Correa, 39
Zayas y Sotomayor, María de, 175
Zeno Gandía, Manuel
    death in works of, 169
    Higiene da la infancia, 141 n. 22, 152 n. 7
    La charca, 125, 137, 162, 170
    life of, 152 n. 7
    as medical doctor, 135
    as Naturalist, 94, 153 n. 8
    Roqué and, 151–52
Zevallos, Angélica, 80
Zola, Émile, 94, 95, 96 n. 12, 97, 169

www.ingramcontent.com/pod-product-compliance
Lightning Source LLC
Chambersburg PA
CBHW031550300426
44111CB00006BA/258